1611 KING JAMES VERSION
APOCR

SCROLLS FOUND IN QUMRAN AND THOSE NOT PRESENT

MW00955599

ApocryphaTest.com

Full Publishing With Torah Test For:

Wisdom of
SIRACH

Prayer of
MANASSEH

The Book of
BARUCH

Letter of
JEREMIAH

With Further Qumran Evidence of:

1ST & 2ND ESDRAS

Text Adapted From The 1611
KING JAMES VERSION
REVISED ENGLISH

Compiled, Edited, Commentary, Maps, Charts, and Research By
Timothy Schwab, Anna Zamoranos and The God Culture Team

LeviteBible.com

NOTE: Why Foreward vs. the traditional foreword? As The God Culture represents an adjusting of traditional history, geography and bible interpretation, they wanted something more from the opening words that sets the tone appropriately. They employ a sort of literary double entendre in using the word Foreward reviving an Old English word far more significant. Foreward means to keep, guard, vanguard, protect, tend, etc. It denotes a warding of evil in a sense. This work also strives to move a people forward out of the Dark Ages which still persist. For this book, that is the title chosen very appropriately in raising the curtain on this work.

To order additional copies of this book, contact:

The Levite Bible By The God Culture
TheGodCulture@gmail.com
Facebook: The God Culture - Original
www.ApocryphaTest.com
www.LeviteBible.com
www.TheGodCulture.com

CONTENTS

The Book of Jubilees:
7" x 10"

First Enoch:
7" x 10"

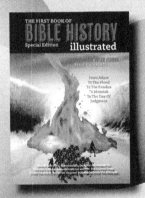

Bible History Illustrated:
7" x 10"

Apocrypha: Vol. 1
7" x 10"

MIND-BLOWING REVELATIONS

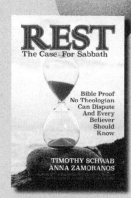

FOREWARD

By Timothy Schwab
*Author, Publisher, Researcher, Speaker, Singer/Songwriter,
Founder of The God Culture, Non-Pharisee and proudly so...*

This classification of apocrypha originates from the Greek apokryptein, ἀπόκρυφος, meaning *"to hide away [83]."* It is a combination of the Greek apo *(away)* and kryptein *(hide or conceal)*. Step back... and think about this title. Most of these books were originally simply known as Bible Canon, we will prove. To classify them into a supposed separate category, serves the exact expressed purpose of this term placing, in some cases, inspired scripture there in deception. They, then, mix it in with occult accounts raising their credibility in fraud, and then, though it remained in Bibles and even some today, keep it separated so that it is marginalized by many as hidden away or concealed from the average believer. That intent becomes obvious when one tests these books. Some have historicity as Canon and others are complete occult fabrications that never even belonged together. Who would even think in such terms? Why are scholars not properly testing it? We will in over two volumes of the Apocrypha in this book and the next.

Though most of these books were included in his Old Testament Latin translation in the Vulgate Bible, it was Jerome who appears to have been the first to apply this term *"apocrypha [83]."* Understand, most of these books labeled apocrypha were not hidden in the Christian Church on such a scale until Jerome treated them as set aside and less significant. This is uneducated ridicule even in Jerome's time *(382 A.D.)*. He had no authority to take books circulated as inspired scripture attacking them as less authoritative which was a slippery slope the Catholic Church and even Protestants later embraced in ignorance. Today, scholarship calls this illiterate paradigm "textual criticism." He also should not have added occult books that never belonged and one became Canon when it never was *(see Testing Esther. Vol. 2)*.

However, though first to use the term perhaps, if true, and certainly a Pharisee pawn in his behavior, Jerome is not the origin of such practice. The Pharisees were. The true battle here was whether Jerome would continue the Bible Canon of the Biblically ordained keepers of scripture for certain texts or change the religion to Pharisaism. When the Qumran/Bethabara Temple Priests established a book as Old Testament Canon as they did, Jerome had no ordination to change it, not one letter and especially entire books. This would lead to our losing knowledge the Bible ekklesia once had. Jerome was abandoning the Bible and confusing it.

> *"That version incorporated a number of works that later, non-Hellenistic Jewish scholarship at the Council of Jamnia (A.D. 90) identified as being outside the authentic Hebrew canon. The Talmud separates these works as Sefarim Hizonim (Extraneous Books)." [83].*

However, were all of these books "extraneous" or extra? No! Most were found in Qumran/Bethabara either in direct fragments or in association with books in which they were considered a part of in the First Century. For instance, Daniel writes of Shadrach, Meshach and Abednego *(Hebrew name, Azaryah)*. Azaryah wrote a very short account of the prayer that he spoke when in the fiery furnace which, at that time and before, was included in the Book of Daniel. Who would then usurp the throne of Yahusha, the Word, and the documented Biblical keepers of Old Testament Canon and claim this book should no longer be part of Daniel? They set it aside and pick it off as they did many, and all to match the Pharisees who influenced that decision in error.

There were no ordained keepers of Bible Canon in Egypt at the time of the Septuagint around 300-200 B.C. Though a useful translation as a secondary source, the Septuagint is not a translation by the Temple Priests who were in Israel in the Temple where they should have been at the time of it's translation into Greek. However, even that publishing includes several of these books. No Pharisee ever qualifies as being ordained to keep Bible Canon to the First Century either but the opposite. This includes especially Josephus, the Pharisee, whose publishing of the Pharisee Canon now proves archaeologically to be a changing of Bible Canon also coalescing with the Pharisee Council of Jamnia oddly the same year. Generally, the Protestant Old Testament Canon today is driven by Jospehus' listing from 90 A.D. or so and one could not be more uneducated especially in the face of the many rebukes of Pharisee doctrines, oral traditions and their Canon *(see "Pharisee Fruits")*.

> *"For we have not an innumerable multitude of books among us, disagreeing from, and contradicting one another: [as the Greeks have:] but only twenty-two books: which contain the records of all the past times: which are justly believed to be divine. (8) And of them five belong to Moses: which contain his laws, and the traditions of the origin of mankind, till his death. This interval of time was little short of three thousand years. But as to the time from the death of Moses, till the reign of Artaxerxes, King of Persia, who reigned after Xerxes, the Prophets, who were after Moses, wrote down what was done in their times, in thirteen books. The remaining four books contain hymns to God; and precepts for the conduct of human life."*
> *– Flavius Josephus, Against Apion 1:8.*

In the arena of law, this serves as a Pharisee written confession of guilt by Josephus, the admitted Pharisee, that they changed the Bible which was the Old Testament of that era. He offers the Pharisee Canon which is missing books already at that time and adds especially Esther not found in the real Temple Priests' library as it never was scripture *(see Testing Esther, Vol. 2)*. This is why Messiah points out that very fact *(John 5:46; Mark 7; Matt. 22:29, etc.)*. He said to beware of their leaven or expanding/ changing of the Word *(Matt. 16:6-12; Mark 8:15; Luke 12:1)*.

Josephus, also, represents the very first publishing of the Book of Esther which he or his fellow Pharisees likely authored at that time. The whole account represents one of the most significant frauds in all of history. They changed the Bible and the modern church, especially Protestants, are relying on this Pharisee Canon as their basis for Bible Canon when we found the actual Bible Canon in Qumran/Bethabara. That is ignored and hidden or kryptein. Fortunately, all of the modern Old Testament Canon was found there except Esther, but it becomes clear, they have been censoring texts also found there. None of those texts were called "apocrypha" by the Bethabara Temple Priests. They were discovered among the exiled Temple Priests, the sons of Zadok, who continued such ordination to the First Century to which these texts are dated then and before essentially. In other words, the proof of their fraud is well established now and really since 1947 or so especially. In order to also conceal or kryptein their illegal acts, they enter even deeper fraud which we offer our research on who lived in Qumran in the Introduction.

Even the 1611 King James Version propagates that false paradigm by setting aside these books as Apocrypha mixed with false books in a genre that never even existed in the time the Old Testament was determined which was long before Pharisees existed in Jerusalem as a party, nor the Catholic Church. That is a Pharisee term for books outside of their already altered Bible Canon and that is what the modern church calls the Bible for the Old Testament today generally. They could not wax more inept. This is a basic foundational principle that undermines the whole of scripture as they censored witnesses to the Bible that the Bible requires, per scripture, as where are the second witnesses especially of some of the most important doctrines of both the Old and New Testaments? Then, the same scoffers calling themselves scholars undermine, at times, in so-called textual criticism, exploiting the very gaps that this censorship of ignorance creates.

> *And when I was about sixteen years old [A.D. 53], I had a mind to make trial of the several sects that were among us. These sects are three: the first is that of the Pharisees; the second that Sadducees; and the third that of the Essens; as we have frequently told you. For I thought that by this means I might choose the best, if I were once acquainted with them all. So I contented myself with hard fare; and underwent great difficulties; and went through them all. Nor did I content my self with these trials only: but when I was informed that one whose name was Banus lived in the desert, and used no other clothing than grew upon trees; and had no other food than what grew of its own accord; and bathed himself in cold water frequently, both by night and by day, in order to preserve his chastity, I imitated him in those things; and continued with him three years [from A.D. 53 to A.D. 56]. (4) So when I had accomplished my desires, I returned back to the city: being now nineteen years old: and began to conduct my self according to the rules of the sect of the Pharisees: which is of kin to the sect of the Stoicks, as the Greeks call them.*
> *– The Life of Flavius Josephus, Flavius Josephus, 1:2 [11]*

Josephus admitted he was a Pharisee in adulthood *(yes, scholars, learn how to read as he said so in his own autobiography)*. He was a royal Hasmonean by blood *(The Life..., 1:1 [11])* which are the enemies of the Temple who conquered it in 165 B.C. The Dead Sea Scrolls have a massive number of rebukes of their factions *(see "Who Were the Pharisees and Hasmoneans According to the Dead Sea Scrolls" chart)*. He was also an Essene in his youth and never mentions them living in Bethabara, nor does Pliny, nor archaeology. We are aware practically all modern Bible scholars do not know that as they read the Dead Sea Scrolls and then, ignore what they say. Those are experts of nothing but willing ignorance in this regard. For it was these very Pharisees and Hasmoneans who defiled the Temple, usurped the Priesthood and daily sacrifices as Daniel predicted in the transgression of desolation *(Dan. 8:13)*.

> *And every member of the House of Separation who went out of the Holy City and leaned on God at the time when **Israel sinned and defiled the Temple**...*
> *– The Damascus Document, Vermes, p. 137*

> *[For the violence done to Lebanon shall overwhelm you, and the **destruction of the beasts**] shall terrify you, because of the blood of men and the violence done to the land, the city, and all its inhabitants (ii, 17).*
> *Interpreted, this saying concerns the **Wicked Priest**, inasmuch as he shall be paid the reward which he himself tendered to the Poor. For Lebanon is the Council of the Community; and **the beasts are the simple of Judah who keep the Law**. As **he himself plotted the destruction of the Poor**, so 5 will **God condemn him to destruction**. And as for that which He said, Because of the blood of the city and the violence done to the land: interpreted, the city is **Jerusalem** where the **Wicked Priest committed abominable deeds and defiled the Temple of God**. The violence done to the land... – Commentary on Habakkuk, Vermes, p. 515*

The Greeks did not defile the Temple and that history never occurs in anything credible to confirm Maccabees' assertions which are proven to represent a fraudulent account, not history *(see Testing 1st & 2nd Maccabees, Vol. 2)*. Maccabees as well, was not found in Qumran but historical documents were that say the opposite and expose those books as lies *(Commentary on Nahum, Vermes, p. 505 [22]; According to Origen and Josephus, Whiston, [82])*.

The Pharisees were their priestly caste of the Hasmonean establishment whom they chose from criminals as they *"...made unto themselves of the lowest of them priests (2Ki. 17:32)."* This is why Rabbinic Judaism continues to refer to their god as Hashem, an etymological derivative of Ashima, the false god *(2Ki. 17:30)* of the Samaritan replacements of the Northern Tribes of Israel when they were taken captive to Assyria and never returned according to scripture *(2Ki. 17:32)*. This infusion in Samaria represents what was installed in Yahudaea by the Hasmoneans replacing the Biblical relationship with Yahuah. They mixed Yahuah's traditions with their occult religions and gods as they forced a Temple Priest to teach them *(2Ki. 17:28)*. They were placating the land that was rejecting them as they were being devoured by lions *(2Ki. 17:25)*.

Earlier in life, Josephus was trained as an Essene by Bannus in the wilderness in Ein Gedi, not Qumran, according to massive archaeological evidence in "The Essene Find," and the location Pliny the Elder pinpoints with incredible accuracy. However, Josephus defines three sects of Pharisaism here in this admission – Pharisees, Hasmoneans and Essenes from which he derives from all three. He includes the Sadducees as a faction he never joined as a fourth really but he was never one of them because the Pharisees were already marginalizing and even eliminating them by his era. He admits in his own autobiography that he was all three culminating in his becoming a Pharisee especially as a mature adult at age 19. He was a Pharisee period. How any scholar can ignore what Josephus says he was to claim he was not a Pharisee, requires witchcraft and represents a lie according to the man himself. Those scholars are dangerous as they prove illiterate placating doctrines of ignorance essentially teaching all of us how not to read. They are trying to replace the historic and Biblical record with their own. How dare they.

When Josephus, then, quotes a list of what is referred to as Bible Canon, he most certainly is not representing the true sons of Zadok who were exiled by these factions to Qumran/Bethabara. That area was where Yahusha launched His ministry and not the defiled Jerusalem Temple in His time. If they think that is the origin of their churches, they clearly are Pharisees no matter what they call themselves and they have a Pharisee Bible Canon as well. The Jewish Encyclopedia defines Pharisaism as morphing into Rabbinic Judaism in foundation after the Second Temple was destroyed. This has never been a mystery and how can the church lose track of their physical enemy called the *"synagogue of Satan, which say they are Jews (Yahudim: there is never a word Jew in the Hebrew, nor Greek, Bible), and are not, but do lie"* by Yahusha Himself in *Rev. 2:9* and *3:9*. Josephus was a liar according to Messiah as were all 3 of his sects *(Hasmoneans included)*.

According to Josephus, who would know as he was one of them, says he, Pharisees are kin to the philosopher sect according to the Greeks, the Stoics which the Bible is clear are the opposite of the Biblical ekklesia *(Acts 17)*. Why would anyone look to them to determine what the true Temple Priests curated as Bible Canon?

Acts 17:16-20 KJV
*Now while Paul waited for them at Athens, his spirit was stirred in him, when he saw the city **wholly given to idolatry**. Therefore **disputed he in the synagogue with the Jews**, and with the devout persons, and in the market daily with them that met with him. Then certain **philosophers of the Epicureans, and of the Stoicks**, encountered him. And some said, What will this babbler say? other some, He seemeth to be a setter forth of **strange gods**: because he preached unto them Jesus, and the*

*resurrection. And they took him, and brought him unto Areopagus, saying, May we know what this **new doctrine**, whereof thou speakest, is? For thou bringest certain **strange things to our ears:** we would know therefore what these things mean.*

These were and still remain the opposite of the Bible paradigm which continued with Messiah and the Prophets, never Pharisees as even a saved Pharisee would be forced to leave that party in time. Josephus defines himself as one of those enemies of scripture, according to scripture, and certainly never represents the Bible paradigm in regard to its books. Only the true exiled Temple Priests kept Bible Canon. The Sanhedrin even opposed Yahusha. Though they did not crucify Him by their own hands, it was Pharisees who captured Him, put Him on trial, found the sinless Son of Yahuah guilty, and when Rome refused to put Him to death, they demanded it even when given an alternative. That is the Pharisee, Talmudic way of trying to claim they were not responsible, yet scripture is clear they were complicit.

This is the reason we find occult philosophy in the Talmud and Rabbinic documents and even today as these were never the Biblical paradigm. They stood against it. They disputed and argued even with Yahusha and the Apostles. They called Yahusha a strange god and the doctrines of Paul, who represented the theology of Yahusha and the entire Bible, as strange things to their ears. Why are Bible scholars listening to Josephus on this topic when he proves to have no credibility and again, rattles off a list that vets an admission of guilt in changing the Bible? Most scholars do not see this at all and that is sad. That is the reason we have been publishing this Levite Bible Series. This is far too important especially in this age of increasing knowledge Daniel predicted *(Dan. 12:4)*.

"The Greek Fathers such as Origen and Clement, who used the Greek Bible, which included these books, frequently cite them as 'scripture', 'Divine scripture', ' inspired,' or the like. Later Greek Fathers x rejected in various ways this conception of the Canon, but it was accepted and maintained in the West by St. Augustine."
– R.H. Charles, 1913, p. 9. [81].

In addition, Josephus exposes himself when he, who was trained as an Essene in Ein Gedi having no association with the Bible's Temple Priests' community of Qumran/Bethabara but the occult, praises the Essenes for their being seers. Seers are not prophets of Yahuah but in their occult world, they are the very seers rebuked by scripture as sorcerers or magicians *(see specific examples in Introduction)*. Notice the New Age sounding emphasis on the soul or the third eye of the occult world. These are not Bible believers and they kept no scripture there as no library of scripture was found in or near Ein Gedi. Their holy books are not the Bible. They are their occult texts known by the Greeks, Babylonians, Assyrians, etc. They are Kabbalists who also believe in reincarnation which only a demon can do so.

"These are the divine doctrines of the Essens (6) about the soul, which lay an unavoidable bait for such as have once had a taste of their philosophy. There are also those among them who undertake to foretel things to come, by reading the holy books, and using several sorts of purifications, and being perpetually conversant in the discourses of the prophets; and it is but seldom that they miss in their predictions."
– Josephus, Of the War, Book II, 8.11b-12

Josephus continued to practice this sorcery or alchemy advancing his Essene training. For he foretold of the ascension of Vespasian to the throne as Roman Emperor and it did indeed occur *[Josephus, Of the War, Book III, 8.9]*. This is, then, confirmed, not by the bible or it's prophets, but by the occult Oracle of the God of Carmel. When was Mt. Carmel known to have the Temple and Yahuah's presence? Not in those days of the replacement Samaritans who practiced infused religions.

"When he consulted the oracle of the god of Carmel in Judaea, the lots were highly encouraging, promising that whatever he planned or wished however great it might be, would come to pass; and one of his high-born prisoners, Josephus by name, as he was being put in chains, declared most confidently that he would soon be released by the same man, who would then, however, be emperor."
– The Twelve Caesars, The Life of Vespasian, 5.6, p. 281. [110]

Carmel was a Samaritan stronghold mountain whom the imposters claimed replaced the Temple in fraud. Their god was never Yahuah. They served Ba'al *(Molech)* and Ashima *(Hashem)* whom they brought from Assyria and Babylon and tried to infuse that with the worship of Yahuah *(2Ki. 17)*. Their reason for doing so was the land and it's lions were destroying them. However, that was not a Prophecy of Yahuah, it was that of an Essene seer in the occult. This led to Josephus' release and unprecedented adoption into the political household of the Flavian Dynasty. Pharisees were now in the family of Roman Emperors. This is very likely where Constantine the Great hailed from in bloodline from the family name change to Flavius Josephus. He was a Flavian but not the bloodline of the Flavian Dynasty somehow. Josephus is likely that key in bloodline as the adopted Flavian.

In this publishing, we wish to catalogue and test books that are identified in a very impertinent way as "apocrypha" according to the 1611 Authorized King James Version which pattern was truly established by the same Pharisees in Josephus' era. We will determine which of these was and still is Bible Canon and which should not be. We will use the Qumran Scrolls as a framework as well as establish historicity continued from there to the Early Church. This will include a Torah Test where some of these books are quoted in the New Testament even by Messiah. This is not to be confused with the other uneducated, propaganda term Pseudepigrapha which is a label of scoffers who can't read in this same vein. May Yahuah give you wisdom in restoring His Word in your life. He gave it to us for a reason. Yah Bless.

INTRODUCTION: Who Lived in Qumran?

In 1947, the voice in the wilderness cried out yet again. Did you hear it? The entire modern Old Testament canon was found in Qumran with the exception of the Book of Esther in what is inappropriately labeled and expanded in scope as the Dead Sea Scrolls as the find was specific to the Qumran area and truly remains so. This included other books as well. For many of these books, these are the oldest copies found and some were complete such as the 24-foot long Isaiah Scroll. After over 70 years, we still know little about this community yet the archaeology, writings of the community and the large compound found there confirm these were the Aaronic Levite Priests, the sons of Zadok, who had been exiled to the Wilderness of Yahudaea by the Hasmoneans and Pharisees. They were the Temple High Priests replaced by a new unbiblical order.

However, today, the world allows the Pharisees who defiled the Temple to teach us about this community. No wonder we know so little about them or at least we are taught so. This was the base of operations for John the Baptist and his disciples, including Andrew, where he baptized Yahusha and was visited by Him later privately. It is among the most well-documented New Testament communities on record and the church does not even know because it is too busy defending a control narrative that the other books found with the Old Testament are somehow cursed when Yahusha, John and the sons of Zadok set this library as a time capsule to preserve His Word.

Note: This "Who Lived In Qumran?" section is a repeat of our previous books. The rest of the book is new.

Photo: Stone Sundial from Qumran site. The Qumran community were the keepers of the Biblical calendar based on the sun and the canon of scripture according to the decrees from Yacob and Moses.

Several other books were found among these scrolls which must be considered and tested. This includes several books erroneously classified as "Apocrypha" in ignorance. Clearly important among that community of Levite priests, this tells us much as the Temple Levites were the keepers of scripture. Yacob entrusted Levi with this role in Jubilees 45:16 and Moses authorized these same Aaronic Levites in Deuteronomy 31:24-26 to do the same. If one truly wanted to know what books were and were not included in the Bible canon at the time of Messiah, they need not look far as this preserved the Old Testament canon of scripture up until His time. There were no books yet, just scroll libraries like the one found in Qumran.

Some attempt to force the books in the Septuagint that can be a useful publishing indeed in comparison but never as a standalone text as inerrant scripture. In fact, it too was a scroll library created in Egypt and the Aaronic Levites were not in Egypt at that time. They were in the Temple where they should be soon to be driven out into the Wilderness of Yahudaea. They would take their Bible, scroll library in that time, with them. This was rediscovered in 1947 and immediately the Catholic Church and Pharisees moved to redefine the Bible that was found to protect the fraud they perpetrated in those days and since. The sect that created the Septuagint Greek translation in Egypt were not Aaronic Levite priests. These were Essenes in their attempt to hijack scripture which they would later write what they would call scripture in the Gnostic Gospels also found in Egypt. Not one Gnostic Gospel was found in Qumran nor do they coalesce with the New nor Old Testaments.

Essene is a name not found in the Bible even in the Greek Septuagint version demonstrating that cult has nothing to do with the Bible. The Qumran community never uses it nor anything similar. It is derived from the writings of Pliny, Josephus and others as ESSENOI, or ESSAIOI. As this is not a Bible word, we must go to an occult source to learn this originates in Egypt. In 2007, the Rosicrucian Digest weighs in on this.

Origins of the Word "Essene"
The word truly comes from the Egyptian word kashai, which means "secret." And there is a Jewish word of similar sound, chsahi, meaning "secret" or "silent"; and this word would naturally be translated into essaios or "Essene," denoting "secret" or "mystic." Even Josephus found that the Egyptian symbols of light and truth are represented by the word choshen, which transliterates into the Greek as essen. Historical references have been found also wherein the priests of the ancient temples of Ephesus bore the name of Essene. A branch of the organization established by the Greeks translated the word Essene as being derived from the Syrian word asaya, meaning "physician," into the Greek word therapeutes, having the same meaning. [9]

Again, this is an occult source and they take credit for the Essenes as a secret cult of sorcerers. To them, that is a good thing where those of us believers know better. However, what they do not connect is the "chsahi" *(kashaph: רשכ: H3784)* were the sorcerers and magicians in which Moses and Aaron faced in Egypt*(Ex. 7:11)*. Some of them exited Egypt in the Exodus and settled in Ein Gedi in ancient times and not Qumran. Pliny notes they are a very ancient cult. This same sorcery and witchcraft is recorded in Canaan*(Dt. 18:10)*, in Israel*(2 Chr. 33:6)* and even in Babylon*(Dan. 2:2)*. It is the enemy of the Bible.

Some even further connect this Aramaic word "asaya" as the origin of the word Hasmonean. These are the conquerors of the Temple in 165 B.C. who exiled the Levite Temple priest system who are rebuked by their Qumran community as the "sons of darkness." What a world in which we live. This word is the origin of the Hasidim or Hasidic Jews of today. They are Essenes. The breakdown of the factions still exists as Rabbinic Judaism generally are Pharisees essentially with a sect of Hasidim, Essenes. Sure, they call themselves pious but they do not even remotely know the relationship of Torah. This is why we find them referring to their god as Hashem. This name is a variant of Ashima, the god of the Samaritans from whom they originate. Who would replace the name of Yahuah 6,800+ times with Lord or Ba'al in Hebrew? These Samaritans would. Any attempt to associate them with Messiah and John the Baptist is ridiculous. We were warned in the end times evil would be called good and good, evil.

One of the main reasons employed by many is this assumption that Essenes lived in Qumran which they never did. Attempts are even exercised claiming Yahusha and John believed in resurrection and somehow that is supposed to be equated to the reincarnation doctrine of the Essenes which is among the most illiterate of positions. The two doctrines are opposites as are the Essenes from the Qumran community. In fact, human spirits cannot reincarnate. The only spirits who do are demons or spirits of Nephilim when they die. They wander the dry places and when invited, they can enter a human and possess it or even an animal as Messiah cast demons into swine *(Matt. 8:28-34; Mark 5:1-20; Luke 8:26-39)*. Reincarnation is literally a doctrine of demons as only they reincarnate possessing the body of another.

Essenes originated from Egypt, though perhaps truly Mesopotamian origins ultimately, thus the Aramaic, where they were known as physicians or alchemists of sort. There, they were called the Therapeutae in Greek. In Biblical terms they were sorcerers such as the false prophet identified as from Yahudaea, Barjesus, an Essene*(Acts 13:6)*, the "child of the devil" according to Paul, Elymus*(Acts 13:8)* and the bewitching Simon the sorcerer*(Acts 8:9)*. In Greek, Paul calls this pharmakeía*(φαρμακεία: G5331)* meaning medication *("pharmacy"),* i.e. *(by extension)* magic *(literally or figuratively):*–sorcery, witchcraft."

Revelation tells us this is the end times deception in fact playing out as *"by thy sorceries were all nations deceived"(Rev. 18:23)*. This same sorcery is exactly what has happened with this entire narrative. Only a fool would claim Essenes lived in Qumran with no evidence, writings identifying themselves as Levites and incredibly significant Essene finds 25 miles South in Ein Gedi matching Pliny's directions to their headquarters. No scholar could logically draw such conclusion yet the mantra is vast. This false story permeates Judaism*(Pharisaism according to the Jewish Encyclopedia)* and those who manage the Rockefeller-funded museum doling out the idiotic control line. The church has bought this especially in seminaries. It is a lie.

The other list of Bible canon immediately thrown out there is that of Josephus who propagated a closed canon according to him of course. Josephus was an admitted Pharisee, Hasmonean and he was Essene trained by Banus in the wilderness*(Ein Gedi) [11: The Life of Flavius Josephus]*. Realize his "closed canon" which some Christians actually cite would mean the entire New Testament is not scripture and was already rebuked as ignoring part of the law or Torah according to Messiah*(Jn. 5:46-47)* and what they did use, they turned against scripture according to Him*(Mark 7:9)*. That is an oxymoron many do not even think through. His listing of what the Pharisees considered scripture educate us all on the paradigm at the time of Messiah and shortly after when the New Testament was just written as it already censored scripture especially.

However, whom did Yacob and Moses entrust with the keeping of scripture, Torah and what we would call Bible? The Temple Levite Priests of Aaron and Josephus was not nor were the Rabbis/Pharisees or Hasidim/Essenes. We have now found this scroll library which is the only which qualifies as the Bible canon for the entire history up until the time the Temple was destroyed. The question is, whom was ever given authority to overrule these Levites? Who was given their responsibility to keep scripture? Who was given authority to overturn Messiah's endorsement of this canon as well? Certainly not Pharisees who already threw out the Book of Jubilees in the days of Messiah. Most certainly not the cowardly general, Josephus, who ordered all of his troops to commit suicide while he failed to do so himself. Josephus is useful for history and geography to a point. However, he was no authority on scripture and his list is a spouting of Pharisee doctrine rebuked by Messiah many times. Only the Levite library records canon. Any Catholic counsel changing that was usurping Biblical authority it never had.

This community left history and scripture behind so that we would all know just what was and was not considered canon. They even include commentaries on different books, additional prophecy especially of the war of the "sons of darkness" versus the "sons of light," hymns, calendars, etc. The Hasmoneans*(Essenes)* and their priests*(Pharisees and Sadducees)* who exiled the true Aaronic Priests from the Temple are called the "sons of darkness" as they conquered the Temple and Yahudaea in 165 B.C. This battle will last until the very end times in their writings. The Temple was the center of worship in Jerusalem. Though the Second Temple no longer housed the ark of the covenant with Yahuah's presence, it still received His blessing until that time. Priestly courses continued such as that of Zacharias, father of John the Baptist, in the course of Abiyah*(Abia)* but the leadership in the Temple, in all of Yahudaea and essentially the world in a spiritual sense had been usurped by these "sons of darkness." This was a fulfillment of the Psalm 83 war in which David predicted the Temple, not even built at the time of his prophecy, would be defiled by neighboring enemies in this exact sense.

For the Hasmoneans did not attack just the Greeks nor did they originate in Yahudaea. They inhabited an area called Modi'in which is across the border into Dan controlled by Samaria and the Philistines. They were not Hebrews, nor Israelites. They were Samaritans who were the replacements of the Northern Tribes of Israel when they were taken captive into Assyria since around 700 B.C. This is why even in Messiah's parable of the Good Samaritan*(Lk. 10:25-37)*, what was unthinkable in the paradigm of that day, was that a Samaritan could be good. These replacements

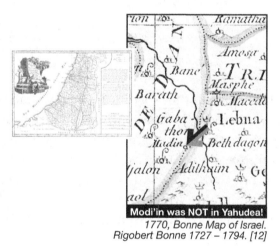

Modi'in was NOT in Yahudea!
1770, Bonne Map of Israel.
Rigobert Bonne 1727 – 1794. [12]

were brought into the Northern Kingdom of Samaria and kept the name. They, then, attempted to infuse the worship of Yahuah into pagan religions of their gods Ashima*(Hashem)*, Adrammelech *(Melech/Molech/Ba'al)* and others. However, this was never a sincere gesture. It was a response to the land that had been rejecting them as they were being attacked by lions. They brought in a Levite Priest to teach them the rituals of the Bible. Yahuah rejected this infusion and always will *(2 Ki. 17)*.

The Pharisees and Sadducees did not exist in Jerusalem until the so-called Hasmonean Revolt in 165 B.C. You will find the Books of Maccabees as well as Esther were not found among the Qumran scrolls because neither are scripture and we will test them *(Vol. 2)*. Both are the stories of what would become Zionism today. This was predicted not only by David but identified in Daniel and Revelation as Messiah discusses the Synagogue of Satan who say they are Yahudim and are not but do lie*(Rev. 2:9, 3:9)*. Even the term Jew is fraud and it never should be used in scripture as it is not of Ancient Hebrew,

Aramaic, Greek, Latin, Old French, Old German nor Old English origin. The name of Yahuah's people includes His own and such tribes would never remove His name from theirs. His people in the Old and New Testament are the Yahudim in Hebrew and Greek really. The shortened form of this word is Yah's, never Jews, as there was no "J" in any of the languages in which the Bible has been interpreted through. The first two letters are YH(יה) and that is Yah, not Jew, or Yah's, not Jews, in short. This fraud wraps into the rest of this false narrative coming from the modern Pharisees and the Catholic Church who changed scripture and attempt to cover it up.

Many do not realize that Qumran is identified in the Bible. However, Qumran is it's Muslim name oddly continued by Pharisees and modern Israel. Why would they do so when the Bible identifies this area by the name as Bethabara*(Greek)* or Betharabah*(Hebrew)*. Joshua*(Yahushua)* identifies the Western coastline of the Dead Sea geographically when he outlines a list in North to South progression of the cities of the Dead Sea wilderness.

> *Joshua 15:61-62 KJV: In the wilderness, **Betharabah**, Middin, and Secacah, And Nibshan, and the city of Salt, and Engedi; six cities with their villages.*

He begins in the North with Betharabah on the Northwestern tip. That is called Qumran today. Joshua continues as he heads South to Middin which is due South of Qumran, then, further South all the way to Ein Gedi. He defined a 25-mile distance from North to South. Notice there are several cities between Betharabah*(Qumran)* and Ein Gedi so even if somehow Pliny meant just North instead of just above in the mountains, which is obvious, he still would not be identifying Qumran as the headquarters of the Essenes. Of course, Ein Gedi has the archaeology called "The Essene Find."

The Madaba Mosaic Map*(below)*, c. 6th century A.D., contains the oldest surviving original map of especially the Dead Sea and right on the intersection where the Jordon meets the Dead Sea, is labeled in Greek as Βηθαβαρά, Bethabara. This is right where Joshua placed it and it is modern Qumran, a new name continued in fraud.

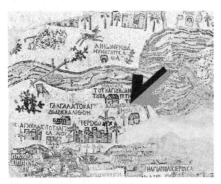

Above: Jordan. Madaba (biblical Medeba) - St. George's Church. Fragment of the oldest floor mosaic map of the Holy Land - the Jordan River and the Dead Sea. [13]

The reason this is important as well is John the Baptist baptized Messiah at Bethabara. This was not some random journey into the wilderness but a visit to the very compound and library designed similar to the Temple where scripture was now kept outside of the Temple. Messiah Himself visited it more than once. Yahusha grew up and initially operated in Galilee*(Mt. 2:22)*. He came from there, and headed South to beyond Jordan. The Jordan is not simply the Jordan River in scripture but the entire Jordan Plain or Jordan Valley *(Gn. 13:10)*. This does not indicate crossing the river but into the Wilderness of Yahudaea at Qumran right on the border.

Luke 3:2-4 KJV: *...the word of God came unto John the son of Zacharias in the wilderness. And he came into **all the country about Jordan**, preaching the baptism of repentance for the remission of sins; As it is written in the book of the words of Esaias the prophet, saying, The **voice of one crying in the wilderness**, Prepare ye the way of the Lord, make his paths straight.*

Matthew 3 KJV: *1: In those days **came John the Baptist**, preaching **in the wilderness of Judaea**...*
*5-6: Then **went out to him Jerusalem**, and all Judaea, and all the region round about Jordan, And were **baptized of him in Jordan**, confessing their sins.*

The Wilderness of Yahudea *(Chambers Map, right)* is very specifically the area along the West coast of the Dead Sea. It is not, nor ever has, referred to the Jordan Plain or Valley, nor River other than before there was a Dead Sea perhaps which was likely created by the destruction of Sodom. This has been known all along even on many maps until the 20th century which physically document it's position *[right]*.

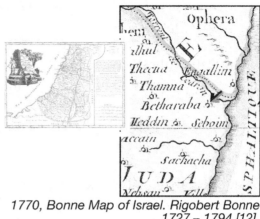

1770, Bonne Map of Israel. Rigobert Bonne 1727 – 1794 [12].

1836, Tanner Map of Palestine, Israel, Holy Land. [14]

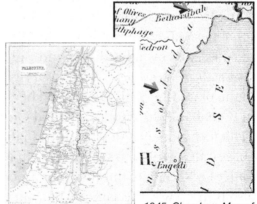

1845, Chambers Map of Palestine, Israel, Holy Land. [16]

Inset of 1852, Philip Map of Palestine, Israel, Holy Land. [17]

Matthew 3:13 KJV: Then cometh Jesus from Galilee to Jordan unto John, to be baptized of him.

Where did Yahusha come from? Galilee. He travels South to Jordan. Where in Jordan? This verse is not specific but the Bible is.

John 1:28 KJV: These things were done in Bethabara beyond Jordan, where John was baptizing.

Now, we have details rather than a general area. Yahusha came from Galilee heading South. He enters the Jordan Valley region and he travels "beyond" the Jordan Valley to a place called Bethabara. Where is this? The Jordan ends to the South at the Dead Sea and on the Northwest corner of the Dead Sea is Bethabara in the Wilderness of Yahudaea where John operated and baptized Messiah. It does not say he crossed the Jordan changing directions to go to the East. It says he travels South beyond Jordan to Bethabara. This is very clear and maps agree. This is Qumran.

The word beyond in Greek here is peran *(πέραν)* meaning "other side, beyond, over, farther side." This is where many scholars go wrong by forgetting the orientation of the region from Galilee South which does not enter the East side of the Jordan which is still the Jordan Valley. It progresses beyond the Jordan Valley to the Wilderness of Yahudaea where John is said to be based. There is a reason.

John was an Aaronic bloodline Levite Priest qualified to be of High Priestly caste. He was not some hermit living under a tree eating locusts and honey. John ties directly to this community in written prophesies, their shared purpose, and even his diet found right there in Qumran documents *(see chart "John the Baptist in Qumran?")*. He was a righteous Aaronic Levite Priest operating in the place where his people had been exiled in the Wilderness of Yahudaea in Bethabara which today is called Qumran.

This forerunner to Messiah, the Elijah come again, wore camel's hair clothing *(Mt. 3:4, Mk. 1:6)* akin to sackcloth as in mourning. He was essentially living the oath of a Rechabite but he was not poor and he did not live under a tree. He also is in no way the same as Banaah from the Talmud though attempts are made as Banaah lived 2-3 centuries later. John the Baptist was no Essene, nor Pharisee, nor was anyone in the Qumran community. John baptized mostly in fresh springs in clean water not the muddy waters of the Jordan River that few would desire to participate. Bethabara *(Qumran)* had fresh water. There is no disputing Qumran is Bethabara where Messiah was baptized and John and the Levite sons of Zadok operated. This was the new location of the Temple practice where scripture was kept, thus Bible Canon.

THE ESSENES OF EIN GEDI

"On the west side of the Dead Sea, but out of range of the noxious exhalations of the coast, is the solitary tribe of the Essenes..."
"Lying below the Essenes was formerly the town of Engedi..." "Next comes Masada..." – Pliny the Elder, Natural History (Book V) [10]

Remnants of a Chalcolithic Temple (4th millennium BCE). [18]

Pliny, a geographer, indisputably located the Essenes in the mountains overlooking Ein Gedi, 25 miles South of Qumran. He even anchors it to Masada just to the South and that is the Southern tip, not near Qumran.

This is affirmed in mass scale archaeology called "The Essene Find" in Ein Gedi. This included a very ancient temple identified as a Chalcolithic Temple, c. 4th millennium B.C., which was not built by the Essenes but likely part of their compound in the mountains matching their religion.

Essene synagogue in Ein Gedi. [18]

Also, archaeologists discovered a synagogue with many symbols identifying these Essenes as the secret cult throughout history fitting to everything we know about the Essenes who never lived in Qumran.

Tile mosaic on synagogue floor in Ein Gedi. [18]

They were obsessed with peacocks as they worship the Peacock Angel *(Persian)* identified by many as the Nephilim deity known as Asmodeus. They etched swastika on the wall, very prominently display an 8-pointed star of Ishtar on the floor in tile, etc. They even offer what appears a very freemasonic warning on the wall.

There is no actual coherent data placing Essenes in Qumran and shame on any "scholar" saying so.

Peacock symbols in Ein Gedi synagogue. [18]

TEMPLE PRIEST ASSOCIATIONS IN THE DEAD SEA SCROLLS

The Biblical keepers of scripture and the Temple marginalized, mischaracterized, and hidden in fraud!

SONS OF ZADOK = 20 TIMES

From the days of King Solomon, these are the Temple Priests. They are Levites and sons of Aaron both. However, they were given charge of the Temple worship and are the only Biblical keepers of scripture to the First Century. They never call themselves Essenes but they identify themselves over 100 times and any scholar confusing the two is no scholar. They remained holy according to Ezekiel:

Ezekiel 48:11 KJV
It shall be for the priests that are sanctified of the sons of Zadok; which have kept my charge, which went not astray when the children of Israel went astray, as the Levites went astray.

They remained faithful when exiled from the Temple to Qumran and they will stand again in the End Times.

"The sons of Zadok are the elect of Israel, the men called by name who shall stand at the end of days."
–The Damascus Document, p. 132 [22]

Scripture was found in their library meaning this was Bible canon kept by the Sons of Zadok as was Biblical tradition. Essenes are never mentioned in scripture and never a Biblical tribe, nor found in or near Qumran. That is blatant fraud!

Moses in Deuteronomy 31:25-26 KJV (Cf. Jubilees 45:16)
That Moses commanded the Levites, which bare the ark of the covenant of the LORD, saying, Take this book of the law, and put it in the side of the ark of the covenant of the LORD your God, that it may be there for a witness against thee.

SONS OF AARON = 16 TIMES
LEVITES = 71 TIMES
SONS OF LEVI = 5 TIMES
SONS OF LIGHT = 27 TIMES
TEACHER OF RIGHTEOUSNESS = 53 TIMES

"...this concerns the Wicked Priest who pursued the Teacher of Righteousness to the house of his exile..." –COMMENTARY ON HABAKKUK, p. 515 [22]

"...the city is Jerusalem where the Wicked Priest committed abominable deeds and defiled the Temple of Elohim. The violence done to the land..." –COMMENTARY ON HABAKKUK, p. 515 [22]

"Words of blessing. The M[aster shall bless] the sons of Zadok the Priests, whom Elohim has chosen to confirm His Covenant for [ever]" – The Blessing of the High Priest, p.388 [22]

"When Elohim engenders (the Priest-) Messiah, he shall come with them [at] the head of the whole congregation of Israel with all [his brethren, the sons] of Aaron the Priests" – The Messianic Rule, p.161 [22]

*From a search of "The Complete Dead Sea Scrolls in English" by Geza Vermes [22]. Some are his mentions in commentary but that further affirms he knew who these were and still ignorantly concluded in fraud that these were Essenes with 0 mentions, 0 archaeology and Pliny indisputably placing them in Ein Gedi confirmed in archaeology.

ESSENES MENTIONED = 0

When groups of scholars make themselves so stupid as to say this group were Essenes, you know they are only offering propaganda.

WHO DEFILED THE SECOND TEMPLE?

The Books of Maccabees, not found in the Dead Sea Scrolls make the claim Greece defiled the Temple. That is a lie!

GREECE DID NOT DEFILE THE TEMPLE

From the account of the Temple Priests which appears within their commentaries of prophetic interpretation of events that had already occurred in their time, they record that Greece did not defile the Temple nor even attack Yahudaea with their military. This is consistent with Greek history that does not mention this Maccabees account which is not history, nor Bible. This is a major problem for modern Judaism which has only this claim to link it to their being Hebrews. They are not.

"Whither the lion goes, there is the lion's cub, [with none to disturb it] (ii, 11b).
[Interpreted, this concerns Deme]trius king of Greece who sought, on the counsel of those who seek smooth things, to enter Jerusalem. [But Elohim did not permit the city to be delivered] into the hands of the kings of Greece, from the time of Antiochus until the coming of the rulers of the Kittim. But then she shall be trampled under their feet..."
–COMMENTARY ON NAHUM, p. 505 [22]

Thus, from the time of Demetrius to the time of Antiochus I including the time of Antiochus Epiphanes and until the time of the Kittim takeover which is the Roman Empire, Yahudaea was not subdued with Greece's military. Even Alexander the Great was welcomed in a peaceful takeover not military conquest especially in the Temple where he even burnt the sacrifice of the Temple. Greece wanted the tax revenues and Israel agreed to that in all accounts, even Josephus, Tacitus, Origen and others agree on that. However, who trampled Yahudaea? Who defiled the Temple? This community did not keep that a secret...

"[For the violence done to Lebanon shall overwhelm you, and the destruction of the beasts] X II shall terrify you, because of the blood of men and the violence done to the land, the city, and all its inhabitants (ii, 17). Interpreted, this saying concerns the Wicked Priest, inasmuch as he shall be paid the reward which he himself tendered to the Poor. For Lebanon is the Council of the Community; and the beasts are the simple of Judah who keep the Law. As he himself plotted the destruction of the Poor, so will Elohim condemn him to destruction. And as for that which He said, Because of the blood of the city and the violence done to the land: interpreted, the city is Jerusalem where the Wicked Priest committed abominable deeds and defiled the Temple of Elohim. The violence done to the land: these are the cities of Judah where he robbed the Poor of their possessions." –COMMENTARY ON HABAKKUK, p. 515 [22]

The Wicked Priest is not one man but the Hasmoneans including their priests, the Pharisees and new Sanhedrin that were new to Jerusalem and neither faction ever mentioned in the entire Old Testament as they did not exist in Jerusalem until installed by the Hasmoneans around 165 B.C. These exiled the Aaronic, Levite Temple Priest leadership of antiquity to Qumran replacing them with a new unbiblical order in Jerusalem. That is the defiling of the Temple, not Greece. They conquered as they maintained control of it and changed the religion to their Samaritan infusion of Persian basis with attempted worship of YHWH that He rejected then and rejects now. This is clear, indisputable and actual history from the First Century ignored and untold by the church generally as they maintain willing ignorance as 2 Peter 3 warned. Who do they listen to? The very ones who defiled the Temple.

*Excerpts from "The Complete Dead Sea Scrolls in English" by Geza Vermes [22]. One will notice multiple injections from Vermes, and many scholars since, of the Maccabees' story as fact when these very writings of this community condemn the Hasmonean Revolt as the defiling of the Temple. That is dishonest and fraudulent!

THE MACCABEES DID!

THE HANUKKAH HOAX

The Feast of Dedication of modern Judaism also originates in the Books of Maccabees, yet Greece did not defile the Temple. However, worse, the Bible gives dates for the Dedication of the First and Second Temples and neither are near December.

FIRST TEMPLE FEAST OF DEDICATION:

Feast of Tabernacles. 7th Hebrew Month (Ethanim)
Modern Calendar: Between Sept. 15 - Oct. 15
1 Kings 8:63, 8:2; 2 Chronicles 5:3

SECOND TEMPLE FEAST OF DEDICATION:

Adar 3 or 23. 12th Hebrew Month (Not December)
Modern Calendar: Between Feb. 15 - Mar. 15
Ezra 6:15-17, 1st Esdras 7:5-8 (Note: March 15 is still Winter)

The Second Temple stood until 70 A.D. Therefore, it's Feast of Dedication remained Late February to Early March *(Winter)*. The history used to redefine this as a rededication proves to be fraud according to the Qumran community *(previous page)*. What the Maccabees did was celebrate their pagan, Persian Winter Solstice Festival and they called it Hanukkah which is the Hebrew word for dedication. However, they defiled the Temple on that date. It is a rather disgusting display in fraud. Some attempt to claim Messiah was celebrating the Hasmonean Hanukkah but that as well is a lie. He was there in the 12th Hebrew Month *(Feb 15-Mar. 15)*.

EXPOSED IN 1ST ESDRAS!

Matthew 15:12-14 KJV
Then came his disciples, and said unto him, Knowest thou that the Pharisees were offended, after they heard this saying? But he answered and said, Every plant, which my heavenly Father hath not planted, shall be rooted up. Let them alone: they be blind leaders of the blind. And if the blind lead the blind, both shall fall into the ditch.

MODERN HANUKKAH IS THAT DITCH!

Messiah Was In The Temple In Adar *(between Feb. 15-Mar. 15)* NOT December!

John 10:22 KJV
*And it was at Jerusalem **the feast of dedication**, and it was **winter**. And Yahusha walked in the Temple in Solomon's porch.*

This is consistent with the Second Temple Feast of Dedication in the Winter in Late February to Mid-March. Messiah did NOT celebrate the Hasmonean Hanukkah nor does He ever embrace their story on any level. He rebukes their priests, their religion and even their lineage. It is time we correct this for good.

PHARISEE FRUITS

These Fruits Match Satan's from John 10:10 not Yahusha's

"Vipers"	"Hypocrites"	"Expand the Word with Leaven"
Matt. 3:7, 12:34, 23:33 Luke 3:7	Matt. 6:2, 6:5, 15:7, 16:3, 22:18, 23:13, 14, 15, 23, 25, 27, 28, 29, 24:51 Mark 7:6 Luke 11:44, 12:56	Matt. 15:6, 16:6, 11 Mark 7:13, 8:15 Luke 12:1
"Lead People to Hell"	"Operate Against His Commandments"	"Blind" "Vain"
Matt. 23:13, 23:15, 24:51 Luke 11:52	Matt. 15:3-6, 23:4, 23 Mark 7:5-13 Rom. 2:17-20	Matt. 15:12-14, 23:16-17, 23-26 Mark 7:7 John 9:39-41 Rom. 1:21, 2:17-20
"Condemned to Hell Generally"	"Unclean" "Self-Righteous"	"Murderers"
Matt. 5:20, 23:13-15, 24:51	Matt. 6:5, 23:5, 15, 23-27, 28 Luke 7:29-30, 36-50, 18:9-14 John 8:39-59, 12:42	Matt. 12:14, 21:45-46, 23:31, 26:4 Luke 6:11, 11:47 John 8:44, 11:45-57 Acts 3:14-15, 7:52

"Pharisaism shaped the character of Judaism and the life and thought of the Jew for all the future."

—Jewish Encyclopedia [60]

ACCORDING TO THE BIBLE

Why Ignore What the Bible Says to Support a False Paradigm?

"Seed/ Synagogue of Satan"	"Devour Widow's Houses/Poor"	"Pray/Give to Be Seen" "Haughty"
John 8:44 Rev. 2:9, 3:9	Matt. 23:14 Mark 12:40 Luke 7:36-50, 20:47, 21:1-6	Matt. 6:2, 5, 16, 23:5-6, 14, 17-22 Mark 12:40 Luke 11:43,16:14, 20:45-47
"Don't Know Prophecy" "Seek Signs"	**"Don't Know Scripture"**	**"Thieves" "Extort"**
Matt. 12:14-37, 16:1-4, 27:40-43 Mark 8:11-12 Luke 7:29-30, 11:29-32 John 5:18, 10:24-39	Matt. 16:6-12, 21:23-27, 22:34-46, 23:23-24 , 26:62-68 Mark 3:6; Acts 1:6 Luke 7:29-30, 22:2 17:20-21 John 5:18, 10:24-39	Matt. 21:13, 23:25 Mark 11:17 Luke 19:46
"Stand in the Way of Knowledge"	**"Accusers and Liars"**	**"Fools"**
Matt. 23:34-35 Luke 11:52, 22:2 John 12:42	Matt. 12:1-2, 13-17, 22-24, 22:15-22, Mark 3:22 Luke 6:7, 7:39, 11:53, 19:39, 20:20-26 John 8:13; Rev. 2:9	Matt. 23:17, 19 Luke 11:40, 24:25 Rom. 1:22, 2:17-20

Pharisaism Became Rabbinic Judaism After 70 A.D. Pharisees Are Modern Rabbis, Modern Jews.

WHO WERE THE PHARISEES AND HASMONEANS?

*Page Number in Paranthesis.

"Sons of Darkness" "Men of the Pit"	"Sons of Belial/ Satan" "Lot of Belial"	"Wicked Priests"
War Scroll, (165-182) Dam. Doc. (134, 144) 4Q548 (573) Comm. Rule (111) 4Q258 (121) Hymn 9 (265)	4Q286 (394), 4Q386 (613) Dam. Doc. (133) Temple Scroll (212) War Scroll (176) Comm. Rule (99) Hymn 7 (263)	4Q394-9 (221) 4Q448 (340) iQpHab (509-515) 4QpPsa (519)
"Defilers of the Temple"	"Theives" "Rob the Poor" "Prey on Widows"	"Unclean"
iQpHab (513, 515) Dam. Doc. (133, 137, 148) 4Q174 (525) Temple Scroll (212)	iQpHab (509-515) Dam. Doc. (134) 4Q163 (499) Hymn 13 (273) Comm. Rule (113)	iQpHab (513) 4Q174 (525) Dam. Doc. (133-134) 4Q286 (394)
"Vain"	"Strangers" "Men of Perdition"	"Flouters of the Law" (Disregard, Despise)
iQpHab (514) Dam. Doc. (134) 4Q174 (526) Comm. Rule (103, 119) War Scroll (171, 176) Hymn 14 (276)	4Q174 (525) 4Q501 (328) Comm. Rule (113) 4Q171 (522)	iQpHab (509-512) Dam. Doc. (133) 4Q163 (499) 4Q174 (525) 11Q13 (533)

"Pharisaism shaped the character of Judaism and the life and thought of the Jew for all the future."
—*Jewish Encyclopedia [60]*

ACCORDING TO THE DEAD SEA SCROLLS

From "The Complete Dead Sea Scrolls in English. Revised Edition" By Geza Vermes. [22]

"Liars" "Spouter of Lies"	"Those Who Seek Smooth Things"	"Scoffers"
4QpPsa (37)	Dam. Doc. (129-130)	Dam. Doc. (129, 137)
iQpHab (510-515)	Thanksgiving Hymns	iQH, 1Q36, 4Q427-32
Dam. Doc. (137)	(262-269)	Hymn 6 (262)
4Q 171 (519, 522)	4Q163, (499)	4Q162 (499)
4Q501 (328)	4Q169, (505-7)	
Hymn 14 (278)	4Q177, (536)	

"Abomination" "House of Guilt"	"Enemies"	"Oppressive" "Overbearing"
iQpHab (511, 513)	iQpHab (514-515)	iQpHab (509-514)
Dam. Doc. (133)	Dam. Doc. (133)	4Q448 (341)
4Q175 (528)	4Q174 (525)	4Q508 (383)
Temple Scroll (212)	War Scroll	4Q504 (378)
4Q387 (603)	(176-177, 184)	4Q 171 (522)
4Q389 (604)	Temple Scroll (215-217)	

"Unfaithful" "Rebellious"	"Vipers, Spiders, Serpents, Dragons"	"Men of Violence" "Instruments of Violence"
iQpHab (509-510, 513)	Dam. Doc. (133)	Hymn 14 (276, 278)
Dam. Doc. (133)	Hymn 14 (275)	Hymn 7 (263)
4Q306 (243), 11Q13 (533)	Hymn 13 (273)	4Q 171 (520-522)
Hymn 14 (278)		Comm. Rule (113)
4Q332 (405)		iQpHab (509-515)
Comm. Rule (99)		4Q175 (528), 4Q379 (585)

Pharisaism Became Rabbinic Judaism After 70 A.D. Pharisees Are Modern Rabbis, Modern Jews

JOHN THE BAPTIST IN QUMRAN?

He Likely Grew Up There (Luke 1:80)

"You may eat [the following] flying [insects]: every kind of great locust, every kind of long-headed locust, every kind of green locust, and every kind of desert locust." (Yes, the insect!)
—The Temple Scroll, P. 207 [22]

JOHN'S RARE DIET FOUND THERE

"And as for locusts, according to their various kinds they shall plunge them alive into fire or water, for this is what their nature requires."
—The Damascus Document, P. 143 [22]

PROPHECY OF JOHN BLESSING MESSIAH

The Blessing of the Prince of the Congregation (100 B.C.) [22]

"The **Master (John the Baptist) shall bless the Prince of the Congregation (Yahusha)** . . . and shall **renew for him the Covenant of the Community** that he may establish the **kingdom of His people for ever**, [that he may **judge the poor** with righteousness and] **dispense justice** with {equity to the oppressed} of the land, and that he may walk perfectly before Him in all the ways [of truth], and that **he may establish His holy Covenant** at the time of the affliction of those who seek Elohim. May the Lord raise you up to everlasting heights, and as a fortified tower upon a high wall! [May you **smite the peoples**] with the might of your hand and ravage the earth with **your sceptre**; may you **bring death to the ungodly with the breath of your lips**! ...The **rulers ... [and all the kings of the] nations shall serve you**. He shall strengthen you with **His holy Name** and you shall be **as a [lion**; and you shall not lie down until you have devoured the] prey which naught shall deliver"
—Calendars, Liturgies and Prayers, p. 389-390.

PREPARE THE WAY IN THE WILDERNESS...

Zacharias' prophecy at John's birth: Luke 1:79

"To Give Light..."

Qumran Identification:

"Sons of Light"
[22]

John baptized Yahusha in Qumran/Bethabara fulfilling these 2 Qumran prophesies and Isaiah. These exiled Temple Priests knew their community would play such a role. This is the link between the Old and New Testaments.

And when these become members of the Community in Israel according to all these rules, they shall separate from the habitation of unjust men and shall go into the wilderness to prepare there the way of Him; as it is written, Prepare in the wilderness the way of..., make straight in the desert a path for our God (Isa. xl, 3). This (path) is the study of the Law which He commanded by the hand of Moses, that they may do according to all that has been revealed from age to age, and as the Prophets have revealed by His Holy Spirit.
—The Community Rule, P. 109. [22]

Is the "Apocrypha" or Portions Scripture, Inspired and Canon?

Criteria set forth by Blue Letter Bible with our stricter additions. [1]

☐ ### 1. Prophetic Authorship

"For a book to be considered canonical, it must have been written by a prophet or apostle or by one who had a special relationship to such (Mark to Peter, Luke to Paul). Only those who had witnessed the events or had recorded eyewitness testimony could have their writings considered as Holy Scripture." Note: The Temple Priests curated scripture and that should matter to scholars too as their library was found in Qumran/Bethabara.

☐ ### 2. Witness of the Spirit, Quoted As Doctrine In Scripture

"The appeal to the inner witness of the Holy Spirit was also made to aid the people in understanding which books belonged in the canon and which did not." BLB quotes Pinnock who claims the canon is a matter of "historical process" (Clark Pinnock, Biblical Revelation, Grand Rapids: Baker Book House, 1973, p. 104). [2] We would agree but Pinnock ignores the most obvious such history. The Levite Library or Bible canon found in Qumran/Bethabara serves as a time capsule for the Old Testament canon long before the Catholic Church, nor counsels, nor even Pharisee party in Yahudaea. Every book in the modern Old Testament canon was found there except Esther. It is Levite Priests, sons of Zadok, who were the keepers of scripture and the Qumran/Bethabara community identifies as such over 100 times.

☐ ### 3. Acceptance

"The final test is the acceptance of the people of God." BLB notes this is to accept Jesus and the Apostles which we agree for New Testament but this would also be to accept His people in the time of the Old Testament.

☐ ### 4. In Agreement With the Whole of Scripture (Our Addition)

Does it agree with scripture in whole? Even the Gospels have minor details to iron out in understanding and reconciliation, but how does it compare? The conclusion may surprise.

1. PROPHETIC AUTHORSHIP: WHO WROTE THESE BOOKS?

For 1st and 2nd Esdras, please see our extensive Torah Test published in 2nd Esdras: The Hidden Book of Prophecy With First Esdras available free in eBook at 2Esdras.org.

Each of these credible books erroneously classified as "Apocrypha" is pretty clear whom authored them. The question comes from scoffers calling themselves Bible Scholars who will claim they can't prove authorship, which remains their shortcoming and not the text itself which they ignore and do not believe. Who ever said these books rely on them to approve? Who do they think they are? It is a false paradigm they establish to ensure failure, yet they have failed us.

When a book tells you who authored it or a prophet known to author similar or the same accounts is included as a main character in the story, only one playing games of willing ignorance would try to reject them on such lame basis. They are removing scripture and that is unacceptable. When those books are also found among the only scroll library endorsed as Bible Canon kept by the exiled Temple Priests or even strongly associated in ancient times as part of another book which was found there, one is not thinking when they claim they have the right to remove them from the Bible or even separate and hide them as "apocrypha." No scholar has such authority and never has. The Old Testament Canon was already established before the Pharisees usurped the Priesthood and religion in Yahudaea in 165 B.C. and long before there was a Catholic Church, nor Counsels. Who cares what they voted when they had no right to vote on the already established Old Testament which we now have firm evidence of its contents in terms of books archaeologically.

WISDOM OF SIRACH:

The Wisdom of Sirach is named for it's authors who were known as Biblical sages, teachers of Bible wisdom in their ages. Some refer to it as Ecclesiasticus as well, though a confusing title. Geza Vermes refers to them as *"sages"* and this is consistent with the office of prophet, sages and priests as documented in Jeremiah 18:18.

> *"In the apocryphal Book of Ecclesiasticus, dated to the beginning of the second century b.c.e., its author, Jesus ben Sira, a sage from Jerusalem..."*
> – Vermes, p. 50 [22]

There are two opening Prologues. The first was written by an uncertain author but regardless identifies really the family of Sirach, a grandfather, his son and the grandson all writing this book of wisdom over time. We have no issue republishing this from the 1611 King James Version as it serves as background and that unknown author is not adding to the book in any sense but validating its historicity.

[A Prologue made by an uncertain Author.]
This Yahusha was the son of Sirach, and grand-child to Yahusha of the same name
with him; This man therefore lived in the latter times, after the people had been led
away captive, and called home again...

We, then, observe a second Prologue, written by the author of this book identifying himself as the grandson, Yahusha ben Sirach, also crediting his father and grandfather. He and his grandfather share the same name but this is a family effort of Biblical sages qualified to write scripture. Thus, there are three consecutive generations of Sirach's who authored or contributed to the content of this book as a grandfather, father and the culmination written by the grandson, *"the son of Sirach"* identifying the wisdom of *"My grandfather Yahusha."*

A fragment of Sirach was found in the Dead Sea Scrolls among some Psalm fragments which were dated to about 200 B.C. In continual fraud, those supposed scholars fail to bother to date the Sirach fragment found with them. The reason they refuse to do so is likely that is actually the era in which Sirach was completed around the Second Century B.C. Though not likely an original but a copy as all Bible texts found in Qumran represent, this date may not be exact but the era fits and leaves little room to question someone else authoring the book when Sirach says he wrote it and it is documented to about that era even by date.

"Three previously unknown poems and an extract from the Hebrew version of Sirach li (51) also feature in the Scroll." – Vermes, p. 307. [22]
The psalms themselves probably belong to the second century b.c.e. at the latest, but they may even date to the third century b.c.e ." – Vermes, p. 308. [22]

Additionally, Sirach himself in his Prologue actually dates the completion of this book in terms of the reign of an Egyptian Euergetes king well documented historically as it reads: *"For in the eight and thirtieth year coming into Egypt, when Euergetes was King..."* Two options exist and only two defining a ballpark which coalesces with the texts with which it was found as very close to the era in that it was written. Either this is Ptolemy III *(246-221 B.C.)* or Ptolemy VII *(145-116 B.C.) [61].* Though the margin note from the 1611 King James Version references likely the latter and we did not change that, this dating may actually indicate the former.

However, we have only an age to determine here and we have a very close match far too close to the time of authorship indicated. If this were any other Bible book, there would never be a question here and there is none with Sirach either. The three Sirachs are responsible for this wisdom and the third of them completed this writing. No one else did. The notion that Temple Priests, whom we found this text among, went around making up scripture and writing it in fraud years later, demonstrates a profound disability in scholarship today.

Finally, Sirach was originally penned in Hebrew most likely as fragments are found in Hebrew as well as Aramaic in Qumran.

> *"On the other hand, the Hebrew poem from Ben Sira li(51) has a patently better chance of reflecting the original than either the Greek translation by the author's grandson, preserved in the Septuagint, or the Hebrew of the medieval Cairo Genizah manuscripts, because the Qumran version alone faithfully reflects the acrostic character of the composition with the lines starting with the successive letters of the Hebrew alphabet, aleph, bet, gimel, etc." – Vermes, p. 16.*

Of course, scholars seem to attempt to insert their own pertinence when Sirach already told us in his Prologue essentially, these words of wisdom were originally in Hebrew. Indeed, they would be translated into Aramaic and Greek to reach a larger audience in time but their origin remains Hebrew and the fragment found clearly identifies this not just spoken but written in Hebrew as well.

> *"For the same things uttered in Hebrew, and translated into another tongue..."*

In the early 1900s, R. H. Charles also records detail of many Hebrew fragments of Sirach being discovered in his time decades before the Dead Sea Scrolls were found *[81, Charles, p. 271-272]*. However, let us not forget this is a false paradigm set by some scholars. There is no scripture that says Yahuah has to preserve His Word in Hebrew on Earth. He does do so in Heaven. Sirach was authored by that family.

THE BOOK OF BARUCH/LETTER OF JEREMIAH (BOOK OF JEREMIAH):

Baruch is an iconic servant of Yahuah in the Book of Jeremiah. Though he served as Jeremiah's scribe, he was also his disciple and mouthpiece at times. This has been so poorly framed by some in scholarship that first, attempt to marginalize his role which is gross negligence on their part. Baruch, being a scribe, wrote this book and said he wrote it while in Babylonian captivity defining the era as well, not centuries later when he was dead and some scholars try to find a false author to fit in ignorance. As to which Baruch, he provides his lineage and it fits that of the same Baruch of Jeremiah.

Baruch met with Yechonias in Jeremiah sharing the words of Jeremiah but he also either met him again or also read his own prophetic words and his own prophetic book to him as well. That should not be a surprise as Baruch is far more than a scribe but a mediator for Jeremiah's word he also wrote down. He even read his book as well as scripture in application to many which he documents right from the opening. For complete understanding, we will review passages from Jeremiah.

Baruch 1:1-4 KJVA

*And these are the words of the book, which **Baruch the son of Neriah**, the son of Maasias, the son of Sedecias, the son of Asadias, the son of Chelcias, **wrote in Babylon**, In the fifth year, and in the seventh day of the month, what time as the Chaldeans took Jerusalem, and burnt it with fire. 3 And **Baruch did read the words of this book**, in the hearing of Yechonias, the son of Yoachim king of Yahuda, and in the ears of all the people, that came to [hear] the book. 4 And in the hearing of the nobles, and of the kings sons, and in the hearing of the elders, and of all the people from the lowest unto the highest, even of all them that dwelt at Babylon, by the river Sud.*

Who Was Baruch?

Let us first establish the character of Baruch who was far more than a scribe alone. He was a disciple of the Prophet Jeremiah who wrote his words. He was extremely skilled in such and holy. It is unthinkable anyone calling themselves a Bible scholar would not be aware of Baruch's standing. Baruch was far more than a mere scribe and no one should be surprised he would have stood up as Jeremiah did in prophecy. He was a disciple of Jeremiah and fellow Prophet even.

Jeremiah 32:13 KJV

*And **I charged Baruch before them**, saying, Thus saith the LORD of hosts, the God of Israel; Take these evidences, this evidence of the purchase, both which is sealed, and this evidence which is open; and put them in an earthen vessel, that they may continue many days.*

Baruch did not just write for Jeremiah, he spoke in his stead as a representative fellow prophet and as a true disciple.

Jeremiah 36 KJV

*5-6: And **Jeremiah commanded Baruch**, saying, I am shut up; I cannot go into the house of the LORD: Therefore go thou, and read in the roll, which thou hast written from my mouth, the words of the LORD in the ears of the people in the LORD'S house upon the fasting day: and also thou shalt read them in the ears of all Judah that come out of their cities. 8: And **Baruch the son of Neriah did according to all that Jeremiah the prophet commanded him, reading in the book the words of the LORD in the LORD'S house.***

Baruch is not a small part of Jeremiah's account at all. For not only did he obey Jeremiah, but others viewed him as an authoritative figure. In delivering the prophesies, he placed his life at risk just as Jeremiah did. That is not a figure who can be marginalized as some scholars attempt. He also shared his own words.

Jeremiah 36:14 KJV
*Therefore all the princes sent Jehudi the son of Nethaniah, the son of Shelemiah, the son of Cushi, **unto Baruch**, saying, **Take in thine hand the roll** wherein **thou hast read** in the ears of the people, and come. So Baruch the son of Neriah took the roll in his hand, and came unto them.*

Jeremiah 36:19 KJV
*Then said the princes unto **Baruch, Go, hide thee, thou and Jeremiah; and let no man know where ye be.***

Jeremiah 36:26-28 KJV
*But the king commanded Jerahmeel the son of Hammelech, and Seraiah the son of Azriel, and Shelemiah the son of Abdeel, **to take Baruch the scribe and Jeremiah the prophet: but the LORD hid them**. Then the word of the LORD came to Jeremiah, after that the king had burned the roll, and the words which **Baruch wrote at the mouth of Jeremiah**, saying, **Take thee again another roll, and write in it all the former words that were in the first roll**, which Jehoiakim the king of Judah hath burned.*

Jeremiah 36:32 KJV
*Then **took Jeremiah another roll, and gave it to Baruch the scribe**, the son of Neriah; who wrote therein from the mouth of Jeremiah all the words of the book which Jehoiakim king of Judah had burned in the fire: and **there were added besides unto them many like words**.*

In fact, speaking to Jeremiah, the proud men complained about Baruch crediting him for setting the Prophet against them to deliver them into the hands of Babylon. Of course, that was not the case. The problem is they did not get it. Yahuah's judgment is righteous and ultimately, those who fled into Egypt ended up facing harsher penalty than those who took their punishment and went into Babylon as they were supposed to. Also, notice additional words were then added as well and that is likely those of Baruch too as these prophets served together.

Jeremiah 43:3 KJV
But Baruch the son of Neriah setteth thee on against us, for to deliver us into the hand of the Chaldeans, that they might put us to death, and carry us away captives into Babylon.

Baruch is a well-established Bible figure who most certainly wrote the book bearing his name and he identifies himself in detail that cannot truly be assailed. Though Baruch 1-5 was not found in Qumran, Baruch 6, retitled in inept confusion as the Letter of Jeremiah was. Thus, Baruch was found there. The so-titled Letter of Jeremiah begins with "A copy of an epistle, which Jeremiah." Baruch was his scribe and discple and was the one who delivered these words to the captives of Babylon as mentioned in the letter. There is no separating the two texts regardless and we will cover the historicity of Baruch considered part of the Book of Jeremiah in scripture since very ancient times.

Regarding Baruch 2 and other additional books attributed to Baruch, these were not found in Qumran and will not be published nor discussed in this writing. In similar fashion to extra books of Enoch which are obvious forgeries not written by Enoch, these must be set aside and tested further. For our Levite Bible Series, we are especially interested in those books found in the Levite Library of Qumran and those quoted there. 2 Baruch was not that we have found.

PRAYER OF MANASSEH

In this one-chapter prayer, we find a continuation and witness to 2nd Chronicles which records the history and Bible account of Manasseh, King of Yahudah. He led many to evil deeds and was led away to captivity *(2Chr. 33:11)*. However, while captive, Manasseh prayed a supplication of repentance that will minister to many. In many cases, the context alone truly waxes Biblical.

> *2 Chronicles 33:12-13 KJV*
> *And when he was in affliction, he besought the LORD his God, and humbled himself greatly before the God of his fathers, And prayed unto him: and he was intreated of him, and heard his supplication, and brought him again to Jerusalem into his kingdom. Then Manasseh knew that the LORD he was God.*

As a result of this repentance, Yahuah heard his petition and Manasseh was spared and returned to Jerusalem where he would do good from there. Though this is only a one-chapter prayer, we find no suspect hinderances in continuing to publish this book with scripture as it was intended. There was a fragment found in Qumran that was labeled "Prayer of Manasseh" that is a fragment that does match this one in content which we will vet in the next section. It is rather odd that some scholars would label it so if they did not believe it was this prayer and it turns out to be consistent in content. However, we see nothing to eliminate it which burden would be the true responsibility as the Temple Priests who kept scripture had this book in their Bible Canon.

Manasseh executed a powerful prayer of which this vets as inspired. It is likely that the Prophet Jeremiah wrote 2nd Chronicles as well according to many scholars and this prayer appears the same though there is no attribution. We see the same dynamic as Jeremiah with Baruch and Letter of Jeremiah *(Baruch 6)* just as we see with the extensions of the Book of Daniel we will vet in Vol. 2. The precedence is there. The likely author of the prayer is the only one who was there, King Manasseh himself in origin, though Jeremiah or Baruch may have written and published it as an addendum to 2nd Chronicles where it was once found and is even referenced as a written prayer *(2Chr. 33:19)*. If only scholars could read...

1611 King James Version
APOCRYPHA

SCROLLS FOUND IN QUMRAN AND THOSE NOT PRESENT

See also, 2nd Esdras: The Hidden Book of Prophecy, free in eBook at 2Esdras.org.

Having proven the exiled Temple Priests who were ordained to keep Bible Canon lived in Qumran/Bethabara, we now have a foundation by which to test ancient texts. As the keepers of scripture left a Library of Bible Canon behind found in 1947 and beyond, this becomes a strong start for a first testing. There is much confusion with many occult books purporting to be inspired scripture. If they are not found in Qumran/Bethabara at least by concrete association, they should be set aside and treated differently until a full test is conducted which no scholar appears to have executed in this age. Scholars continue to treat this find with gross negligence using classifications such as Apocrypha and Pseudepigrapha. They ignorantly declare the holy Temple Priests kept fraudulent writings which has always been a lie. They did not need to create new stories to scare people.

Even this erroneous category of Apocrypha is mixed. The term merely refers to books outside of the Pharisee Canon which is meaningless and exposes the church is generally using that Pharisee Canon for the Old Testament today. However, those scholars fail to ask why they are following the Pharisees whom Yahusha outright rebuked regarding their ignorance of scripture. Their leaven and oral traditions *(Talmud)* transform Torah into anti-Torah *(Mark 7:9)*. How do we determine which is inspired and which is not? Though each requires a more extensive Torah Test we will execute for each next, the first criteria we can apply to root out truly false books is whether the text is found at least in fragments or quoted in content in the the Levite Library of Qumran/Bethabara. That is where the only scripturally-ordained Bible Canon was kept to the First Century. We will complete this testing for the remaining books in Volume 2 next.

BOOK:	QUMRAN TEXT FOUND:
FOUND IN QUMRAN:	....
√ 1ˢᵗ Esdras *(Proto-1stEsdrasᵃˢ)*	*100 B.C.: 4Q550 (4QProto-Estherᵃˢ). Cave 4. Aramaic. Are All 1ˢᵗ Esdras NOT Esther, [Vermes, pp. 619-20] [22][88]*
√ 2ⁿᵈ Esdras *(Used In Interpretation)*	*100 B.C.: 1QpHab, Cave 1 [Vermes, pp. 510-11] ; 100 B.C.: 1QSb, Cave 1 [22: Vermes, pp. 389-390] [22]*
√ Wisdom of Sirach *(Ecclesiasticus)*	*73 B.C.-4 A.D.: 2QSir/2Q18: Cave 2: Hebrew; 11Q5 (11QPsa): Cave 11. Sir. 51. Mas1H (MasSir). [Vermes, pp. 307, 641], 4Q416 VI 5, 13. [22][93]*
Wisdom of Solomon *(Used In Interpretation)*	*See Vol. 2 For Details.*
Book of Tobit	*See Vol. 2 For Details.*
Book of Susanna	*See Vol. 2 For Details.*
√ Prayer of Manasseh	*50 B.C.: 4Q381: 33, 8: Cave 4. Titled "Prayer of Manasseh" which is a match in content to the KJVA; 2 Chr. 33:19 cites Manasseh's prayer was "written among the sayings of the seers (prophets)." Hebrew. [Vermes, p. 319] [22]*
√ Letter of Jeremiah	*100 B.C.: 7Q2: Cave 7: Greek but closer to Hebrew tradition. [Vermes, p. 472] [22]*
BY ASSOCIATION:	....
Once Part of Jeremiah: √ Baruch *(Chapter 6 found in Qumran)*	*Letter of Jeremiah is the 6ᵗʰ Chapter of Baruch. Thus, Chapters 1-5 tie to Qumran as well. These were one book as an addendum to Jeremiah in that age. [81, 76, 78, 84, 79, 77, 80] 7Q2: Cave 7 [22]*
Once Part of Daniel: Prayer of Azariah *(Abednego - The Song of the Three Young Men)*	*See Vol. 2 For Details.*
Bel and the Dragon *(Daniel's exploits)*	*See Vol. 2 For Details.*
NOT FOUND IN D.S.S.:	....
Judith	*See Vol. 2 For Details.*
Book Of Esther *Purim & Additions*	*See Vol. 2 For Details.*
1ˢᵗ & 2ⁿᵈ Maccabees *Hanukkah & Additions*	*See Vol. 2 For Details.*

2. WITNESS OF THE SPIRIT: THE HISTORICAL PROCESS, QUOTED AS DOCTRINE IN SCRIPTURE

1611 KJV APOCRYPHA FOUND OR QUOTED IN QUMRAN AND HISTORICITY BY BOOK:

The books of the 1611 Apocrypha prove mostly to have been treated by the true Temple Priests as inspired scripture at least by association in the cases of certain small books such as Susanna which actually belonged to the end of Daniel in the First Century era. By reclassifying those separately, scholars did not do anything but confuse the issue in willing ignorance. The truly odd thing is these credible texts, the ones that prove so, really do not offer any offensive doctrine except especially Maccabees and Esther which we will test those with Judith in Volume 2 and they prove not credible in whole. They were not found in Qumran and highly offensive if you truly research them.

Let's assess the thinking in an analogy of more modern terms. One's great, great grandfather wrote an account of their family history in 1850 in what was called the Wild West. He compiled this data in the form of letters and diaries written by himself, his son, a brother, 2 cousins, some unidentified authors, his mother, and other family. He left the documents in his barn in clay pots. If he were fortunate enough to have had a printing press as a modern scoffer would demand, he would have bound them all into one book but he was not. By placing them together in his library and the topic coalescing, it is obvious, this is one book in essence regardless. He passes away leaving the house including the history to the next generation.

This next great grandfather is attacked by thieves and the barn is burned down. The clay pots mostly survived, but portions are charred on the edges and incoherent. However, he also loses his only son. He rebuilds the barn and years later, he wills the estate to his nephew as he has no direct heirs. That nephew sold the house with barn to another family not related. He fails to understand the value of the information inside the clay pots and leaves them there in that barn.

The new owner notices the pots but, in his lifetime, never addresses them leaving them to his next of kin, an academic scholar, who becomes curious and opens the pots in 2020. When he does, he discovers portions charred, others rotting away and only small portions remain that are legible. However, there is enough to determine this is the legacy of the family who first built this ranch back in 1850. There are also other copies of these letters and diaries that survived with other family members who moved away which confirm these in whole though they were copies, not originals, from years later. If he were a scholar in the Dead Sea Scrolls today, he would take these writings from this same family and disconnect them. He would assume they were written by different families perhaps even from different states. In the case of the cousins, they must be speaking of some other mountains because they could not possibly represent the ones in full view of the ranch, of course. Some wrote in broken English which must mean they were foreigners of a completely different family not even connected. Of course, they were actually the same family, just some less literate in terms of writing.

One mentioned a stream that is not there anymore so he must have lived in another area though he did not. The grandmother could not have written in that age, which would be a lie but one they would propagate, and therefore, hers is written by a false author a century later than when she lived. They would know that because she would mention something that appears a refrigerator and they would, of course, ignore that history records the first refrigerators in the 1850s or so and claim it must be later in willing ignorance because the scholar doesn't actually know nor represent history. She mentions violence as well and that must be WWI because to a scholar, no violence ever occurred before WWI. They do that with these texts often on a host of topics they remain ignorant in order to claim they were all written during the era of Hellenism which is ridiculous and not even logical. Their reasoning is that no sin nor idols ever existed in any history of Israel or the patriarchs prior until the era of Greek Hellenism which is illiterate.

For one fragment, he would question whether the great, great grandfather was really who he said he was or perhaps someone else wrote that letter too. For the pot in which it was found is from a century later. It was found in a different cabinet in the barn as well. Even though it is the history of that same family in content with the author identified with date even, they would ignore that there was a fire that may have damaged that pot and it was replaced with one constructed at a later date but they cannot think in such common sense terms it appears. The pot does not determine when those contents were written other than at least to that era of the pot's dating. We observe that in scholarship all the time in ignorance.

In a writing later in the great, great grandfather's life, the scholar would assail that as a different author and not the same man because it was more intellectual reading more like what they wish to define as history which in their view must be written by an academic because of course, no other humans are allowed to write their observances without degrees. That is stupidity yet common place in academia. If they did, we are to ignore them because they were not good enough nor smart enough to tell the true events. That is ridiculous.

Another text by perhaps the brother, mentioned a creature akin to Big Foot thus, that must be discredited because modern scholars cannot capture and prove there is such a creature. Again, that is their paradigm and their shortcoming they then, apply to everyone else in a false paradigm blocking knowledge. That is as Pharisee as any behavior could be. They would ignore even former President Teddy Roosevelt as not academic enough nor credible enough for them when he wrote of an account of a Big Foot-like creature in Idaho and Montana in The Wilderness Hunter published in 1893. Another scholar would pile on in consensus noting that there were no known Big Foot legends in that area in 1850 but not until 1912.

In other words, that scholar would be claiming this could not be the first legend because other scholars already decreed the 1912 was the first. Do they even know that? No. Did Big Foot, or whatever creature this may have been mistaken, come into existence in 1912? Would not the very fact that it is reported in that area in 1912 prove this family history credible whether it was Big Foot himself or not? How could one call themselves academic and even think that way? They do.

This is the case with some who ridicule texts like Bel & The Dragon or even Tobit claiming dragons did not exist completely overlooking mass history defining dragons existed as even Alexander the Great had such encounters which he recorded. In the 1800s, science changed the name of many ancient historic dragons and they now call them dinosaurs in fact. Once again, they would scoff that even Roosevelt, nor Daniel, nor Tobit were academic enough to contribute to their paradigm of stupid and well, maybe that is a good thing for all of us. It exposes their agenda.

For Tobit, many forget or cannot actually research that fish bile and that of other animals was used as a remedy for certain types of blindness specifically that which originates from bird droppings even for thousands of years from the B.C. era even to the late date of 1949 in an encyclopedia even. They render that antibiotics is a better treatment, which is not even a point. Perhaps it is today but for thousands of years, we did not have it and doctors treated it with bile in many documented cases. It is unthinkable just how far some will go to dismiss credible knowledge. When they call themselves a scholar and demand we listen to them above everyone else including written history, yet they offer uneducated propaganda instead of logic, we would all be foolish to accept their rhetoric without testing it. It fails.

Therefore, because no one else wrote of it, that the scholar knows of, but he clearly knows little on the topic, he would conclude that portion was false because Big Foot cannot have existed until someone wrote the legend later and this could not possibly be an earlier account of the same. Why? Because he says so.

The mother's writing seemed more contemporary as she wrote as one who lived in the 1920s because the poverty was so overwhelming it had to indicate the Great Depression. The scholar would forget some experienced a depression without even having a stock market. She mentioned a tribe of Indians she encountered who were friendly and the scholar cannot understand how this could be in that era because there was a band within that tribe recorded by the early American soldiers as unfriendly, yet he forgets, they were soldiers who posed a threat and this family was no such. So, he concludes she lived in the 1920s and that portion must be the fabrication of another author who threw it in to confuse people because this scholar says so but can't actually read with comprehension. The same will call others conspiracy theorists when they spin such as a matter of routine.

By the time our new owner, an academic scholar, has assessed all in the clay pots, he determines this is not the family history of one family but thirty-one different families who some did not even live in the same state, nor the same time. Though they all truly lived together in reality. Others weren't writing the family story because they did not have the same writing style as the grandfather whose style changed later in age so those fragments must not even be the same author either. Absent any scientific dating and ignoring history, this scholar deduces some were written far earlier than they even date themselves in the words and none of the authors were the actual authors because he doesn't believe the family could be literate in that area in that age because no other books were found in the home, and no others in any ranches nearby. He forgets and does not bother to research that there were no other ranches in that area during that time but speaks to it as an expert in willing ignorance. Not being historians, he would claim they had no right to write history and thus, all must ignore everything these documents say, except the ones that fit his paradigm of thinking of course which he will selectively use. Are we the only ones who observe the doctrine of Pharisee agitation in such scholarship which applies to those today same as this analogy?

Finally, his friends in consensus would disassemble the pots into the works of 180 authors from criteria set in one paradigm after another that forgets the actual history of this family who lived together in the same area, actually wrote all of these and on the dates they claim. That is an entire complex paradigm of illiteracy created instead replacing actual facts with inept, unacademic speculation. This was a family history that any normal person could read and understand yet now becomes a jumbled mess incoherent and unbelievable. This is what modern scholars have done to the Bible and its texts and they have done even worse with the fragments found in Qumran.

No matter how intelligent this approach appears on the surface, it requires what seems insanity to even think in such a manner. This whole time, this was a consistent, preserved family history of one family and by the time they are done spinning it, it is some unconnected useless letters of no significance. That is no different from their marginalizing the Zadok family of Temple Priests and forgetting whom they were and what they represented. Of course, the actual family descendants who want to know their history, would read it and accept it at face value. When one of them reads all these letters and puts them together connecting them, as they should be, they realize this is a beautiful account. They could have understood this long ago if the man claiming to be a scholar did not confuse everything.

However, as they share their connected affirmed history, they are ridiculed for claiming their great, great grandfather compiled all this, and marginalized for trying to read for themselves when a scholar had already told them stupidly how they are supposed to read these or better, not to read them. Universities would shun this family's interpretation of a straight reading in common sense and they would produce consensus that the scholarly findings were the only truth when the entire time, it was the lie and incredibly inept. But they had consensus... Indeed!

This is why we are publishing this series in layman's terms as we have had enough of the so-called academic rhetoric that surrounds the Dead Sea Scrolls, and really the entire Bible. These supposed scholars cannot even connect the history of the community in Qumran even though there was a massive amount of local writings that identify this as the Temple practice continued by the Sons of Zadok exiled there who would prepare the way for the coming Messiah in the wilderness. Their writings directly admit that was their purpose and scholars ignore it calling them Kabbalist Essenes in the dumbest scholarship ever. That mission included preserving the Bible canon of the Old Testament and archaeology proves they did well. Immediately, upon these discoveries, the propaganda began. This is especially true of what is termed the "apocrypha" which is not even an accurate assessment.

DID YAHUSHA QUOTE ANY OF THESE BOOKS IN THE APOCRYPHA?

One can read so many conflicting writings from scholars claiming that Jesus did not quote the Apocrypha. This is a lie and extremely poor research not even bothering to look at the margin notes of the 1611 King James to see if that anchor is there. In this Torah Test, we will cover those in which the 1611 KJV translators anchor certain New Testament passages only to these apocryphal works and nothing else. That includes the words of Yahusha and means they are the only scriptural origin according to them.

In fact, we had one pastor attempt to argue vehemently that he owned a facsimile of the Original 1611 Authorized King James Version, and it does not have a margin note anchoring Yahusha quoting 2nd Esdras 1:30 in Matthew 23:37. He then, posted that page absent the margin, of course, which was cut off yet still there. We corrected that posting a photo of the actual page for him from the 1611 King James Bible themselves which shows that margin note in 1611. It anchors Yahusha's words specifically to 2nd Esdras and only 2nd Esdras for that passage which a quick reading is apparent to anyone who can read.

That pastor is a good man not intending to deceive people in our opinion but that does not absolve the fact that he was peddling control lines from seminaries without having done an ounce of research for himself. This is the behavior of many, if not most pastors as it is what they are taught. Thus, he and all pastors who do so are unqualified to even render an hypothesis as they are not educated on this topic and thus, it is just a poor guess at best. Any layman could do better. This was another "King James Only" pastor who needs to adjust his title to "King James Edited Centuries Later Only" as he does not know the original 1611 King James, even how to read margin notes, and does not embrace it. Again, it is not him. It is the scholars he has submitted to instead of proving their writings. If he did test their work, he would find, as we have, many poorly formed positions in ignorance.

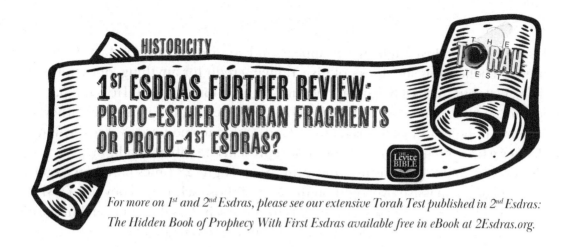

1ST ESDRAS FURTHER REVIEW: PROTO-ESTHER QUMRAN FRAGMENTS OR PROTO-1ST ESDRAS?

For more on 1st and 2nd Esdras, please see our extensive Torah Test published in 2nd Esdras: The Hidden Book of Prophecy With First Esdras available free in eBook at 2Esdras.org.

We have already fully published 2nd Esdras: The Hidden Book of Prophecy With 1st Esdras in which one can download the eBook free at 2Esdras.org. There is a thorough Torah Test there we will not repeat. Upon deeper research for our 26-week Teaching Series, Answers in 2nd Esdras, we uncovered additional evidence to further support the tie between 1st and 2nd Esdras and Qumran/Bethabara. These are extremely obvious when one vets these.

In Qumran, fragments are labeled "Proto-Esther" in fraud as every one of these fragments align far more directly to 1st Esdras that originated in that same era. We find it dumfounding that one calling themselves a Bible scholar could make such as massive error. This is forced propaganda and it would be laughable if it were not so blatantly evil. In The Complete Dead Sea Scrolls In English By Geza Vermes, he asserts in the Introduction: *"It is suggested that the Aramaic fragments of 4Q550 derive from a proto-Esther."* However, the gross negligence of not realizing this was the time of 1st Edras and assuming that Priest Ezra is Esther among many other things, is one of the worst pieces of "scholarship" we have ever witnessed. When such intelligent men are willing to make themselves look as clowns to protect the paradigm of Pharisaism *(Rabbinic Judaism)* and the changing of the Bible, it is obvious they are more committed to their Zionist agenda than to Yahuah. Such a person can hardly be in relationship with the Father nor Son and conduct themselves so poorly. In the first fragment they completely misidentify, they miss that Esther does not know nor use the Most High, there is no one with a similar name to Bagasro which would have to be Mordecai and 1st Esdras shares this same decree regarding one far closer to the name. In other words, nothing of this fragment is Esther.

4Q550: Proto-Esther^d, Cave 4 [Vermes, 620]:
*III **The Most High** whom you (Jews) fear and worship rules o[ver the whole e]arth. Everyone whom He wishes (comes) near. **Bagasro** ...*
***Whoever speaks an evil word against Bagasro** [will be] put to death for there is no-o[ne to destroy h]is good for [e]ver....*

First, the title "Most High" never appears in Esther even once. In fact, Esther is not even a believer as she does not give Yahuah credit for anything, does not pray to Him, fasts but that is a pagan practice and no mention of Him as He is not part of her story. Even the name of YHWH does not appear even once in the text either. In fact, other popular titles such as Elohim (God), Adonai, and Lord escape the writer of Esther who is no believer and does not represent the Bible paradigm.

However, 1st and 2nd Esdras use this term "Most High" 28 times based on a quick search. That is a massive oversight on the part of those scholars. They use YHWH, Yahuah, over 200 times verses Esther, 0. Why these scholars did not even bother to test 1st Esdras from the same time period, is simply gross negligence.

> *1 Esdras 6:31-34 KJVA*
> *That offerings may be made to the **Most High Elohim**, for the king and for his children, and that they may pray for their lives. And he commanded, that whosoever should transgress, yes, or make light of any thing afore spoken or written, out of his own house should a tree be taken, and he thereon be hanged, and all his goods seized for the king. **Yahuah therefore whose Name is there called upon**, utterly destroy every king and nation, that stretches out his hand to hinder or damage that house of Yahuah in Yerusalem. I Darius the king have ordained, that according unto these things it be done with diligence.*
>
> *1 Esdras 8:19 KJVA*
> *And I, king Artaxerxes, have also commanded the keepers of the treasures in Syria and Phoenicia, that whatsoever Ezra the priest, and the reader of the law of the **Most High Elohim** shall send for, they should give to him with speed,*

The account of reference in this fragment is a far better match to that of Zerubbabel from 1st Esdras, not Esther. He was a guard in the palace in Persia who participated in a contest of wisdom decreed by the king. He was found the wisest and gained the favor and protection treated as family of the king.

> *1 Esdras 4:42-43 KJVA*
> *Then said the king unto him, **Ask what you will, more than is appointed in the writing, and we will give it to you**, because you are found wisest, and you **shall sit next to me**, and **shall be called my cousin**. Then he said unto the king, Remember your vow which you have vowed to build Yerusalem in the day when you came to the kingdom,*

This would lead to his return to Yahudaea with the first wave of Lost Tribes to begin the rebuilding of the Temple which is why some refer to it as Zerubbabel's Temple. Esther slept with the king and used that to gain position and favor and her uncle is Mordecai, not Bagasro. However, when one reviews 1st Esdras, there are some words which somehow have become scrambled and even backwards in letters perhaps due to the original Hebrew being rendered left to right instead of right to left by some. In this case, there is a far greater affinity with the name Z-R-B-B-L (Zerubbabel), than MDKY (Mordecai).

> זרבבל: *(Z-R-B-B-L) Z^{e}rubbâbel, zer-oob-baw-bel'; from H2215 and H894; descended of (i.e. from) Babylon, i.e. born there; Zerubbabel, an Israelite:–Zerubbabel.*

Notice, when you break this down, it is essentially Zerub (Zeroob, Z-R-B) was born in Babylon basically. This makes sense as the Southern Kingdom of Israel was captive there in the days in which Zerubbabel was born. Now, look at the name Bagasro and there is a far greater similarity than trying to insert Esther's Uncle Mordecai in illiterate ignorance especially when this account matches 1st Esdras far better than Esther. Just review the word as any scholar should know better and this is an obvious failure for Esther especially when only one letter of Mordecai even matches. A child could do better. There is a Mordecai recorded by Ezra but that one returned with the Southern Kingdom which is not remotely Esther's story. She and her uncle were in Persia after the last wave of Lost Tribes returned and immediately reeks of fiction as a result.

> מרדכי: *(M-R-D-K-Y): Mord^{e}kay, mor-dek-ah'-ee; of foreign derivation; Mordecai, an Israelite:–Mordecai. "little man" or "worshipper of Mars"*

Some align this name with the false Sumerian/Akkadian god, Marduk and Esther with their moon goddess, Ishtar. Both are far too much of a coincidence to ignore especially when the Book of Esther has no Bible story within at all.

However, Zerub (Z-R-B) is easily identified in Bagasro in similarity as it appears to be spelled backwards as B-G-S(Z)-R adding a 'G" as well. This is established in other names rendered backwards in Ezra's accounts as well.

Finally, even the content of the account is 1st Esdras, and not Esther. The king of Persia decreed this protective warning that anyone who would make light of Zerubbabel's Temple and his Elohim would be hanged and his goods seized. That fits this fragment far better than Esther.

> *1 Esdras 6:32-34 KJVA*
> *And he commanded, that whosoever should transgress, yes, or make light of any thing afore spoken or written, out of his own house should a tree be taken, and he thereon be hanged, and all his goods seized for the king. Yahuah therefore whose Name is there called upon, utterly destroy every king and nation, that stretches out his hand to hinder or damage that house of Yahuah in Yerusalem. **I Darius the king have ordained**, that according unto these things it be done with diligence.*

Note, this account is specifically affirmed by Origen around 200 A.D. as he quotes First Esdras with attribution in his response to the scoffer, Julius Africanus who sounded like many modern scholars. Origen wrote he was reading 1st Esdras as historical and Biblical fact one would call inspired. He confuses Nehemiah and Zerubbabel which is a simple mistake as both were involved in the rebuilding.

185-254: Origen:
"Again we read in Esdras, that Neemias, a cup-bearer and eunuch of the king, of Hebrew race, made a request about the rebuilding of the temple, and obtained it..."
– Origen's Letter to Africanus [75]

However, the next so-called "Proto-Esther" Fragment requires one lacking all intellect in scholarship to overlook. For it bears Ezra's name as Priest (Father, same in the Persian culture) Ezra which is so very obvious and the notion that could ever be Esther is utterly illiterate. She is no male. Very clearly those managing the Dead Sea Scrolls are propagandists, not Bible scholars and neither should remain in charge of a single interpretation, nor dig. They have tainted the entire narrative in the largest lies that no sane person could possibly deduce.

However, Christian scholars fall in line assuming these true Temple Priests were Kabbalistic Essenes. Not only is it a ludicrous notion, the evidence bears out that those who created such theories are not educated in the slightest in regards to these scrolls. There is not a single fingernail of Essene archaeology in Qumran but found 25 miles South in Ein Gedi even titled "The Essene Find." There is not a single mention of Essenes in any terms but especially not in the community writings yet they identify themselves as the sons of Zadok, exiled Temple Priests, sons of Aaron, sons of Levi, Levites, sons of Light, etc. over 100 times. Only a lunatic could then assume they were Essenes when they were the very keepers of scripture ordained by Moses and really, Yacob. However, this is the same with this fragment. Their assumption that Esther was a male especially is an oversight a child would not make and we will not excuse them for such negligence.

100 B.C.: 4Q550: 4QProto-Esther^a*: Cave 4 [Vermes, 619]:*
*... [and they li]sten to **Patireza (Patir Ezra), your father** ... and amid the officials of the royal apparel... to work in the service of the king in accordance with all that you have received ... In that hour the **king could not go to sleep** (literally, his spirit was stretched) [and he commanded that the b]ooks of his father be read before him. And among the books there was a scroll [the mou]th of which [was] s[ealed] with seven seals by the signet-ring of his **father Darius** the heading of which ... [Dar]ius the king to the officials of the kingdom, Peace. It was opened and read and in it was found: [... Dar]ius the King to the kings **who will reign after me** and to the officials of the kingdom, Pe[ac]e. It should be known to you **that every tormentor and liar** ...*

First, there are many who take the word Patireza and try to assume that this must be Esther. A Bible scholar should well know Patir or Pater is the title for "Father" or 'Priest" – a male. Esther was no male, no father and no priest. Can they read at all? This is a Bible word used over 400 times for a male and they overlook that?

> πατήρ: *patḗr*, pat-ayr'; apparently a primary word; a "father" (literally or figuratively, near or more remote):–father, parent. Strong's G3962. 419x: Father (268x), father (150x).
> 1. generator or male ancestor 2. C. a title of honour i. teachers, as those to whom pupils trace back the knowledge and training they have received... ii. the members of the Sanhedrin..

Very clearly Eza is Ezra, never Esther, rendered as Father or Priest Ezra. In Persia, it was common to call a priest Father as that is the origin of the Catholic Father even. However, Strong's affirms this word pater as a father or a priest as well including teachers and even members of the Sanhedrin or religious leaders.

> The **Mithraic Pater Patrum** *was the* **high priest** *of the* **Persian rock god.**
> *This* **high priest** *had a* **See on Vatican Hill** *and had the power to "bind and loose."*
> – Catholic Answers [87]

Indeed, the Pope and Catholic Priests bear these same Mithraic titles today from Persia. Mithraism was a cult of its own very prominent also in the Roman Empire even for Constantine the Great but it's origins are in Persia especially as Mithra is a god in Zoroastrianism. It was a Persian religious practice to refer to a Priest as Pater or Father and this is the same in the Greek. Certainly, Yahusha said to call no man pater or father referring to this cult which continues in Catholicism today. However, this fragment is not Ezra writing, it is clearly the Persian king or similar writing in similar Persian terms. Thus Father/Priest Ezra is appropriate.

Why would Ezra be referred to as Pater or Father in what appears to be a decree of the Persian king? This is extremely obvious in 1st Esdras and no match to Esther. Ezra was a father or priest literally as a Son of Zadok. His family ran the Temple when it stood for the 1st and 2nd Temple eras until it was defiled in 165 B.C. They continued to keep Bible Canon to the First Century, and we have now discovered that evidence in Qumran/Bethabara to where they were exiled from the Temple. How can one calling themselves a Bible scholar not know this and illiterately insert Esther as a male... a priest even?

Not only did the Persian King know Ezra, he honored him as Ezra was an expert in the Law of Moses, a scribe as well, and he found grace in the sight of the king. This is whom this fragment discusses, never Esther. It is 1st Esdras.

1 Esdras 8:1-4 KJVA

*And after these things, when **Artaxerxes the king of the Persians** reigned, came **Ezra** the son of Seraiah, the son of Azariah, the son of Hilkiah, the son of Shallum, The **son of Zadok**, the son of Ahitub, the son of Amariah, the son of Uzzi, the son of Memeroth, the son of Zaraias, the son of Sauias, the son of Bukki, the son of Abishua, the son of Phineas, the son of Eleazar, **the son of Aaron the chief Priest.** This Ezra went up from Babylon, **as a Scribe being very ready in the Law of Moses,** that was given by the Elohim of Israel, And **the king did honor him: for he found grace in his sight in all his requests.***

However, this small fragment has other details that once again affirm this is 1ˢᵗ Esdras. For instance, what does ...*amid the officials of the royal apparel....* mean. It is only a fragment in phrase and says very little really. This does not say, such as in the case of Esther (5:1) nor Mordecai (6:8, 8:15), that he or she were arrayed in royal apparel, but the officials were. This is consistent with 1ˢᵗ Esdras. Zerubbabel and the contestants were brought before all the Princes, governors, etc. who were the ones arrayed in royal attire. We already cited 4:32 earlier where the King affirmed this ask on the part of the contestants. However, even so, the contest winner would also be arrayed in royal apparel clothed in purple, sitting next to King Darius as his cousin. The only portion that may have even led to Esther fails and fits 1ˢᵗ Esdras.

1 Esdras 3:5-7 KJVA

*Let every one of us speak a sentence: he that shall overcome, and whose sentence shall seem wiser than the others, unto him shall the **king Darius** give great gifts, and great things in token of victory: As to be **clothed in purple**, to drink in gold, and to sleep upon gold, and a chariot with bridles of gold, and an head-tire of fine linen, and a chain about his neck: And he shall sit **next to Darius**, because of his wisdom, and **shall be called, Darius his cousin.***

1 Esdras 3:13-15 KJVA

*Now when the king was risen up, they took their writings, and delivered them unto him, and so he read them. And sending forth, **he called all the Princes of Persia and Media, and the governors, and the captains, and the lieutenants, and the chief officers,** And sat him down in the royal seat of Judgment, and the writings were read before them:*

The next portion reads: "*to work in the service of the king in accordance with all that you have received...*" This does not appear in either story specifically but would make sense for either. It can only be assumed, and logically so, of either.

Then, there is a portion that almost makes sense they would assume Esther but once again, not if they could read. The fragment reads: "*In that hour the **king could not go to sleep** (literally, his spirit was stretched) [and **he commanded that the b]ooks of his*** *father be read before him."* Indeed, this is similar in both accounts, but Esther fails. In Esther, the King does not command the books of his father be read before him, he had the recent books of his own chronicles brought to him and he read about Mordecai's recent events which saved the king. The king then, asks how Mordecai was rewarded. That is not what this fragment refers to.

> *Esther 6:1-3 KJV*
> *On that night could not the king sleep, and he commanded to bring the book of records of the chronicles; and they were read before the king. And it was found written, that Mordecai had told of Bigthana and Teresh, two of the king's chamberlains, the keepers of the door, who sought to lay hand on the king Ahasuerus. And the king said, What honour and dignity hath been done to Mordecai for this? Then said the king's servants that ministered unto him, There is nothing done for him.*

The king could not sleep in both stories so that tells us nothing. He commanded the book of records in both accounts, but Esther's records are of his own as he reads of Mordecai's saving him in his time, not his father's.

> *1 Esdras 3:3-4 KJVA*
> *And when they ate and drank, and being satisfied were gone home, then Darius the king went into his bed chamber, and slept, and soon after awakened. Then three young men that were of the guard, that kept the kings body, spoke one to another:*
> *1 Esdras 6:21-24 KJVA*
> *Now therefore if it seem good unto the king, let search be made among the records of King Cyrus, And if it be found, that the building of the house of Yahuah at Yerusalem has been done with the consent of King Cyrus, and if our lord the king be so minded, let him signify unto us thereof. Then commanded king Darius to seek among the records at Babylon: and so at Ecbatana the palace which is in the country of Media, there was found a rule wherein these things were recorded. In the first year of the reign of Cyrus, king Cyrus commanded that the house of Yahuah at Yerusalem should be built again where they do sacrifice with continual fire.*

It does become a bit confusing understandably. However, Darius and Cyrus are confused in 1st Esdras and the Book of Ezra. The writer knew what he meant but the confusion originates in kings named the same which is rather typical of Persia in that era. For instance, Cyrus's son is Cambysses yet also bears a second name of Ahasuerus. This fragment seems to indicate a father [ ] IUS and a son [ ] IUS very oddly. That could fit Cyrus and Ahasuerus (Cambysses). However, it does not fit Darius I The Great and his son Xerxes which doesn't equate to IUS. It could even be Cyrus and Darius as Darius would consider Cyrus his father (pater) as former king in the Persian mindset and literally, it appears Cyrus the Great was his uncle by blood. However, the monumental find in the books was that Cyrus had ordered the Jerusalem Temple to be rebuilt. That is what this fragment is about not Mordecai saving the king from a plot to kill him.

1st Esdras fits this whereas Esther cannot. Ahasuerus (Xerxes), who ruled in the time of Esther, would not find the story of Mordecai in the writings of his father Darius because it happened under his own reign. He was reading his own chronicles, not his father's. This is far more likely Cyrus' decree of the Temple's reconstruction and Darius' order to have the book of the records of King Cyrus read to confirm that. That is 1st Esdras and in no way Esther. The two books have the same era and it is gross negligence for a scholar to review Esther and forget about 1st Esdras in this regard.

There are eight criteria in this fragment. The Book of Esther could only fit three of the eight including royal apparel yet not a direct fit in context though it could be assumed, Mordecai would serve the king but so did Zerubbabel in 1st Esdras, and the king could not sleep but of course the wrong books are brought in Esther and there is no match. 1st Esdras matches eight out of eight criteria for ProtoEsther[a] and fully fits the mislabeled ProtoEsther[d] as well. This is not a contest especially not when Pater Ezra is identified by name and title and that male title could never be Esther nor is the name similar.

Further confusion abounds in the Dead Sea Scroll agitators who cannot seem to read basic language in Hebrew, Greek, nor English. New claims that Esther was found in Qumran continue yet every single fragment they identify leads to 1st Esdras, and not to Esther. For fragment 4Q550[b], Line 3 reads Patireza or Father/ Priest Ezra, son of "Ja[ir..." [88] This is fraud as there is no" J" in ancient Hebrew, but "Y" and the "[ir...]" is added in poor assumption. This is "son of Ya..." and there are no other letters in the name present to read nor do we need them. Ezra is a son of the Yahudim, a son of Yahudaea (Judaea). Not only that, Esther was not even Hebrew likely as she should not have been in Persia after the final wave of Lost Tribes returned to Yahudaea. Ezra's father was Seraiah or actually, SeraYAHU who was Chief Priest of the Temple when Babylon sacked it.

Another newer release is labeled 4Q550[c] *[88]*. Line 5 has the word *"purple"* fitting 1st Esdras as well as Esther but that's the only word there with no context. However, scholars again try to stretch Line 2 which reads *"Patireza [your] father, from Hama' who arose concerning the service of [...] before the king [...]."* This blows the lid off of this whole thing as once again this is not Esther, this is definitively Ezra in 1st Esdras.

We, again, have Pater Ezra here identified not only by name and title but the territory from which his father was killed. We know Ezra was in the service of the king and the king honored him. Ezra's father, Serayahu, was killed in Hamath. Indeed, his father was killed or from Hama' as it says.

2 Kings 25:18-21 KJV
*And the captain of the guard **took Seraiah the chief priest**, and Zephaniah the second priest, and the three keepers of the door: And out of the city he took an officer that was set over the men of war, and five men of them that were in the king's presence, which were found in the city, and the principal scribe of the host, which mustered the people of the land, and threescore men of the people of the land that were found in the city: And Nebuzaradan captain of the guard took these, and brought them to the king of Babylon to Riblah: And **the king of Babylon smote them, and slew them at Riblah in the land of Hamath**. So Judah was carried away out of their land. [Riblah in Hamath is affirmed in 2Ki. 23:33; Jer. 39:5, 52:9, 27.]*

Reading this new fragment interpretation and measuring it with Ezra's father's account in 2nd Kings, we now know this is even more firmly Priest Ezra and his father Serayahu who was killed at Hama... which is clearly Hamath.

When we return to fragment 4Q550[b], there is more detail available on Line 4 which reads *"fear of the house of Saphra fell on him [..."* [88]. Once again, this has nothing to do with Esther. However, what did Ezra fear? Note, Esther is not a him and Mordecai fits nothing here. There is no family house of Saphra of note in anything here. Author Crawford notes of Saphra [88]:

> The "him" would appear to be Patireza (although the king is also a possible antecedent), but who or what is the house of Saphra? Saphra, which governs the construct bet ("house), may be either a proper name or a common noun, "scribe."

This is the house of the Scribe from the very words of this scholar trying to force Esther which cannot fit again. It could not be simpler when one tests this with Ezra, which they fail to do. Instead, another scholarly attempt is made to fit Esther, who was not a male nor a scribe, or Mordecai who also was no scribe. He worked at the palace gate and was given a government position later, but not as a scribe. More so, Ezra is from a house, a lineage of scribes and priests as a Son of Zadok and this is fully recorded. *"This Ezra went up from Babylon, as a Scribe being very ready in the Law of Moses... (1Esd.8:4)"* Ezra was not just any scribe, but the very scribe used to restore scripture as much was destroyed. Indeed, the *"fear of the house of Saphra (scribe) fell on him (Pater Ezra)."* This prophetic scribe would be used to restore the Law of which his knowledge excelled.

The next fragment with more information is labeled 4Q550[d] and it adds a few lines of text that are notable but again, not for Esther. In Line 1, it mentions *"because the error of my fathers"* which is specifically Ezra's prayer most certainly and Esther never even prays to Yahuah for her people. Her fasting is also a pagan ritual and she doesn't credit nor thank Yahuah nor mention His name even once. This is clearly the prayer of a Priest like Ezra and Esther and Mordecai have no such office. Where is the repentance of Esther? There is none. This is very close to 1st Esdras.

1 Esdras 8:76-77 KJVA (Ezra's Prayer)
*For ever **since the time of our fathers** we have been and are **in great sin**, even unto this day: And for **our sins and our fathers**, we with our brethren, and our kings, and our priests, were given up unto the Kings of the earth, to the sword, and to captivity, and for a prey with shame, unto this day.*

In Line 3, *"Judah, one of the leaders of Benjam[in...] an exile is standing to be received [...] goo[d..."* has no new significance as both stories are from this same era in which these conditions existed. However, Line 5 offers: *"that a Cuthite man is responsible [... your ki]ngdom, holding power instead of you holding power [..."* On the surface, this appears to reference Haman, the enemy of Israel in Esther. Of course, there are far too many other details that disprove that connection already. However, this is also very firmly 1st Esdras. In their return, Israel was rebuilding the Temple and this was successfully halted by their enemies who were the Cuthites or Samaritans.

It is incredibly illiterate for a scholar to assert this refers to Haman as he was an Agagite *(Esther 3:1)*. King Agag for whom the tribe is named was an Amalekite. They lived South of the Dead Sea. That is not Samaria. This scholar knows better yet somehow still tries to inject the Book of Esther into this fragment erroneously.

"Does "Cuthite" fit into this scheme? The term refers to the Samaritans, (16) inhabitants of northern Israel, who became enemies of the Jews in the late Persian and early Hellenistic periods, with a rivalry stretching back to the time of Nehemiah." [88]

This scholar does not connect this even a little as they forget where Samaria is and where the Amalekites/Agagites were from on two opposite sides of Israel. They try to stretch that since Esther's story is the time of the rebuilding of the Second Temple that somehow it fits simply due to that. Once again, they are ignoring the actual source of this story which is 1st Esdras in which most of the book is about the rebuilding of the Second Temple from the first decree of Cyrus to its completion and the final migration of the Southern Kingdom with Ezra who returned before Esther even entered the palace. The real question is why were Esther and Mordecai still in Persia? They would not be, and the story is false. The assumption made here is that since the Samaritans are enemies all Haman had to be was an enemy to qualify in this ineptitude. They are stretching and this fails.

Finally, of the newer interpretations, 4Q550f also brings in additional information. Line 1 is right out of 1st Esdras, and not Esther: *"behold from the North comes evil [..."* As we just covered in fragment d, Samaria is North of Yahudaea and they are the ones who petitioned Persia to stop the building of the Temple in 1st Esdras. Esther did not care about the Temple or would have returned to Jerusalem with the final wave she missed. Haman's Agagite tribe are the Amalekites to the South of Israel and that fails. Line 2 identifies the Temple in fact: *the building of Zion and in her shelter all the poor of [the] people [...]*" Notice, Esther is not about the Temple and this also serves to prove this is not Esther. It is not even part of its message. However, it is at the forefront of 1st Esdras throughout. How can scholar miss that?

Line 4 reads: *come up upon it. They swell up between Medea and Persia and Assyria and the [Great] Sea...*" The territory defined here again is not Haman from Esther. He is in Persia, but this is a reference to Israel's enemies who are after the Temple. They want it stopped or destroyed and that is very specific to 1st Esdras. Psalm 83 defines these same. If you draw a border from Media, Persia, and Assyria on the East and the Mediterranean Sea, there are many enemies who hated Yahudaea. In 165 B.C., they will finally join forces and overthrow the Temple, usurp the Priesthood and exile the true Temple Priests.

This is very fitting in reference to the Jerusalem Temple, the main topic of 1st Esdras, yet, never mentioned in the Book of Esther. Not one of these fragments coalesces with the Book of Esther and all match 1st Esdras. What kind of scholars are running the Dead Sea Scroll information or disinformation?

Right column of p. 575 of the Greek Uncial MS. Codex Vaticanus, from the Vatican Library, containing 1 Esdras 1:55-2:5. 4th century. Plate XXI. The S.S. Teacher's Edition: The Holy Bible. New York: Henry Frowde, Publisher to the University of Oxford, 1896. Public Domain.

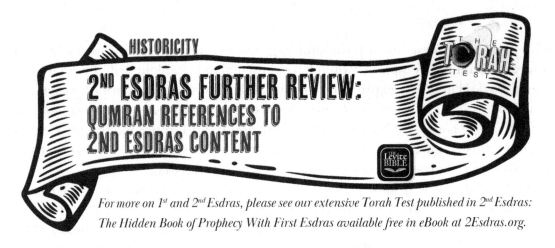

2ND ESDRAS FURTHER REVIEW: QUMRAN REFERENCES TO 2ND ESDRAS CONTENT

For more on 1ˢᵗ and 2ⁿᵈ Esdras, please see our extensive Torah Test published in 2ⁿᵈ Esdras: The Hidden Book of Prophecy With First Esdras available free in eBook at 2Esdras.org.

Just as 1ˢᵗ Esdras is found in so-termed "Proto" fragments in Qumran, so is 2ⁿᵈ Esdras being used in the prophetic interpretations by the local community there. In this case, 2ⁿᵈ Esdras is the only possible origin as in two fragments, Ezra's Eagle Empire is definitively apparent. This is the Prophet Ezra's continuation of Daniel's fourth beast leading to the End Times and Daniel neither recognizes it as an Eagle, nor offers this detail being quoted in interpretation. 2ⁿᵈ Esdras is the origin.

> *100 B.C.: 1QpHab, Cave 1 [Vermes, 510-11]:*
> *Their horses are swifter than leopards and fleeter than evening wolves. Their horses step forward proudly and spread their wings; they fly from afar like an eagle avid to devour. All of them come for violence; the look on their faces is like the east wind (i, 8~9a).*
>
> *[Interpreted, this] concerns the **Kittim who trample the earth with their horses and beasts**. They come from afar, from the islands of the sea, to **devour all the peoples like an eagle** which cannot be satisfied, and they address [all the peoples] with anger and [wrath and fury] and indignation. For it is as He said, The look on their faces is like the east wind.*

In his continuation of Daniel's fourth beast, the Prophet Ezra defines this final Empire as one, long continuous rising of the Final Eagle Empire. There is no other passage which identifies this as an eagle including Daniel who merely refers to it as a "beast, dreadful and terrible *(Dan. 7:7).*" This Eagle is so well defined over 2,000 years by Ezra including smaller feathers, wings and even opposing feathers which are all still part of this same construct of governments. Then, the Eagle has three heads which sleep until the last days and rise culminating in a one-world empire. We interpret this in major detail in our full publishing of 2ⁿᵈ Esdras: The Hidden Book of Prophecy as well as in our 26-Week Video Teaching Series on YouTube, Rumble, Playeur, Odysee with podcast available on most major podservers. Ezra defines this Eagle Empire over Chapters 11 and 12 from the time of the Roman Empire to its continuation as the Holy Roman Empire with change noted even with matching criteria, to the time of the End including it's doom. That is clearly what is being referenced here and in the next fragment, even more so.

> *2 Esdras 11:1-2 KJVA*
> *Then I saw a dream, and behold, there came up from the Sea an Eagle, which had twelve feathered wings, and three heads. And I saw, and behold, she spread her wings over all the earth, and all the winds of the air blew on her, and were gathered together.*
> *2 Esdras 12:3 KJVA*
> *And I saw, and behold, they appeared no more, and the whole body of the Eagle was burnt, so that the earth was in great fear:*
> *2 Esdras 12:24 KJVA*
> *And of those that dwell therein with much oppression, above all those that were before them: therefore are they called the heads of the Eagle.*

In a far more substantial match to 2ⁿᵈ Esdras 11-13, we see direct confirmation of the role of the exiled Temple Priests in Qumran/Bethabara as those preparing the way in the wilderness for the coming Messiah. We find a prophecy of their leader, John the Baptist, as a son of Zadok blessing Yahusha, known throughout the Qumran Scrolls as the Prince of the Congregation. This occurred in Bethabara which is Qumran *(see Introduction)*. This is definitive with multiple markers that fit.

> *The Blessing of the Prince of the Congregation (1QSb, 100 B.C.) [56]*
> *"The Master (John the Baptist) shall bless the Prince of the Congregation (Yahusha) . . . and shall renew for him the Covenant of the Community that he may establish the kingdom of His people for ever, [that he may judge the poor with righteousness and] dispense justice with {equity to the oppressed} of the land, and that he may walk perfectly before Him in all the ways [of truth], and that he may establish His holy Covenant at the time of the affliction of those who seek God. May the Lord raise you up to everlasting heights, and as a fortified tower upon a high wall! [May you smite the peoples] with the might of your hand and ravage the earth with your sceptre; may you bring death to the ungodly with the breath of your lips! [May He shed upon you the spirit of counsel] and everlasting might, the spirit of knowledge and of the fear of God; may righteousness be the girdle [of your loins] and may your reins be girdled [with faithfulness]! May He make your horns of iron and your hooves of bronze; may you toss like a young bull [and trample the peoples] like the mire of the streets! For God has established you as the sceptre. The rulers ... [and all the kings of the] nations shall serve you. He shall strengthen you with His holy Name and you shall be as a [lion; and you shall not lie down until you have devoured the] prey which naught shall deliver"*
> *– Calendars, Liturgies and Prayers, p. 389-390.*

John the Baptist, the son of Zadok through his mother's bloodline, and priestly line of Abiyah through his father's *(Luke 1:5)*, lived and operated in Bethabara *(see Introduction)* as a leader or master. He baptized Messiah in the place where Yahusha launched His ministry in Bethabara, not in the Jerusalem Temple *(Jn. 1:28-36)*. Only Messiah fits this Prince of the Congregation as he is judge of all *(2Esd. 12:33, 8:18, 7:33, 7:44, 7:69, 8:18, 13:37, 11:46)*. He has a kingdom established forever *(2Esd. 9:1-8)* and He established His covenant which fits no prophet *(2Esd. 13:38)*. Yahusha is the Scepter in prophecy *(Gn. 49:10, Nm. 24:17, Hb. 1:18)* who smites the ungodly peoples in the end *(2Esd. 9:9-13)* and all kings will only serve Messiah and no one else *(Psalm 72:11, Is. 45:22-25, Phil. 2:10, Rom. 14:11)*. Literally, He came in the name of Yahuah *(Yahusha, Jn. 5:43)* and no one can deliver those whom He judges and condemns to Hell *(2Esd. 7:45, 13:38)*. Only Yahusha brings death spiritually and in finality to the ungodly *(2Esd. 13:11, 49)* and with His breath, or as 2nd Esdras is being represented there, with fire from His mouth *(2Esd. 13:4, 10, 27, 38)*. Remember, Revelation is not written yet. This is quoting 2nd Esdras in large part with a clear understanding of prophecy in general. Even the Lion Messiah is mentioned prominently in 2nd Esdras *(2Esd. 11:37, 12:31-32)*.

This is overwhelmingly 2nd Esdras content in whole being used by the Temple Priests to interpret prophecy. One of the most telling is the manner in which Yahusha consumes the wicked on the Day of Judgment which is very specific to 2nd Esdras though the whole passage coalesces with 2nd Esdras.

> *2 Esdras 13:9-11 KJVA*
> *And lo, as he saw the violence of the multitude that came, he neither lift up his hand, nor held sword, nor any instrument of war. But only I saw that **he sent out of his mouth, as it had been a blast of fire, and out of his lips a flaming breath, and out of his tongue he cast out sparks and tempests**, And they were all mixed together; the **blast of fire**, the **flaming breath**, and the **great tempest**, and fell with violence upon the multitude**, which was prepared to fight, and burnt them up every one, so that upon a sudden, of an innumerable multitude, nothing was to be perceived, but only dust and smell of smoke: when I saw this, I was afraid.*
> *2 Esdras 13:38 KJVA*
> *And shall lay before them their evil thoughts, and the torments wherewith they shall begin to be tormented, which are **like unto a flame**: and he shall **destroy them without labor, by the law which is like unto fire.***

Though Yahusha is certainly denoted as the Lion of Judah or Yahudah in scripture. This prophecy of the Eagle includes the lion Messiah who comes out of the woods to condemn this terrible beast in the end. A perfect contextual match.

2 Esdras 11:37 KJVA
And I beheld, and lo, as it were a roaring Lion, chased out of the wood: and I saw
that he sent out a man's voice unto the Eagle, and said, Hear you, I will talk with
you, and the Highest shall say unto you, Are you not it that remains of the four
beasts, whom I made to reign in my world, that the end of their times might come
through them?

This Eagle Empire continues to the very Day of Judgment in what will be a one world empire of sort as much prophecy affirms. This is the same Eagle consumed by the lion Messiah in the end.

2 Esdras 11:31-32 KJVA
And behold, the head was turned with them that were with it, and did eat up the
*two feathers under the wing that would have reigned. But **this head put the whole***
***earth in fear**, and bare rule in it over all those that dwelt upon the earth, with*
*much oppression, and **it had the governance of the world more then all the wings***
that had been.

There is no doubt both of these fragments align with the content of 2nd Esdras 11-13 and nothing else could coalesce as perfectly. 2nd Esdras was indeed quoted and used in written interpretation around 100 B.C. in the Qumran community. This means it was written before that and used as inspired scripture in Qumran whether we have direct fragments or not. These are very direct interpretations using the Book of 2nd Esdras period. We also know historically, there was a practice among the very early church that included 2nd Esdras as the same book as 1st Esdras.

"Origen, in his Commentary on Ps. i, gives the second list that we know of, which
belongs to a time not later than A.D. 231 ; he reckons as belonging to the Canon
the twenty-two books of the Hebrew Old Testament. But, strange to say, Origen
includes in his list the First Book of Esdras (he treats 1, 2 Esdras as one book) and
the Epistle of Jeremiah, neither of which had ever been regarded as canonical by
*the Jews. Origen's list is adopted by **Athanasius, Cyril**, and **Epiphanius**, as well as*
*in the **Laodicean Canon**, in each case with the addition of **Baruch**.*
*Furthermore, as Dr. Swete goes on to say {op. cit., p. 222), '**Amphilochius***
*mentions two books of Esdras, and it is at least possible that the Esdras of **Gregory***
*of **Nazianzus** is intended to include both books, and that the Epistle, or Baruch*
and the Epistle, are to be understood as forming part of Jeremiah in the lists both
of Gregory and Amphilochius.' The point of importance which these facts reveal
*is that 'an expansion of the Hebrew Canon, which involved **no addition to the***
***number of the books**, was predominant in the East during the fourth century.'"*
[81, Charles, p. 298] [91]

Scholars noting that some quote or kept 1st Esdras but not 2nd Esdras because they do not break it out in the ancient mindset, do not represent the ancients and do not understand the pattern associated with how they kept scripture. This also included the Book of Jeremiah which incorporated Baruch and Letter of Jeremiah *(Baruch 6)* as addendums as well as the Book of Daniel which attached Susanna as Chapter 13, Bel & The Dragon as Chapter 14, and Prayer of Azaryah inserted after 3:23 historically. Those scholars ignoring such are not Bible scholars especially in light of the Qumran scrolls they have marginalized and ignored in illiteracy. 1st and 2nd Esdras were used in 100 B.C. in Qumran. That makes them inspired Bible Canon and we further prove this in 2nd Esdras: The Hidden Book of Prophecy With 1st Esdras available free in eBook at 2Esdras.org.

Illustration of the three-headed eagle from Ezra's vision of Daniel's fourth beast.
Head-piece to second book of Esdras, vignette with three headed eagle flying above a wave; letterpress in two columns below and on verso. 1812, published 1815. Inscriptions: Lettered below image with production detail: "J Landseer fecit/Crouch end 1812", "P J de Loutherbourg delt", and publication line: "Published 3 July 1815 Mess Cadell & Davies". Print made by John Landseer. Dimensions: height: 490 millimetres (sheet); width: 393 millimetres (sheet). Public Domain.

WISDOM OF SIRACH: ECCLESIASTICUS

Wisdom of Sirach, known especially since Jerome as Ecclesiasticus, was also present in the fragments found in Qumran. The Temple Priests included this in their Bible Canon. There is no modern scholar who can ignore nor override that with any credibility. The Temple Priests did not make a mistake as to what was scripture and no scholar has the right to second guess something so important with ridicule and scoffing they call textual criticism.

> *"Psalms Scroll from Cave 11 contains seven apocryphal poems, including chapter li(51) of the Wisdom of Jesus ben Sira, not annexed to, but interspersed among, the canonical hymns." – Vermes, p. 16[22].*

> *"...the Wisdom of Jesus ben Sira or Ecclesiasticus in Hebrew. Part of the latter, chapters xxxix-xliv (39-44), has also survived at Masada, and hence cannot be later than 73/4 c e, the date when the stronghold was captured by the Romans, and two medieval manuscripts, discovered in the storeroom (genizah) of a synagogue in Cairo in 1896, have preserved about two thirds of the Greek version. – Vermes, p. 11 [22].*

In addition to direct fragments *2QSir, 11Q5* and *MasSir* attributed to Sirach, there are some portions within 4Q Instruction, the Wisdom Literature that no doubt originate in Sirach as well.

> *"The deuteronomic phrase is used by both (Sir 9:1; 4Q416 VI 5, 13). Further, both books have an interest in family matters and surety. They can use similar terminology on the risk involved in surety: Sir 29: 15"for he offers his very life for you"; 4Q416 IV 5 "you have giv]en away all your life for him". [94]*

> *"In its opening lines, 4QInstruction projects a message that one is better able to understand the nature of God by understanding the regularity and structure of the cosmos, an idea also encountered in Ben Sira (Sir 39:12–15; 42:15–43:33; cf. 4Q417 1 I, 27)." p. 335. [96]*

The first and sole true judge of historicity is whether or not a text was found affirmed in the Dead Sea Scrolls where the Temple Priests were who kept the only official Bible Canon to the First Century. We have established that with Sirach.

Sirach is legitimately dated as written around 200 B.C. or so which is the time of the grandson. These fragments date very close to that era in fact within about a century. Thus, we would not expect to find it quoted in the Old Testament of course. However, we do find it in the New Testament and especially from James who was very clearly steeped in the theology and wisdom of Sirach. These are similar and R.H. Charles *[81]* even notes that the Greek at times is even closer than the English translations.

THE GREEK VERSION AND THE SECONDARY GREEK TEXT INCLUDING SIRACH EARLY:

R.H. Charles accurately notes that Sirach was written very close to the time it was first translated into the Greek Septuagint which included it as canon. As he was an adept translator, he recognized Sirach was originally written in the Hebrew even evident in the Greek translation. With Hebrew portions being discovered in his time and the finding of Hebrew fragments in the Qumran Scrolls decades after Charles died, this becomes further entrenched. The tradition of Sirach in the church originates in the Greek Septuagint largely but Sirach was originally written in Hebrew. Though we do not have a specific date it began to be included in the Septuagint, we already know Sirach was written around 200 or so B.C. and then, appears shortly after in Qumran and in copies of the Greek Septuagint. The Qumran community did not write Sirach but kept it from the 165 B.C. exile through the first century. What was found there was a copy.

> Among the versions of Sirach this is the most important as being the earliest. As the Prologue tells us, the Greek translation was made from the original Hebrew by the author's grandson; there was, therefore, **not a long period of time between the original writing and its Greek translation. The Greek form of the book was that in which it was first officially received by the Church.** Another fact which enhances the importance of this version is that in a number of instances **the text represents a purer form of the original Hebrew than that contained in the manuscripts of the Hebrew text recently discovered.** This fact makes the use of the Greek version extremely valuable, and indeed indispensable, for the reconstruction of the Hebrew text. [81, Charles, p. 280]

SIRACH IN THE NEW TESTAMENT, FIRST CENTURY:

First, James (Yacob), the brother of Yahusha, was clearly not just familiar but emerged in the Wisdom of Sirach. The scholarly litmus test sets a false paradigm when it demands that James identify every word of scripture he uses, attributing the book of origin. He did not need to and who are they to say he did? They have no right to demand such. That is the opposite of scholarship. It is bullying propaganda. The words of wisdom here are attributed to Sirach because Sirach was in the Bible or scroll library James used. These are incredibly similar, and no doubt originate in Sirach whether any scholar wishes to ignore the obvious or not. R.H. Charles really nailed this down in his compilation of the apocrypha.

Sirach:	*James: New Testament: Charles, p. 295. [81]*
18:18, 20:15, 41:22 wisdom given, upraid not	*James 1:5 wisdom given, upraid not*
1:28 Disobey not the Lord ; and come not unto Him vilh a double heart	*1:6,8 that doubteth is like the surge of the sea driven by the wind and tossed...*
2:12 Woe unto fearful hearts, and to faint hands, and to the sinner that goeth two ways ; woe unto the faint heart, 7:10 Be not fainthearted in... prayer	*a doubleminded man unstable in all his ways*
2:1 if thou comest to serve the Lord, prepare thy soul for temptation	*1:2-4 Count it all joy, my brethren, when ye fall into manifold temptations*
15:11-20 Say not thou, It is through the Lord that I fell away. . . . Say not thou, It is He that caused me to err, For He hath no need of a sinful man	*1:13-15 Let no man say when he is tempted, I am tempted, of God : for God cannot be tempted with evil, and He Himself tempteth no man,*
5:11 Be swift to hear	*1:19 Let every man be swift to hear*
12:11 And thou shall be unto him as one that hath wiped a mirror	*1:23 he is like unto a man beholding his natural face in a mirror*
27:13 The discourse of fools is an offense, and their laughter is in the wantonness (pleasure) of sin	*5:5 Ye have lived delicately on the earth, and taken your pleasure*
38:9-15 My son, in thy sickness be not negligent, but pray unto the Lord and He shall heal thee	*5:14 Is any among you sick? let him call for the elders of the church;and let them pray over him, anointing him with oil in the name of the Lord.*

The Book of Hebrews, likely written by James who loved Sirach's wisdom, uses the terminology *"weak hands"* or *"hands which hang down"* and *"feeble knees"* which originates from Sirach as well.

> ***Hebrews 12:12 KJV:*** *Wherefore lift up the **hands which hang down**, and the **feeble knees**;*

*Sirach 25:23: A wicked woman abates the courage, makes a heavy countenance, and a wounded heart: a woman that will not comfort her husband in distress makes **weak hands**, and **feeble knees**.*

R.H. Charles sums up that James was well versed and influenced by the Wisdom of Sirach.

"If these examples are not sufficient to establish a relation of direct dependence, they are sufficient to justify the inference—which is confirmed by the general character of the Epistle and its relation to other books of the Wisdom-Literature—that the author of St. James was well acquainted with, and was influenced by, Sirach.
*– **R.H. Charles, Apocrypha, p. 295. [81]***

Charles identified other New Testament passages that had origins in Sirach as well. This leads to Yahusha quoting Sirach multiple times.

Sirach:	*New Testament: Charles, p. 295. [81]*
25:23	*Heb. 12:12*
31:3, 11:18-19	***Luke 12:15 ***Yahusha Quoted Sirach******
28:2	*Matt. 6:14 ***Yahusha Quoted Sirach****
29:12	*Matt. 6:19 ***Yahusha Quoted Sirach****
32:24	*Matt. 16:27 ***Yahusha Quoted Sirach****
48:10	*Luke 1:17* **Yahusha Quoted Sirach****

One of the better examples here is Yahusha quoting Sirach in very similar form in Luke 12:15 especially. For those that require Messiah to always attribute every word He spoke to the book from where it originated, that is one of the most illiterate of false paradigms. The content is a match and Yahusha quoted Sirach.

Luke 12:15 KJV
And he said unto them, Take heed, and beware of covetousness: for a man's life consisteth not in the abundance of the things which he possesseth.
Sirach 31:3 KJVA
The rich have great labor in gathering riches together, and when he rests, he is filled with his delicates.
Sirach 11:18-19 KJVA
There is that waxes rich by his wariness, and pinching, and this is the portion of his reward: Whereas he says, I have found rest, and now will eat continually of my goods, and yet he knows not what time shall come upon him, and that he must leave those things to others, and die.

Is there ancient precedence for Yahusha's famous statement about knowing men by their fruits? This is extremely significant as he was quoting the Wisdom of Sirach, not creating new doctrine. Yahusha says: "Ye shall know them by their fruits." This is worded even more closely in the NRSV Sirach as "...the fruit discloses the cultivation." Yahusha quoted the Wisdom of Sirach. Why would any church avoid it? The scoffer may exclaim these are different because Yahusha editorializes as if the Son of Yahuah is not allowed to do so. We all know that is just plain stupid.

> *Matthew 7:16-20 KJV: Even so every good tree bringeth forth good fruit; but a corrupt tree bringeth forth evil fruit. A good tree cannot bring forth evil fruit, neither can a corrupt tree bring forth good fruit. Every tree that bringeth not forth good fruit is hewn down, and cast into the fire. Wherefore by their fruits ye shall know them. (Cf. Luke 6:43-47)*
>
> *Sirach 27:6 The fruit declares if the tree has been dressed: so is the utterance of a conceit in the heart of man. NRSV: "...the fruit discloses the cultivation."*

Messiah expresses He is the vine and we are the branches. He speaks of the sinner's heart representing rocky soil in which good seeds cannot take root. The sinner does not bring forth many branches as a result and bad fruit, if any. This is all wrapped up together with the previous wisdom that you shall know them by their fruits. Believers bear good fruit and are pruned and flourish. The wicked will be cut off and burned in the fire. This entire analogy is not original to Yahusha. He read and understood the Wisdom of Sirach. One of the most important passages in all of the New Testament where Yahusha defines salvation, derives from the Wisdom of Sirach. He quoted it and editorialized in deeper explanation. Though Charles and the 1611 KJV did not catch this, this is definitive.

> *Mark 4:5 KJV: And some fell on stony ground, where it had not much earth; and immediately it sprang up, because it had no depth of earth: 16-17: And these are they likewise which are sown on stony ground; who, when they have heard the word, immediately receive it with gladness; And have no root in themselves, and so endure but for a time: afterward, when affliction or persecution ariseth for the word's sake, immediately they are offended. (Cf. Matt. 13:18–23; Luke 8:11–15; John 15:1-11)*
>
> *Sirach 40:15: The children of the ungodly shall not bring forth many branches: but are as unclean roots upon a hard rock.*

Additionally, one cannot get a better witness to the Wisdom of Sirach than the Holy Spirit Himself. While pregnant with Yahusha in the womb, Mary visited Elizabeth. In response to Mary's news of Messiah, John the Baptist leapt in the womb and Elizabeth was filled with the Holy Ghost *(Luke 1:41)*. In response amid this Holy Spirit encounter, Mary, also guided by the Holy Spirit, cites Sirach.

Luke 1:52 KJV (Mary speaking to Elizabeth): He hath put down the mighty from their seats, and exalted them of low degree.
Sirach 10:14-16: Yahuah has cast down the thrones of proud princes, and set up the meek in their stead. Yahuah hath plucked up the roots of the proud nations: and planted the lowly in their place. Yahuah overthrew countries of the heathen: and destroyed them to the foundations of the earth.

We all know the scriptures that Yahuah is no respecter of persons or shows no partiality. In terms of salvation, we are in a relationship with Him, or we are not. We are born again (saved), or we are not. This line that is drawn in the New Testament is not new. It likely originates in the Wisdom of Sirach which both Peter and Paul were reading and applying in doctrine as inspired scripture. In this case, it is Sirach which editorializes further, and Peter and Paul very clearly understood this.

*Acts 10:34 KJV: Then Peter opened his mouth, and said, **Of a truth I perceive that God is no respecter of persons:***
*Romans 2:11 KJV: For **there is no respect of persons with God.***
*Galatians 2:6 KJV: But of these who seemed to be somewhat, (whatsoever they were, it maketh no matter to me: **God accepteth no man's person:**) for they who seemed to be somewhat in conference added nothing to me:*
*Sirach 35:12-16: **Do not think to corrupt with gifts,** for such **he will not receive:** and trust not to unrighteous sacrifices, for Yahuah is judge, and **with him is no respect of persons.** He will not accept any person against a poor man: but will hear the prayer of the oppressed. He will not despise the supplication of the fatherless: nor the widow when she pours out her complaint. Do not the tears run down the widow's cheeks? And is not her cry against him that causes them to fall? He that serves Yahuah, shall be accepted with favor, and his prayer shall reach unto the clouds.*

One can read many commentaries and books which note Yahusha's words that one who will not forgive their brother will not be forgiven. Oddly, most of those scholars do not research the origin of such a paramount statement which better come from scripture with a second witness. There are even some who will assert this was Messiah creating new doctrine which is illiterate. For Yahusha was quoting Sirach 28 in this regard.

Matt. 6:14-15 KJV
For if ye forgive men their trespasses, your heavenly Father will also forgive you: But if ye forgive not men their trespasses, neither will your Father forgive your trespasses.
Sirach 28:2 Forgive your neighbor the hurt that he has done unto you, so shall your sins also be forgiven when you pray.

We also find Paul's dissertation against gluttony in 1 Cor. 6:12-13 and 10:23-26, truly aligns with Sirach 36:18 and 37:28-30. Again, Sirach was published first so there is no wiggle room for scholars against Sirach. Also, Acts 20:35 credits Yahusha for saying "It is more blessed to give than to receive." That is not a quote documented of Yahusha Messiah. This is a quote from Yahusha Ben Sirach 4:31 exactly.

These especially are not minor doctrines in any sense, yet these bedrocks of the New Testament originate in the Wisdom of Sirach from centuries earlier proven in archaeology and not debatable. This should be no surprise but what is, is the number of scholars who are uneducated on this topic yet dare to position themselves as experts in ignorance. Is the Wisdom of Sirach found in the New Testament in application? Indeed, it is even quoted more than once by Yahusha Himself with significance. Who is any scholar to override Him and His Apostles?

1611 KJV ANCHORS NEW TESTAMENT ORIGINS TO SIRACH:

When it comes to the Original 1611 Authorized King James Version, Ecclesiasticus *(Wisdom of Sirach)* was translated into the English just like the canonical books. That is far too significant of an effort for any church to try to ignore this book because it was classified as outside the Pharisee Canon, an impertinent point that every pastor and scholar should be aware. However, the 1611 King James identifies and anchors portions of Sirach as the origin of verses found in the New Testament and we will only cite those margin notes that do not recognize any Old Testament anchor in that same note. That proves a very significant test.

Scholars try to then, marginalize even this fact yet they cannot overcome it. Some of these are right out of the words of Yahusha meaning He quoted Sirach according to the 1611 KJV, not us. If one is especially "KJV only" or they are looking for Sirach in their Bible, it was there in 1611 and with New Testament content anchored to it as the origin of the words of Messiah and the Apostles. That is no small thing. Here are some of those examples as further evidence. We did not include any of those references which also include Old Testament at the same time as either could be the origin. In these cases, it is Sirach that is the likely origin and there are far too numerous to ignore. You can look these up for yourself on *KingJamesBibleOnline. org* directly. They even have a photo of the exact page and you can read it in the Original 1611 Authorized King James Version for yourself. It is there.

Sirach:	New Testament: 1611 KJVA Anchor to NT:
2:1 ***Yahusha Quoted Sirach***	Matt. 4:11; 2Tim. 3:12; 1Pet. 4:12
2:15 ***Yahusha Quoted Sirach***	John 14:20
3:18	Phil. 2:3
5:1 ***Yahusha Quoted Sirach***	Luke 12:15
5:11	James 1:19

6:25 ***Yahusha Quoted Sirach***	Matt. 11:29
7:14 ***Yahusha Quoted Sirach***	Matt. 6:5, 7
8:2 ***Yahusha Quoted Sirach***	Matt. 5:25
8:5	Gal. 6:2; 1Cor. 2:6
11:4	Acts 12:21
11:19 ***Yahusha Quoted Sirach***	Luke 12:19
11:20 ***Yahusha Quoted Sirach***	Matt. 10:22
14:1	James 3:2
14:13 & Tobit 4:7 *(One or the other is the origin)*	Luke 14:13 ***Yahusha Quoted Sirach or Tobit***
17:23 ***Yahusha Quoted Sirach***	Matt. 25:35
17:24	Acts 3:19
18:10	2Pet. 3:8
18:20	1Cor. 11:28, 31
Sirach:	*New Testament: 1611 KJVA Anchor to NT:*
18:30	Rom. 6:6, 13:14
19:16	James 3:2
24:17 ***Yahusha Quoted Sirach***	John 15:1
25:8	James 3:2
27:6 ***Yahusha Quoted Sirach***	Matt. 7:17
31:1	1Tim. 6:9, 10
31:8 ***Yahusha Quoted Sirach***	Luke 6:24
32:23	Rom. 14:5
35:9	2Cor. 9:7
40:18	Phil. 4:12; 1Tim. 6:6

We then find some of the so-called "Early Church Fathers" continuing to quote the Wisdom of Sirach as that is an already established New Testament practice which began with the original curators of Bible Canon – the exiled Temple Priests in Qumran very close to the time Sirach was written to the First Century. No beat is missing here. These only have value in this spectrum as support as these serve only as secondary affirmation and are not our position. Some attempt to only use these as evidence by itself and we agree that is not within itself good enough. One needs more precedence, and the primary evidence of the Qumran scrolls fully establish this along with the New Testament quotes.

We do not care who disagrees with a certain passage in connection as that is not our position and no way to attempt to debate it. It does not matter what Early Church Fathers were against it either as they clearly did not represent the Bible paradigm if they thought they had the authority to remove scripture the ordained keepers of scripture as well as the Apostles and Messiah Himself already established. They do not get a vote and neither does any modern scholar. That is scoffing, not scholarship. All this evidence works together to prove the Wisdom of Sirach was and remains inspired scripture from the experts whose opinion mattered rather than from modern scholars whose does not. This is the ancient precedent already established but the pattern continues in 80 A.D. to 570 A.D. and beyond. There is no debate and once again, notice how tight the window is here. There is only a century between the Qumran dating and the original composition and now, there is less than a century, as early as 80 A.D., Sirach was still used as scripture. It takes an incredibly inept scholar to attempt to debate that.

SIRACH: 80-570 AND BEYOND: AFTER THE APOSTLES:

80: Didache 4:5-6: References Sirach 4:31 and 4:36. [84][81]

177: Tertullian: Contra Gnostic 8, De Exhort. Castit. 2, De Had. Mnl. 3 cites Sirach as canon. [81]

198: Clement of Alexandria: The Instructor 2.8 quotes Sirach 39:26 as the "Scripture says..." [89] The Instructor 2:1 cites Sirach 18:32, 31:25, 26, 27, 29, 26:8, 31:20, 21:20, 20:5, 8, 31:31, 14:1, 9:9, 31:16-18, 32:11, 9:15, 18, 39:13-14, 26-27, 23:18-19, 18:30, 11:4. [90] The Instructor, 1:8 quotes Sirach 21:6. [81]

248: Origen: Contra Celsum 6.7 cites "Jesus the son of Sirach, who has left us the treatise called Wisdom..." [84][Against Celsus, 7:12 quotes Sirach 21:18 as "sacred scripture." [81]

252: Cyprian of Carthage: Treatise 7.9 quotes Sirach 2:1,4 5. Testimonia (e.g. 3.95, 96) (258 A.D.) and in his letters (e.g. Ep. lix. 20), has many quotations from Sirach. [81]

265: Dionysius the Great: On Nature, 3 quotes Sirach 16:24-25. [81]

305-384: Pope Damasus I: Divine Scriptures included Ecclesiasticus. [84]

310: Lactantius: Institutions, 4:8 quotes Sirach 24:3-5. [81]

311 : Methodius: Bishop of Lycia "quotes without reserve from Sirach, Wisdom, and Baruch, treating them all as 'Scripture.'"[81]

315-403 : Epiphanius of Salamis: Adversus Haereses (Against Heresies), 76.5 cited "...the books of Wisdom, that of Solomon and the Son of Sirach as inspired scripture." [84]

324: Alexander of Alexandria: "To brother Alexander, fragment in Theodoret of Cyrus' Ecclesiastical History 1:3 quotes Sirach 1:2 and 3:21." [81]

337-397: Ambrose of Milan: De Fide Bk. 1.6.47 quotes Sirach 28:28. [84]

345: Aphraates the Persian Sage: Demonstrations, 22:7 quotes Sirach 29:17. [81]

347-407: John Chrysostom: Sirach 9:15 quoted in Homilies on First Corinthians, 15.10 [81]

350: Cyril of Jerusalem: Catechetical Lectures, 6:4 quotes Sirach 3:20,21. [81]

362: Athanasius: Discourses Against the Arians, 2:79 quotes Sirach 1:8,9. [81]

368: Hilary of Poitiers: Prol. in libr. Psalm "cites Ecclesiasticus and Wisdom as prophets, 'an expression which seems to imply his belief in their canonicity." [81]

370: Basil: Hexaemeron, 6:10 ""What Scripture says is very true, 'As for a fool he changeth as the moon' [Sirach 27:11].” He defined Sirach true scripture. [81][84]

376-444: Cyril of Alexandria: Commentary on Isaiah, Chap. 6: Sirach 15:9. [84]

382: Council of Rome: Decree of Pope Damasus listed the Old Testament to include Wisdom... Ecclesiasticus [Sirach]... Jeremias one book (with Baruch 1-6)... Daniel one book (with Susanna, Bel, and Azaryah)... Tobit... [81]

387: John Chrysostom: Homily 35 on Acts quotes Sirach 15:9 [89] Homilies on John, 48 (391 A.D.) quotes Sirach 1:19, 10:9. [81]

387-493: St. Patrick of Ireland: Letter to Coroticus 8: Sirach 34:24. [84]

391: Ambrose: Duties of the Clergy, 1:2:5 quotes Sirach 20:6. [81]

393: Council of Hippo: Sirach was specially mentioned as being one of the canonical books. [81]

397: Council of Carthage: the 'five books of Solomon', i.e. Proverbs, Ecclesiastes, Canticles, Wisdom, and Sirach, are reckoned among the canonical Scriptures. [81]

397: Philastrius of Brescia: De Haeres. 88 quotes Sirach as the work of a 'prophet'. [81]

400: Apostolic Constitutions: 47:85 endorses Sirach as “And besides these, take care that your young persons learn the Wisdom of the very learned Sirach.” [81]

404: Jerome: To Eustochium, Epistle 108 cites Sirach as scripture: “[D]oes not the scripture say: 'Burden not thyself above thy power' [Sirach 13:2]?” [81]

419: Council of Carthage: Affirmed 397 canon including Sirach.

420: Jerome: First to use the term “apocrypha” it appears including Sirach as such. In his Commentary on Isaiah (2:3) he prefaces quotations from Sirach and Wisdom with 'sicut scriptum est,' [81]

426: John Cassian: The Institutes, 4:37 quotes Sirach 2:1. [91] De Inst. Caen. 4:8 (450 A.D.) cites Sirach 2:1 as Scripture. [81]

430: Augustine: De Doctr. Christiana, 2:8 and Speculum include Sirach as canonical. [81]

434-445: Vincent of Lerins: Commonitory for the Authenticity and Universality of the Catholic Faith, 21:51 quotes Sirach 8:14. [81][84]

461: Pope Leo the Great: Sermon 49:6 quotes Sirach 3:29 as “Scripture.” [81]

480-547: Benedict of Nursia: Rule of St. Benedict: 7 quotes Sirach 18:30. [84]

550: Pseudo-Gelasian: His list of canon includes Sirach and Wisdom... [81]

570: Cassiodorus: “...in his enumeration of the books of the Bible {De inst. Div. litt. 14) also includes Sirach and Wisdom among the books of Solomon, and therefore regards them as canonical; so also Tobit...” [81]

The Wisdom of Sirach has always remained Bible Canon. No scholar can undermine it. The fact that they have attempted for so many centuries proves their denomination does not fully represent scripture especially when they do not even know who kept the Bible canon to the First Century which is inexcusable. This was established long before that church existed and before there was ever a Pharisee party usurping the power over the worship of Yahudaea. Even at that time, the true Bible Canon was preserved in a time capsule in Qumran/Bethabara. In the category of historicity, the Wisdom of Sirach is inspired scripture and Bible Canon which no one can derail.

Jesus Ben Sirach, 1860 woodcut by Julius Schnorr von Karolsfeld, a Lutheran. Public Domain.

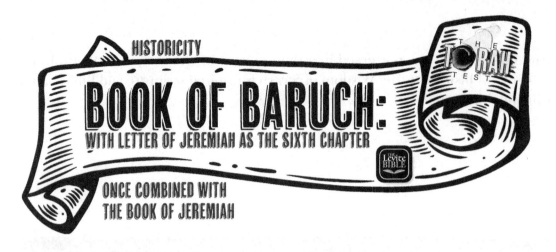

HISTORICITY
BOOK OF BARUCH:
WITH LETTER OF JEREMIAH AS THE SIXTH CHAPTER

ONCE COMBINED WITH THE BOOK OF JEREMIAH

QUMRAN, FIRST CENTURY B.C.:

When Paul was quoting the words of Baruch, which he did, it was still included in the Book of Jeremiah not a separate book as history did not treat it that way. When fragments of Jeremiah were found in Qumran, Baruch was there as it was part of it whether direct fragments of those chapters were found or not. However, one needs no conjecture because Letter to Jeremiah was found in Qumran, and it is Chapter 6 of Baruch not a separate book either. You can see the extent that scholars have gone to in order to disconnect this inspired scripture from its place in the Bible Canon. It is not scholarship, but propaganda.

In fact, you will find the Book of Baruch confused with Jeremiah often in ancient times because it was once part of the Book of Jeremiah in treatment. The Letter of Jeremiah was also included as Baruch Chapter 6 as well. That is historical fact according to many of the so-called early church fathers such as Athenagoras *(177)* who called the words written in Baruch the words of the Prophet Jeremiah, but they match Baruch *[81][78][84]*. He was not confused, modern scholars are when they simply do not get it. Irenaeus *(180)* cites Baruch 4:36-5:9 as being from the Book of Jeremiah *[79][81]* because it was, though today it is treated as separate in error. Clement of Alexandria *(198)* references several passages from the Book of Baruch as the words of Jeremiah, yet they are Baruch's words which is consistent and the two cannot be separated really *[81]*. In 244, Origen records *"Jeremiah, with Lamentations and the epistle (Baruch 6) in one, Jeremiah [81]*.

Even in the Fourth Century when many Greek fathers separated books of the apocrypha, Baruch served as the exception as it was an appendix to the Book of Jeremiah *[81]*. For instance, Lactantius *(305)* "cites Baruch 3:36 as the words of Jeremiah along with citations from Isaiah and the Psalms *[81]*." Pope Damasus I *(305-384)* documents the "Divine Scriptures included... Jeremias, one book" (including Baruch and Letter of Jeremiah) *[84]*. At the Council of Laodicea *(343-380)* "Jeremiah is listed with Baruch and Lamentations, though all three are named [77]." In 350 A.D., Jeremiah is treated as one book by Cyril of Jerusalem, not three separate ones: *"of Jeremias, one, along with Baruch, Lamentations and the Letter [of Jeremiah]"* *[77]*. Athanasius *(367)* lists **"Jeremias, and along with it, Baruch, Lamentations, and the Letter"** *[77][84]* also treating the three books as Jeremiah all in one. Hilary of Poitiers *(359)* quotes Bar. 3:36–38 citing *"Jeremias"*, about which Jurgens states: **"Baruch was secretary to Jeremias, and is cited by the Fathers mostly under the name of Jeremias"** *(Jurgens §864)*.

In the Council of Rome *(382)*, the Decree of Pope Damasus listed the Old Testament to include Jeremiah as one book with Baruch 1-6, and Chapter 6 being the Letter of Jeremiah. The Councils of Hippo and Carthage *(393-397)*, treat the Book of Jeremiah to include Baruch 1-5 and the Epistle *(Letter)* of Jeremiah *(Baruch 6)* as one book *[77]*. Even as late as 1442 and 1546, the Councils of Florence and Trent continued to include: *"Jeremias with Baruch" as stated as canonical; but the Letter of Jeremiah is not specified, being included as the sixth chapter of Baruch in late medieval Vulgate Bibles"* [84]. *[See Baruch/Letter of Jeremiah: 132-1550: After the Apostles.]* This practice continues in some circles to this day.

This was never a mystery. These supposed three books are one in the same historically all penned by the hand of the famous scribe and prophet, Baruch including Jeremiah's words and his own. They were partners in prophecy and Baruch was the disciple and mouthpiece of Jeremiah even. To dismiss that synergy and endorsement is illiterate. As Letter of Jeremiah, which they separated out later erroneously, was actually Baruch Chapter 6, the finding of fragments of its contents in Cave 7 of Qumran proves that the Book of Baruch was directly found in Qumran. Baruch 6 was, and it matters not that scholars have attempted to separate it as Letter of Jeremiah as if Baruch was not his scribe and did not write it. That is truly willing ignorance. It also proves the Septuagint Greek version likely included Baruch even before 100 B.C. thus, from the date of its first translation between 300-200 B.C., it was Bible canon. It certainly was in Qumran/Bethabara and it should still persist in our modern Bibles.

> *"Among the nineteen, minute fragments found in Cave 7 - which contained only Greek texts - two have been identified as relics of Exodus 28:4-7 (7Q1) and the Letter of Jeremiah, verses 43-44 (7Q2 or papLXXEpJer). The former is said to be closer to the traditional Hebrew text than to the LXX (Septuagint). Both are dated to about 100 b.c.e."* – Vermes, p. 572. *[22]*

The find at Qumran also produced a portion of the actual Book of Jeremiah in 2QJer or 2Q13. Again, that included Baruch 1-5 and 6 (Letter of Jeremiah) at that time according to historical tradition. No one discards the other chapters of Jeremiah not found. Either way, the Book of Baruch is tied to the Dead Sea Scrolls indisputably. This means it was included in the only Old Testament Bible canon endorsed by the Bible and even Messiah Himself to the First Century.

JEREMIAH IN BARUCH:

R.H. Charles noticed the cohesion of the Book of Jeremiah and portions of Jeremiah borrowed from the same scribe who wrote the prophet's words in the Book of Baruch. Though this is not our position, it serves as secondary evidence of the synergy well documented.

> *"Another point to which the same writer calls attention is the close connexion between LXX on Jeremiah and our own text in those cases where borrowings from Jeremiah have taken place"* [81]

Baruch:	Borrowed From Jeremiah: Charles, p. 577 [81]
1:9	24:1
2:3	19:9
2:4	42:18
2:11	32:21
2:13	42:2
2:21, 22	34:9-10
2:23	25:10-11

In addition, R.H. Charles catalogues several very close similarities between Baruch and Song of Solomon *(See margin notes)*. Solomon's writing would come first of course. Jeremiah would as well though portions written likely at the same time.

NEW TESTAMENT ORIGINS FROM BARUCH/LETTER OF JEREMIAH:

The 1611 Authorized King James Version only includes one cross-reference with 1 Corinthians 10:20 originating in Baruch 4:7 thus, documenting that Paul quoted Baruch. One is enough when the book is rather small and found in the Bible Canon of the Qumran Temple Priests. Bear in mind, the KJV tradition comes down to us through the Greek and these, in part, read essentially as the same wording. That is quite significant.

> *1 Corinthians 10:20 KJV*
> *But I say, that the things which the Gentiles sacrifice, **they sacrifice to devils, and not to God:** and I would not that ye should have fellowship with devils.*

> *Baruch 4:7 KJVA*
> *7 For you provoked Him that made you, by **sacrificing unto devils, and not to Elohim.***

BARUCH/LETTER OF JEREMIAH: 90-1550: AFTER THE APOSTLES:

However, beyond the New Testament and into the next era, we find the Book of Baruch treated as inspired Bible canon still. That was not the new practice as we find it used in Qumran/Bethabara by the Temple Priests as well as by Paul. Any scholar claiming it was new at that point or any era after, as we have even seen some claim that practice new in the 1500s, is ignorant of the Qumran Scrolls and what Baruch is. For most, that already settles this test. Baruch was in the Greek Septuagint which was originally created in 300-200 B.C. but scholars would then, question that it was not added because they don't have an index of books from that period, nor a full copy. However, we know it was treated as scripture in that era by the use of Baruch in Qumran near that time and Paul in the First Century.

The Syriac version in 132 A.D. continued this tradition as Baruch was treated as scripture. That is extremely close in era. However, even closer in 90 A.D., Josephus, who was a Pharisee who did not include Baruch in his Pharisee Bible which is impertinent to any discussion, well knew the skill of Baruch, not just as Jeremiah's scribe but as the mouthpiece of the prophet. He is sly to ignore naming Baruch's book but he most certainly included Baruch's content without attribution. For those scholars requiring that Pharisee to tell the truth in quoting Baruch, perhaps someday they will mature to elementary levels where we could allow them to participate in discussion. For now, many undermine their own credibility. Some even claim the Talmud or Midrash as origins, yet both are later. What that also proves, and we will not cover because they are an impertinent religion to the Bible, the Rabbis also used Baruch as it was first in those instances they try to forge.

> *90 A.D.: Josephus:*
> *Accordingly Jeremiah abode in a city of that countrey which was called Mispah; and desired of Nebuzaradan that he would set at liberty **his disciple Baruch, the son of Neriah; one of a very eminent family; and exceeding skilful in the language of his country (Hebrew).***
> *– Flavius Josephus, Antiquities of the Jews, Book 10:1, 90 A.D. [76]*

> *"Baruch, his own disciple…"*
> *"Accordingly both the people, and Johanan disobeyed the counsel of God, which he gave them by the Prophet, and removed into Egypt; and carried **Jeremiah and Baruch** along with him." – Flavius Josephus, Antiquities of the Jews, Book 10:1, 90 A.D. 10:6, 90 A.D. [76]*

This passage is followed up with a more recent footnote by the translator which identifies that the Book of Baruch, labeled "apocrypha" inappropriately, is Bible Canon, genuine and serves as an addition to and part of the Book of Jeremiah. Of course, Josephus did not write that nor would he. No Pharisee would. Instead, he lied misrepresenting the words of Baruch as his own. That is unacceptable in any age of scholarship.

> *"Of this character of **Baruch**, the son of Neriah, and the genuineness of his*
> *Book, that stands now in our apocrypha; and that it is really a canonical book,*
> *and an appendix to Jeremiah, see Authent. Rec. Pt I. pag. 1–11."*
> *– Flavius Josephus, Antiquities of the Jews, Book 10:1, Footnote 22 by*
> *William Whiston: University of Cambridge. London. 1737. [76]*

As usual Josephus was not honest enough to credit his very obvious use of books like Jubilees which he certainly did use for geography without crediting the book several times. R.H. Charles noted several such occurrences in which it appears Josephus quoted Baruch or the details thereof in 90 A.D. without offering honest intellectual sourcing since Baruch was not in his Pharisee Canon. He used it regardless. In fact, in 2:13, etc. *[below]*, Charles used the language those passages *"are fully attested by Josephus."* Again, no attribution is made by Josephus but that is clearly his character flaw, not Baruch's which he quoted period. If Josephus used even its historical numbers, he only demonstrates a conflict of interests in any credible determination of the canonicity of a book he quoted and used without even honestly divulging such. It proves he was no authority on Bible Canon as he was not even honest. Baruch remained powerful enough for him to refer to its content several times and no one can conceal that, or at least not any longer. This is a major problem for most scholars holding this view against Baruch as inspired Canon. 90 A.D. is during the time the New Testament was being written still and Baruch was being used for history and truly as scripture by Josephus though he fraudulently did not credit whom he was copying.

Baruch:	Quoted By Josephus, 90 A.D.: Charles, p. 575 [81]
2:21	*Wars of the Jews, 2.17.3*
2:2, 3, 24	*Wars of the Jews, 6.3.4 and 4.5.1-2*
2:25	*Wars of the Jews, 6.9.2-3*
2:13, 14, 23, 29 ; 3:8	*Wars of the Jews, 6.9.3*
1:2, 2:26	*Wars of the Jews, 1.7.4f ; Jos., ibid., 6.4.*

According to R.H. Charles, Origen *(231)* also references, with centuries of tradition following him, that Baruch and the Epistle of Jeremiah continued to be treated as part of the Book of Jeremiah and Bible Canon.

*Origen, in his **Commentary on Ps. i**, gives the second list that we know of, which belongs to a time not later than **A.D. 231** ; he reckons as belonging to the Canon the **twenty-two books** of the Hebrew Old Testament.3 But, strange to say, Origen includes in his list the **First Book of Esdras** (he treats 1, 2 Esdras as one book) and the **Epistle of Jeremiah (Letter of Jeremiah)**, neither of which had ever been regarded as canonical by the Jews. Origen's list is **adopted by Athanasius, Cyril, and Epiphanius,4** as well as in the **Laodicean Canon**, in each case with the addition of Baruch.*

*Furthermore, as Dr. Swete goes on to say {op. cit., p. 222), '**Amphilochius** mentions two books of Esdras, and it is at least possible that the **Esdras of Gregory of Nazianzus** is intended to include both books, and that the Epistle, or Baruch and the Epistle (Letter of Jeremiah), are to be understood as forming part of Jeremiah in the lists both of Gregory and Amphilochius.' The point of importance which these facts reveal is that '**an expansion of the Hebrew Canon, which involved no addition to the number of the books, was predominant in the East during the fourth century** '. – Charles, p. 298. [81]*

The Book of Baruch 1-5 with Baruch 6, known as Letter or Epistle of Jeremiah, were quoted by many so-called Early Church Fathers and considered in ancient Bible Canons after the era of the Apostles from 90 A.D. forward. No supposed "Church Father" had the right to change what the Temple Priests already established as Old Testament and though they did in some cases, the Book of Baruch and its Chapter 6 *(Letter of Jeremiah)* were included in the Book of Jeremiah as the ancient tradition passed down as reliable, inspired scripture. Already found in Qumran dated to 100 B.C. as a Greek text likely from the original Hebrew, part of the original Septuagint of 300-200 B.C. most likely, and quoted in the First Century at least by Paul, we find Baruch continued in practice as inspired.

90 A.D. Josephus: [see chart, left]
132: Syriac version: Baruch was included as scripture. [81]
177: Athenagoras of Athens: Plea for Christians 9 cites Baruch in the same arena of prophetic testimony as Jeremiah. [78][84] "Athenagoras, in his Apologia, addressed to the emperor, M. Aurelius, cites (§ 69) Bar. 3:35 as the words of an inspired prophet in close connexion with passages from Isaiah." [81]
177: Melito of Sardes: Quotes "Bar. 3:38 in his Commentary on St. John's Gospel, and also Bar. 3:9-13 in his Jerem. Homil. 7:3." [81]
180-190: Theodotion's Greek Version: Baruch was considered canonical. [103]
180: Irenaeus of Lyons: Adversus Haereses (Against Heresies): 5.35.1 draws extensively on Baruch 4:36 to 5:9. Irenaeus cites these readings as being from the Book of Jeremiah. [79][81]
198: Clement of Alexandria: The Instructor Bk. 2.3 quotes Bar. 3:16-19. [84] and in "Paean for Wisdom (217 A.D.)" (Jurgens §410a) [81] The Instructor,

1:8 quotes Baruch 3:9. Paedag. 1:10.91-2 cites several passages from the Book of Baruch as the words of Jeremiah. [81]

*205: **Tertullian:** Scorpiace, 8, quotes Bar. 6:3. Adv. Praxean 16 references Bar. 3:37. [81]*

*210: **Hippolytus:** Against the Noetus, 2 quotes Baruch 3:25-38. [81]*

*244: **Origen:** Canon of the Hebrews, Fragment in Eusebius' Church History, 6:25 "canonical books" included "Esdras, First and Second in one" "Jeremiah, with Lamentations and the epistle in one, Jeremiah [Baruch 6]." [81]*

*252: **Cyprian:** Test, adversus Jud. 2:6 quotes Bar. 3:35-37. [81]*

300: "Yet in fact many Greek Fathers of the fourth century separated the Apocryphal (or so-called Deutero-Canonical) writings from the Canonical. Baruch, however, formed an exception, since it was treated as an appendix to Jeremiah..." [81]

*305: **Lactantius:** Inst. 4.38 cites Bar. 3:36 as the words of Jeremiah along with citations from Isaiah and the Psalms." [81]*

*305-384: **Pope Damasus I:** " Divine Scriptures included... Jeremias, one book" (included Baruch and Letter of Jeremiah). [84]*

*311: **Methodius:** Bishop of Lycia quotes without reserve from Sirach, Wisdom, and Baruch, treating them all as 'Scripture.' [81]*

*311: **Dionysius of Alexandria:** Apost. Const cites Bar. 4:4 and Bar. 3:14-15. [81]*

*343-380: **Council of Laodicea:** "Jeremiah is listed with Baruch and Lamentations, though all three are named [77]."*

*350: **Cyril of Jerusalem's** 4th Catechetical Lecture: Jeremiah is treated as one book: "of Jeremias, one, along with Baruch, Lamentations and the Letter [77]." Catechetical Lectures, 9:15 quotes Baruch 3:36-38. [81]*

*350: **Ephrem the Syrian:** "regarded Bar., as well as the other Apocrypha, as Scripture." [81]*

*350: **Codex Vaticanus:** Canon placed "...in the order Jeremiah, Baruch, Lamentations, Letter of Jeremiah..." [104]*

*351: **Athanasius:** Defense of the Nicene Faith, 2:12 quotes Baruch 3:12. Discourses Against the Arians, 1:4 (A.D. 362) quotes Baruch 4:20,22. [81]*

*367: **39th Festal Letter of St. Athanasius:** Lists "Jeremias, and along with it, Baruch, Lamentations, and the Letter." The "Letter" refers to the Letter of Jeremiah, which is appended as the sixth chapter of Baruch in Catholic Bibles and other Bibles, including the King James Version , although the latter doesn't place it in the biblical canon." [77][84]*

*359: **Hilary of Poitiers:** (Bar. 3:36–38) citing "Jeremias", about which Jurgens states: "Baruch was secretary to Jeremias, and is cited by the Fathers mostly under the name of Jeremias" (Jurgens §864). Prol. in libr. Psalm Epistle of Jeremiah included as canon. [81]*

*375: **Basil:** On the Holy Spirit, 6:15 quotes Baruch 3:3. [81]*

382: Council of Rome: Decree of Pope Damasus listed the Old Testament to include Wisdom... Ecclesiasticus [Sirach]... Jeremias one book (with Baruch 1-6)... Daniel one book (with Susanna, Bel, and Azaryah)... Tobit... [81]

384: Gregory of Nyssa: Against Eunomius, 6:4 quoted Baruch 3:38. [81]

384: Ambrose: Concerning Repentance, 1:9:43 quoted Baruch 5:1. [81]

*393-397: Councils of Hippo and Carthage: "In addition, Steinmueller says: "Modern scholars also point out that **one and the same translator translated Jeremias, Baruch, and the Epistle of Jeremias from the Hebrew into the Greek,** and thus these three books had been considered as one, a fact that is also confirmed by early church documents" (Ibid., emphasis added). The canonical lists of the Councils of Hippo (A.D. 393) and Carthage (A.D. 397) would be such examples." [77]*

399: Jerome: To Oceanus, Epistle 77:4 quotes Baruch 5:5. [81]

400: Codex Alexandrinus: Canon placed "...in the order Jeremiah, Baruch, Lamentations, Letter of Jeremiah..." [104]

400-500: Eritrean/Ethiopian Orthodox Bible: Included Baruch as canonical. [103]

403: John Chrysostom: Against Marcionist & Manicheans cites "And Baruch in the book of Jeremiah says... yet quotes Baruch 3:35-37 as Jeremiah." [81]

404: Rufinus of Aquileia: The Apostles Creed, 37-38: Baruch 3:36-38. [81]

430: John Cassian: The Incarnation of Christ, 4:13: Baruch 3:37,38. [81]

*519 and 553: Anonymous Latin Scholar: "...contains a **list of books of Scripture presented as having been declared canonical by the Council of Rome (382 AD).** Again this list asserts the canonicity of Jeremiah without reference to Baruch." [80]*

676-749: John Damascene: Exact Exposition of the Orthodox Faith Bk. 4.6 quotes Baruch 3:38. [84]

*1442 & 1546: Council of Florence and Council of Trent: "Jeremias with Baruch" is stated as canonical; but the **Letter of Jeremiah is not specified, being included as the sixth chapter of Baruch** in late medieval Vulgate Bibles. [84]*

The tradition is clearly documented. No scholar has the right to change what the Temple Priests kept found in archaeology to at least 100 B.C. That was continued in the New Testament and quoted by Josephus during that same time in the First Century. Then, Baruch and Letter of Jeremiah (Baruch 6) were found as Canon, included as the Book of Jeremiah with massive precedence as inspired scripture, shortly after still in 132 A.D. and passed to the next generations for more than one thousand years including the tradition. The number of poorly written commentaries on this are astounding. This is simple research, easy to reproduce and check. Baruch is inspired Bible Canon.

PRAYER OF MANASSEH:

ONCE COMBINED WITH 2ND CHRONICLES IN THE ACCOUNT OF KING MANASSEH'S REPENTANCE

2 Chronicles 33:12-13 KJV (King Manasseh Repents in Captivity)
*And when he was in affliction, he besought the LORD his God, and humbled himself greatly before the God of his fathers, And **prayed unto him**: and he was intreated of him, and **heard his supplication**, and **brought him again to Jerusalem** into his kingdom. Then Manasseh knew that the LORD he was God. **33:19: His prayer also, and how God was intreated of him**, and **all his sin**, and **his trespass**, and the places wherein he built high places, and set up groves and graven images, before he was humbled: behold, **they are written among the sayings of the seers.***

QUMRAN, B.C. ERA:

Chronicles defines Manasseh's prayer was *"written among the sayings of the seers"* with information found in the Original 1611 Authorized King James Version of the Prayer of Manasseh. Many scoffers love to think those in history had nothing better to do than to make up writings. In this case, its a prayer written by one who very clearly was connected to this event being King Manasseh himself. However, this account reads exactly as one would expect. A liar could not have written this as an imposter and the contents of this prayer are Biblical. Not only is there nothing to fear in reviewing this, it vets as inspired.

A fragment labeled "Prayer of Manasseh" that even begins with such text, same as the 1611 King James, was found in Qumran in Cave 4 – 4Q381 33, 8 [22]. However, after titling the fragment appropriately as it gives that title in its text, there are scholars who actually back up and claim the content is another account. One must wonder, can they read? This is far too common among scholars who are incapable of reading two texts and affirming the similarities, when they do not wish to, of course. This is Apocrypha. So, they are not motivated to find it in the Dead Sea Scrolls, yet it is there. The content, however, though it is worded differently indeed, is incredibly similar to the point of becoming a definitive match to the 1611 KJVA Prayer of Manasseh. The 1611 tradition comes to us from the Greek translation in origin and this fragment is in Hebrew. Thus, how could scholars be surprised the wording is different without bothering to test the content? Remember, that was centuries before the Dead Sea Scrolls were discovered.

However, it does not just bear the title the same in the text, a head on comparison with the Qumran fragment and the 1611 KJVA concur in content indeed.

TEST: PRAYER OF MANASSEH: DEAD SEA SCROLLS, 4Q381 33, 8 *(Vermes, p. 324-325.) [22]*
VS. 1611 KJV APOCRYPHA VERSION: *[Bold In Brackets]*

D.S.S. 8a. "Prayer of Manasseh, King of Judah when the King of Assyria gaoled him.
[Apocrypha Subtitle from 1611 KJVA 400+ years before the Dead Sea Scrolls were found:
The prayer of Manasseh, King of Yahudah, when he was held captive in Babylon.] MATCH!

D.S.S. 8b. . . . [my G]od . . . my salvation is near in Thine eyes . . .
[Apocrypha 1:1: O Yahuah, Almighty Elohim (God)... 1:14: ...for you will save me that am
unworthy, according to your great mercy. 1:7b: and of your infinite mercies have appointed
repentance unto sinners that they may be saved....] CONTENT MATCH!

D.S.S. 9a. I wait for Thy delivering presence, and I feel faint before Thee because of my s[in].
[Apocrypha 1:8b-9a: ...but you have appointed repentance unto me that am a sinner: for I have
sinned above the number of the sands of the sea.] CONTENT MATCH!

D.S.S. 9b. For [Thou hast] enlarged [Thy mercies(?)], and I have multiplied guilt.
*[Apocrypha 1:9b: My transgressions, O Yahuah, are **multiplied:** my transgressions are **multiplied,***
*and I am not worthy to behold and see the height of heaven, for the **multitude of mine iniquity.** 1:7b:*
and of your infinite mercies have appointed repentance unto sinners that they may be saved....]
CONTENT MATCH!

D.S.S. 10a. And thus . . . from eternal joy and my soul shall not see goodness . . .
[Apocrypha 1:12-13: I have sinned, O Yahuah, I have sinned and I acknowledge my iniquities:
wherefore I humbly beseech you, forgive me, O Yahuah, forgive me, and destroy me not with my
iniquities. Be not angry with me forever, by reserving evil for me, neither condemn me into the
lower parts of the earth.] CONTENT MATCH!

D.S.S. 10b. He has lifted me up on high above a nation . . . And I did not remember thee [in Thy
plac]e of h[oliness];
[Apocrypha 1:10: I am bowed down with many iron bands, that I cannot lift up my head, neither
have any release: For I have provoked your wrath, and done evil before you, I did not your will,
neither kept I your Commandments: I have set up abominations, and have multiplied offenses.]
CONTENT MATCH!

D.S.S. 10c. I did not serve [Thee] . . ."
[Apocrypha 1:10b: I did not your will, neither kept I your Commandments: I have set up
abominations, and have multiplied offenses. 1:12: I have sinned, O Yahuah, I have sinned and
I acknowledge my iniquities...] CONTENT MATCH!

It is dumfounding that a scholar would actually claim these are not the same account based on their confusion of the Hebrew vernacular verses the Greek which is the origin of the KJVA. They would go out of their way to explain this acceptable difference if it were a text they wanted to defend. However, no one needs their consensus as it remains illiterate at present for many. These are indeed the same account as the content is practically a complete match from the title down to even small fragments. This is not something anyone can debate.

In the case of Baruch and Letter of Jeremiah *(Baruch 6 historically)*, we find that Jeremiah, just like Daniel, is documented as having addendums in practice even in Qumran. Baruch 6 *(Letter of Jeremiah)* was found there. Baruch was the scribe and fellow prophet with Jeremiah and here we have the same practice with a famous prayer recorded as written scripture in 2nd Chronicles 33:19. Someone wrote it and published it somewhere as Canon says the Bible. Where else would it be placed other than as an addendum to the book that references this account and written prayer. Most scholars attribute Jeremiah or his scribe, Baruch, as the writer of 1-2 Kings and 1-2 Chronicles. This is a sensible connection especially now that we know firmly, this text was affirmed in Qumran to 50 B.C. or so. Also, Prayer of Manasseh is documented in the ancient Greek Septuagint. This addendum is not strange in the Septuagint. They were "welded together" in the LXX Greek Septuagint.

> *"Then follow extracts from the LXX of 2 Kings 21:1-18 and 2 Chron. 33:1 ff., which are welded together and expanded by four Additions, to which there is nothing corresponding in the Hebrew text (Charles did not have the benefit of the Dead Sea Scrolls decades later which proves this wrong essentially). The order in which these extracts follow one another is as follows:*
>
> | | |
> |---|---|
> | *(1) 2 Kings 21:1-4.* | ***(7) Addition B., followed by 'The Prayer of*** |
> | *(2) 2 Chron. 33:5-8.* | ***Manasses'.*** |
> | *(3) 2 Kings 21:9-16.* | *(8) Addition C.* |
> | *(4) 2 Chron. 33:11.* | *(9) 2 Chron. 33:13^b.* |
> | *(5) Addition A.* | *(10) Addition D.* |
> | *(6) 2 Chron. 33:12-13^a.* | *(11) 2 Chron. 33:15, 16."* |
> | *– Charles, p. 613. [81]* | |

Though it was added into the Vulgate in later editions, this text was already being censored or lost for more than a thousand years to many. That, however, cannot overcome the fact it was Bible Canon in Qumran kept by the Temple Priests who are the only ordained to curate Bible Canon to the First Century. Prayer of Manasseh was found included in Didascalia *(200)*, Apostolical Constitutions *(300-400)*, Codex Alexandrinus *(400)* and Codex Turicensis *(600)* *[81]*. There is enough evidence here to determine that Prayer of Manasseh was and remains inspired Bible Canon.

3. ACCEPTANCE

For more on 1st and 2nd Esdras, please see our extensive Torah Test published in 2nd Esdras: The Hidden Book of Prophecy With 1st Esdras available free in eBook at 2Esdras.org.

As they all represent Old Testament times, all six of these mislabeled "apocryphal" books fit well into the Biblical paradigm in the identity of Israel especially. One cannot get more Israelite than these books. However, there are also prophesies of Messiah as well.

IDENTITY OF BIBLICAL ISRAEL:

1st Esdras:

As it is the story of the return of the Southern Tribes to Israel in the days of Ezra, this book restores the Law and sees the return of Biblical Israel to their homeland. Much of the content overlaps with the Book of Ezra and it not only follows Biblical Israel even by families, but 1st Esdras identifies Israel's enemies in their home region which is critical.

2nd Esdras:

The prophet Ezra defines Daniel's fourth beast, the coming enemy Eagle Empire, to its transition over thousands of years all the way to its destruction in the End Times. It is the true believers who oppose this foe, and it is destroyed in the End really bringing the Old and New Testaments together. Ezra laments the destruction of Jerusalem and the Temple in his era of captivity but sees the rebuilding of the Temple, the restoration of the Law, and even the Word as much was damaged in the fire. Ezra's position is that of a prophet and scribe who affirms Biblical Israel as the rest of the Bible has always viewed it.

Wisdom of Sirach:

In Chapter 36 especially, Sirach prays for the deliverance of Israel. He, also, honors the patriarchs of Israel's past (44:1-50:29) and one cannot separate Sirach from the scriptural view of Biblical Israel.

Baruch /Letter of Jeremiah:

As Jeremiah's scribe, disciple, spokesperson and fellow prophet, Baruch wrote the Book of Jeremiah and also, shares his own prophecy. His view of Biblical Israel is just as Jeremiah's, and one cannot wax more scriptural in this regard.

Prayer of Manasseh:

In the time of King Manasseh, the critical issue for Israel as a whole was that of sin and idol worship. He was guilty of propagating that lifestyle rebelling against Yahuah. This prayer, documented as a published writing in 2ⁿᵈ Chronicles 33:19, is a precious repentance for himself and Biblical Israel representing a return to the ways of Yahuah. Yahuah heard his prayer and restored him as a result. In the end, Manasseh repented and returned to Yahuah's ways blessing Biblical Israel.

YAHUSHA AND THE APOSTLES TO COME:

Of course, not all Old Testament books contain prophecy of the coming Messiah. One can force archetypes or types of Christ as some attempt, but there is never a need to do so and we will not in this testing in which all six of these texts already pass as identifying with Biblical Israel. It is notable, however, that some of these have strong prophesies on Yahusha coming in the flesh as well as His Second Coming.

1ˢᵗ Esdras:

As this is a two-part book sometimes even treated as one, prophecy is reserved generally for the second book.

2ⁿᵈ Esdras:

This book has an incredible amount of End Times revelation as to the roll of Yahusha in His Second Coming. However, the Prophet Ezra directly predicts the coming of Messiah in 400 years in his time about 400 B.C. and He knew His name would be called Yahusha (7:28). He foresaw Yahusha's death and ascension as well. 2ⁿᵈ Esdras is used to interpret multiple fragments in Qumran documented in the local writings there to about 100 B.C. before Messiah and thus, proves accurate prophecy even. His view of Yahusha is repeated in Revelation, by Yahusha Himself even according to the 1611 KJV Margin, and by the Apostles.

Wisdom of Sirach:

The Apostles and Yahusha quote Sirach in content numerous times. In 47:11, this book is a clear prediction of the coming Messiah. It foreshadows Yahusha's taking away the sins of the world and was given the covenant of kings and a throne of glory. Also, His horn is exalted forever which is a direct elusion to First Enoch's Animal Dream Vision (1 En. 89-90) in which Messiah is viewed as a ram with one horn of power that the Pharisees could not break until the timing was right for His sacrifice. Sirach identifies with Yah's people.

Baruch /Letter of Jeremiah:

Baruch prophesied Messiah would come from Jacob's bloodline and live among men (3:36-37). He speaks of Israel giving away their honor to a strange nation consistent with Messianic prophesies (4:1-4).

Prayer of Manasseh:

Though there are not any references in this one-chapter prayer to Messiah specifically, this is the Old Testament and an addendum to 2nd Chronicles with no need to express such prophecy.

4. IN AGREEMENT WITH THE WHOLE OF SCRIPTURE (OUR ADDITION)

For more on 1st and 2nd Esdras, please see our extensive Torah Test published in 2nd Esdras: The Hidden Book of Prophecy With 1st Esdras available free in eBook at 2Esdras.org.

We find most of these books quoted in content in the New Testament several times. Messiah and the Apostles generally read them and taught them. Anyone claiming that Yahusha taught scripture with which He did not agree, is not a scholar of anything Biblical.

1st Esdras:

When one reads the Book of Ezra and 1st Esdras in parallel, they will find a great affinity. The content of this book agrees and vets as inspired scripture.

2nd Esdras:

Serving as the foundation for the Book of Revelation on many doctrines especially, 2nd Esdras is proven inspired scripture. This book vets as accurate prophecy and used far too often for significant doctrine by the Apostles to be ignored and shoved aside into a category in a false paradigm. Messiah also directly quoted a paragraph from 2nd Esdras even according to the 1611 KJV.

Wisdom of Sirach:

As our largest book in this Apocrypha series, Sirach is packed with wisdom akin to the other wisdom texts throughout the Bible and even in the Dead Sea Scrolls. It does not truly introduce anything new in theology that would shatter in any comparison to other scripture. It shares so much because it belongs with the rest of what we call Bible Canon with which it agrees.

Baruch /Letter of Jeremiah:

It is rather difficult to pinpoint another writer who could be as credible as Jeremiah's scribe, disciple, mouthpiece and fellow prophet. This account tests as accurate and inspired in content and historicity.

Prayer of Manasseh:

Not only is this prayer documented as published according to 2nd Chronicles 33:19, it is a clear match to that found in Qumran as consisting as part of Bible Canon in antiquity in the only history that matters. As a true prayer of real repentance, this is a must read for all of us. Nothing in this prayer persists against scripture.

All six of these texts vet as inspired Bible Canon in every category. Authorship is not truly a problem for either. They have historic support since the Dead Sea Scrolls and a continued historicity into the Early Church. All six view Biblical Israel and ultimately the ekklesia of Messiah consistent with the rest of scripture and they have no real conflicts in content with the rest of the Bible. We will complete this Torah Test for the rest of the 1611 King James Apocrypha in Volume 2 coming very soon after this publishing. It will be announced on our many platforms, but all can check ApocryphaTest.com for an update.

Certainly, there will be some scholar who will claim but what about...? And what about fragment...? How about they use their brain and begin to reconcile anything they view as a discrepancy with all of scripture, as they do this with Bible Canon too. Everything we have found them trying to treat as discrepancies, prove in a reconcile to be disinformation of illiterate children. Even the Gospels and Torah have been torn apart by some scholars and it is illiterate anti-Biblical, satanic behavior unbecoming of anyone calling themselves a Bible scholar.

There is truly nothing left for debate. The reason there is argument today among scholars is that most do not even know whom the Bible ordained to keep Bible Canon to the First Century. Shame on them. In losing track of these holy priests who were the curators of the original Bible, they also lose sight of the synagogue of satan who replaced them since 165 B.C. usurping the Priesthood and the Temple even, but never legitimately. The fact that those call themselves Bible scholars and yet, follow the Pharisees is practically the dumbest paradigm in world history. These are literally the opposite of the Temple Priests and keepers of Canon. They were rebuked so many times on this topic by Yahusha and somehow Bible scholars do not seem to even know it *(See "Pharisee Fruits" Chart)*. Instead, they are trained by Pharisees to sit in the seat of the scornful. They scoff, change the Bible, insert occult and Pharisee doctrine far too often and it is a sad state. This is exactly what we were warned in the coming "strong delusion" which has been with us for centuries. The Dark Ages never passed away and began long before the Catholic Church, though it continues to propagate that delusion today.

2 Thessalonians 2:11-17 KJV
And for this cause God shall send them strong delusion, that they should believe a lie: that they all might be damned who believed not the truth, but had pleasure in unrighteousness. But we are bound to give thanks alway to God for you, brethren beloved of the Lord, because God hath from the beginning chosen you to salvation through sanctification of the Spirit and belief of the truth: whereunto he called you by our gospel, to the obtaining of the glory of our Lord Jesus Christ. Therefore, brethren, stand fast, and hold the traditions which ye have been taught, whether by word, or our epistle. Now our Lord Jesus Christ himself, and God, even our Father, which hath loved us, and hath given us everlasting consolation and good hope through grace, comfort your hearts, and stablish you in every good word and work.

1611 King James Version
APOCRYPHA
SCROLLS FOUND IN QUMRAN
AND THOSE NOT PRESENT

See also, 2ⁿᵈ Esdras: The Hidden Book of Prophecy, free in eBook at 2Esdras.org.

CONCLUSION:

6 Texts Are Inspired Scripture By Direct Reference And Used In Interpretation In Qumran Fragments Thus, Not Apocrypha Ever!

For the Remaining Books, See Vol. 2 For Test Completion.

A Book That Is Not Pharisee Is The Wrong Measure To Begin With. A Pharisee Canon Is No Way To Determine What Is Inspired!

Criteria set forth by Blue Letter Bible with our additions. [1]

THE
TORAH
TEST

BOOK	1. Prophetic Authorship	2. Witness Historicity	3. Yah's People Acceptance	4. Agreement w/ Scripture
FOUND IN QUMRAN:				
1st Esdras	✓ Prophet Ezra	✓	✓	✓
2nd Esdras	✓ Prophet Ezra	✓	✓	✓
Wisdom of Sirach *(Ecclesiasticus)*	✓ Family of Sages	✓	✓	✓
Wisdom of Solomon	☐ Test In Vol. 2	☐	☐	☐
Book of Tobit	☐ Test In Vol. 2	☐	☐	☐
Book of Susanna	☐ Test In Vol. 2	☐	☐	☐
Prayer of Manasseh *(Addendum to 2 Chronicles)*	✓ Baruch For Jeremiah	✓	✓	✓
Letter of Jeremiah *(Baruch 6 Historically)*	✓ Baruch For Jeremiah	✓	✓	✓
BY ASSOCIATION:				
Once Part of Jeremiah:				
Baruch *(Addendum to Jeremiah. Ch. 6 found)*	✓ Baruch W/ Jeremiah	✓	✓	✓
Once Part of Daniel:				
Prayer of Azariah *(Abednego - The Song of the Three Young Men)*	☐ Test In Vol. 2	☐	☐	☐
Bel and the Dragon *(Daniel's exploits)*	☐ Test In Vol. 2	☐	☐	☐
NOT FOUND IN D.S.S.:				
Judith	☐ Test In Vol. 2	☐	☐	☐
Book Of Esther *& Additions*	☐ Test In Vol. 2	☐	☐	☐
1st & 2nd Maccabees *& Additions*	☐ Test In Vol. 2	☐	☐	☐

See Testing The Book of Esther & Purim, Testing The Book of Judith, and Testing 1st & 2nd Maccabees & Hanukkah in Volume 2.

THE NAME OF GOD IN "APOCRYPHA"

One revealing sign that portions of "apocrypha" may yet as legitimate is their use of the name of YHWH though more testing must be done. In a quick search of this book, we find over 450 uses of YHWH in what we will prove to be credible texts. However, the Book of Esther never addresses, prays to, fasts for, or even thanks or credits YHWH in the entire story which should raise many red flags. The Bible does not use an acrostic of the name of YHWH, it spells it out over 6,800 times directly in the Hebrew Old Testament. It is never hidden and always has been pronounced.

We learn from Jubilees Hebrew is the language of Creation thus it must be simple and somehow for thousands of years, it was written with just consonants and a couple of vowels *("A" and "U")* yet spoken without ever needing vowel points. Those were added in about 1000 A.D. by the Masoretes and at times serve to offer more confusion than clarity as they clearly were not honest about the name of Yahuah since it was their Pharisee practice to hide His name. Therefore, this must be a phonetic language requiring no vowels and no fancy rules especially those changing even within a word illogically. What we call Hebrew today is Yiddish-infused.

Phonetically, YH is simple. H is AH *(see chart to right)*. That's YAH. The next combination is HW which we know by the names of the prophets is HU. Thus, it's YAHU as with the prophets. Finally, we add the last H or AH for YAHUAH.

We recognize there is a whole church out there which stakes it's claim on the name Jehovah. Here's the largest problem with that word. It is not Ancient Hebrew, Aramaic, Greek, Latin, Old French, Old German nor Old English. In other words, every language in which the Bible has been interpreted through in origin cannot render" J" nor "V" until the Renaissance *(1500s or so)*. The Bible was already thousands of years old and never used "J" nor "V" in any ancient text. There is a Pharisee out there deceiving many by trying to make this fit, but we have the Dead Sea Scrolls dating to as early as 300 B.C. with even entire books such as the Isaiah scroll of about 25 feet in length which never renders a "J" nor a "V" even once.

This leads us to the name of Messiah as the same first 3 letters YHW or YAHU as set by Yahuah. Yes, He literally meant He came in His Father's name. His name ends with SH - SHIN, A - AYIN which is SHA. He is Yahusha with Yahushua also appearing as a variant in scripture. Joshua has this same name in Hebrew. His people are the YAHUdim, never Jews but YAH's.

Finally, some focus on the one time in scripture that Yahuah says His name is HYH, HAYAH as His only name ignoring the 6,800 times it is recorded as YHWH, Yahuah. However, modern Yiddish renders this as EHYEH and similar in fraud. Ancient Hebrew is HA YAH or THE YAH. It is the same name. Yahuah is being specific in saying I am The Yah, not to be confused with any other. He is still invoking His name Yahuah in that passage which matches. In fact, YAH is rendered in the Old Testament 45 times on a standalone basis. Scripture is clear and abundant on this.

FATHER **YAHUAH**

יהוה

HEY　WAW　HEY　YAD

H_AU H_AY

YAHUAH

SON **YAHUSHA**

"YAHU IS SALVATION"

יהושע

AYIN　SHIN　WAW　HEY　YAD

NO "J"

NO "V"

NO VOWEL POINTS

_AH S U H_AY

YAHUSHA

Yeshua Is Missing Letters and of Pharisee Origin

				Ancient Semitic/Hebrew		
Early	Middle	Late	Name	Picture	Meaning	Sound
𐤀		א	El	Ox head	Strong, Power, Leader	ah, eh
		ב	Bet	Tent floorplan	Family, House, In	b, bh(v)
		ג	Gam	Foot	Gather, Walk	g
		ד	Dal	Door	Move, Hang, Entrance	d
		ה	Hey	Man with arms raised	Look, Reveal, Breath	h, ah
		ו	Waw	Tent peg	Add, Secure, Hook	w, o, u
		ז	Zan	Mattock	Food, Cut, Nourish	z
		ח	Hhet	Tent wall	Outside, Divide, Half	hh
		ט	Tet	Basket	Surround, Contain, Mud	t
			Yad	Arm and closed hand	Work, Throw, Worship	y, ee
		כ	Kaph	Open palm	Bend, Open, Allow, Tame	k, kh
		ל	Lam	Shepherd Staff	Teach, Yoke, To, Bind	l
		מ	Mem	Water	Chaos, Mighty, Blood	m
		נ	Nun	Seed	Continue, Heir, Son	n
		ס	Sin	Thorn	Grab, Hate, Protect	s
		ע	Ghah	Eye	Watch, Know, Shade	gh(ng)
		פ	Pey	Mouth	Blow, Scatter, Edge	p, ph(f)
		צ	Tsad	Trail	Journey, chase, hunt	ts
		ק	Quph	Sun on the horizon	Condense, Circle, Time	q
		ר	Resh	Head of a man	First, Top, Beginning	r
		ש	Shin	Two front teeth	Sharp, Press, Eat, Two	sh
		ת	Taw	Crossed sticks	Mark, Sign, Signal, Monument	t
			Ghah	Rope	Twist, Dark, Wicked	gh

AH U

Y

Ancient Hebrew Research Center　26

YAHUdim יהודים
Yah's People (Never Jews, Yah's)

Ha YAH היה
I AM or THE YAH

YAHUdah יהודה
"Yahu Be Praised" (Tribe of Judah)

EliYAHU אליהו
"My God Is Yahu"

YAHUAH TOLD US HIS NAME IS YHWH, YAHUAH MANY TIMES:

Isaiah 42:8: I am YHWH (יהוה): **that is my name**...

Exodus 20:2-4: I am YHWH (יהוה) thy God (Elohim)...

Exodus 6:6: I am YHWH (יהוה)

Leviticus 19:12: I am YHWH (יהוה)

Jeremiah 16:21: ...and they shall know that **my name is YHWH** (יהוה)

Exodus 3:15: And God (Elohim) said... **YHWH** (יהוה) God (Elohim) of your fathers, the God (Elohim) of Abraham, the God (Elohim) of Isaac, and the God (Elohim) of Jacob, hath sent me unto you: **this is my name for ever**, and this is my memorial unto all generations.

Zechariah 13:9: "**They will call on My name**, And I will answer them; I will say, 'They are My people,' And they will say, '**YHWH** (יהוה) **is my God (Elohim).**'"

Ezekiel 39:6: And I will send a fire on Magog, and among them that dwell carelessly in the isles: and they shall know that **I am YHWH** (יהוה)

YHWH PRONOUNCED IN THE BIBLE AS A PRACTICE:

Genesis 4:26: And to Seth, to him also there was born a son; and he called his name Enos: **then began men to call upon the name of YHWH** (יהוה)"

1 Samuel 7:5-9: Then Samuel said, "Gather all Israel to Mizpah and **I will pray to YHWH** (יהוה) for you."

1 Kings 18:36-37: At the time of the offering of the evening sacrifice, Elijah the prophet came near and said, "**O YHWH** (יהוה), **the God** (Elohim) **of Abraham**, Isaac and Israel..."

Jonah 2:2 and he said, "I **called out** of my distress **to YHWH** (יהוה)

Genesis 12:8: ...he builded an altar **unto YHWH** (יהוה), and **called upon the name of YHWH** (יהוה)

Genesis 26:24-25: And **YHWH** (יהוה) **appeared** unto him the same night, and said, **I am** the Elohim of Abraham thy father: fear not, for I am with thee, and will bless thee, and multiply thy seed for my servant Abraham's sake. And he builded an altar there, and **called upon the name of YHWH** (יהוה)

1 Chronicles 16:8: Give **thanks unto YHWH** (יהוה), **call upon his name**...

Psalm 105:1: O give **thanks unto YHWH** (יהוה); **call upon his name**:

Zephaniah 3:9: For then will I turn to the people a pure language, that they may **all call upon the name of YHWH** (יהוה), to serve him with one consent.

Lamentations 3:55: I **called upon thy name**, **O YHWH** (יהוה)

2 Samuel 22:4: I **call upon YHWH** (יהוה), who is worthy to be praised...

Psalm 18:3: I **call upon YHWH** (יהוה), who is worthy to be praised...

1 Kings 18:24: "Then you call on the name of your god (Elohim), and **I will call on the name of YHWH** (יהוה)

2 Kings 5:11: ...Naaman was furious and went away and said, "Behold, I thought, 'He will surely come out to me and stand and **call on the name of YHWH (יהוה) his God** (Elohim)...

Psalm 18:6: In my distress **I called upon YHWH (יהוה)**

Psalm 28:1-2: To You, **O YHWH (יהוה), I call**...

Psalm 55:16: As for me, **I shall call upon God** (Elohim), **And YHWH (יהוה)** will save me.

Psalm 120:1: In my trouble **I cried to YHWH (יהוה)**, And **He answered me**.

Isaiah 58:9: Then **you will call, and YHWH (יהוה) will answer**...

Joel 1:19: To You, **O YHWH (יהוה), I cry**...

Joel 2:32: "And it will come about that **whoever calls on the name of YHWH (יהוה)**

Psalm 99:6: Moses and Aaron were among His priests, And Samuel was among those **who called on His name**; **They called upon YHWH (יהוה) and He answered**...

Numbers 21:7: So the people came to Moses and said, "We have sinned, because we have **spoken against YHWH (יהוה)** and you; **intercede with YHWH (יהוה)**

1 Samuel 12:19: Then all the people said to Samuel, "**Pray for your servants to YHWH (יהוה) your God** (Elohim)...

Genesis 13:4: ...to the place of the altar which he had made there formerly; and there **Abram called on the name of YHWH (יהוה)**

Exodus 32:11-13: Then **Moses entreated YHWH (יהוה) his God** (Elohim), **and said**, "**O YHWH (יהוה)**

Deuteronomy 9:26-29: "**I prayed to YHWH (יהוה) and said**, 'O YHWH (יהוה)GOD (Elohim) do not destroy Your people...

Numbers 14:13-19: But **Moses said to YHWH (יהוה)**, "Then the Egyptians will hear of it, for by Your strength You brought up this people from their midst, and they will tell it to the inhabitants of this land. **They have heard that You, O YHWH (יהוה)**, are in the midst of this people, for **You, O YHWH (יהוה)**, are seen eye to eye... *(and there are many more as this name appears over 6,800 times)*

YHWH WILL BE RESTORED IN THE LAST DAYS SAYS YHWH:

Isaiah 52:6: Therefore **my people shall know my name**: therefore they shall know in that day that I am he that doth speak: behold, it is I.

Jeremiah 16:21: Therefore, behold, I will this once cause them to know, I will cause them to know mine hand and my might; and **they shall know that my name is YHWH (יהוה)**

Ezekiel 39:7: So **will I make my holy name known** in the midst of my people Israel; and I will **not let them pollute my holy name any more**: and the heathen **shall know that I am YHWH (יהוה)**, the Holy One in Israel.

All passages from the KJV.

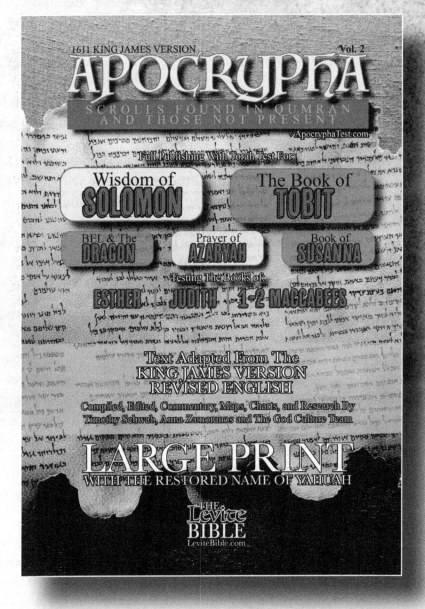

THE WISDOM OF
SIRACH
ECCLESIASTICUS

WITH THE RESTORED
NAME OF YAHUAH

THE
Levite
BIBLE
LeviteBible.com

PROLOGUE 1:

[A Prologue made by an uncertain Author.]

This Yahusha was the son of Sirach, and grandchild to Yahusha of the same name with him; This man therefore lived in the **latter times**, after the people had been led away captive, and called home again, and almost after all the Prophets. Now his grandfather Yahusha (as he himself witnessed) was a man of great diligence and wisdom among the Hebrews, who did not only gather the grave and short sentences of wise men, that had been before him, but himself also uttered some of his own, full of much understanding and wisdom. When as therefore the first Yahusha died, leaving this book almost perfected, Sirach his son receiving it after him, left it to his own son Yahusha, who having gotten it into his hands, compiled it all orderly into one Volume, and called it Wisdom, titling it, both by his own name, his father's name, and his grandfather's, alluring the hearer by the very name of Wisdom, to have

Latter times of the Southern Kingdom after the return from Babylon during the Second Temple period. However, this is before the so-called Hasmon-ean Revolt (165 B.C.) which defiled the Temple and never returned the Priesthood they usurped.

a greater love to the study of this Book. It contains therefore, wise sayings, dark sentences, and parables, and certain particular ancient godly stories of men that pleased Elohim. Also his Prayer and Song. Moreover, what benefits Elohim had promised his people, and what plagues he had heaped upon their enemies. This Yahusha did imitate Solomon, and was no less famous for Wisdom, and learning, both being indeed a man of great learning, and so reputed also.

i.e. prophecy including rebuke.

PROLOGUE 2:

[The Prologue of the Wisdom of Yahusha the son of Sirach]

Whereas many and great things have been delivered unto us by the Law and the Prophets, and by others that have followed their steps, for the which things Israel ought to be commended for learning and Wisdom, and whereof not only the Readers must become skillful themselves, but also they that desire to learn, be able to profit them which are without, both by speaking and writing: My grandfather Yahusha, when he had much given himself to the reading of the Law, and the Prophets, and other Books of our fathers, and had gotten therein good judgment, was drawn on also himself, to write something pertaining to learning and Wisdom, to the intent that those which are desirous to learn, and are addicted to these things, might profit much more in living according to the Law. Wherefore, let me entreat you to read it with favor and attention, and to pardon us, wherein we may seem to come short of some words which we have labored to interpret. For the same things uttered in Hebrew, and translated into another tongue, have not the same force in them: and not only these things, but the Law itself, and the Prophets, and the rest of the Books, have no small difference, when they are spoken in their own language. For in the eight and thirtieth year coming into **Egypt**, when **Euergetes was King**, and continuing there some time, I found a Book of no small learning, therefore I thought it most necessary for me, to bestow some diligence and travail to interpret it: Using great watchfulness, and skill in that space, to bring the

"(ευεργέτης, benefactor). A title of honor born by two of the Ptolemaic kings, Ptolemy III (246-221 b.c.) and Ptolemy VII (145-116 b.c.). The author... dates his work with reference to his coming "to Egypt in the thirty-eighth year of the reign of Euergetes." Although he is not specific about which of the two men with this title he refers to, it is apparent that he has in mind the second." [61] Applying actual reason, this book fails to mention the Hasmonean Assult of 165 B.C. in the age it was completed and there is no way this author would have missed that. It is the 246-221 B.C.

Book to an end, and set it forth for them also, which in a strange country are willing to learn, being prepared before in manners to line after the Law.

CHAPTER 1:

1 All wisdom is from Elohim. 10 He gives it to them that love Him. 12 The fear of Yahuah is full of many blessings. 28 To fear Yahuah without hypocrisy.

1 All wisdom comes from Yahuah, and is with him forever. 2 Who can number the sand of the sea, and the drops of rain, and the days of eternity? 3 Who can find out the height of heaven, and the breadth of the earth, and the deep, and wisdom? 4 Wisdom has been created before all things, and the understanding of prudence from everlasting. 5 The word of Elohim Most High, is the fountain of wisdom, and her ways are everlasting commandments. 6 To whom has the root of wisdom been revealed? Or who has known her wise counsels? 7 [Unto whom has the knowledge of wisdom been made manifest? And who has understood her great experience?] 8 There is one wise and greatly to be feared; Yahuah sitting upon

Cf. 1Ki. 3:9.

Cf. Rom.11:3.

Note: v5 and 7 are missing from the Catholic version (NJB). Another assault on the commandments.

His Throne. 9 He created her, and saw her, and numbered her, and powered her out upon all his works. 10 She [is] with all flesh according to his gift, and He has given her to them that love him.

11 The fear of Yahuah is honor, and glory, and gladness, and a crown of rejoicing. 12 The fear of Yahuah makes a merry heart, and gives joy and gladness, and a long life.

13 Who so fears Yahuah, shall be blessed with Him at the last, and he shall find favor in the day of his death. 14 To fear Yahuah, is the beginning of wisdom: and it was created with the faithful in the womb. 15 She has built an everlasting foundation with men, and she shall continue with their seed.

16 To fear Yahuah, is fullness of wisdom, and fills men with her fruits. 17 She fills all their house with things desirable, and the gatherers with her increase. 18 The fear of Yahuah is a crown of wisdom, making peace and perfect health to flourish, both which are the gifts of Elohim: and it enlarges their rejoicing that love him.

19 Wisdom rains down skill and knowledge of understanding, and exalts them to honor that hold her fast. 20 The root of wisdom is to fear Yahuah, and the branches thereof are long life. 21 The fear of Yahuah drives away sins: and where it is present, it turns away wrath. 22 A furious man cannot be justified, for the sway of his fury shall be his destruction. 23 A patient man will bear for a time, and afterward joy shall spring up unto him. 24 He will hide his words for a time, and the lips of many shall declare his wisdom.

25 The parables of knowledge are in the treasures of wisdom: but godliness is an abomination to a sinner. 26 If you desire wisdom, keep the commandments, and Yahuah shall give her unto you. 27 For the fear of Yahuah is wisdom, and instruction: and faith and meekness are his delight.

28 Distrust not the fear of Yahuah when you are poor: and come not unto him with a double heart. 29 Be not an hypocrite in the sight of men, and take good heed what you speak. 30 Exalt not yourself, lest you fall, and bring dishonor upon your soul, and so Elohim discover your secrets, and cast you down in the midst of the

Cf. Prov. 1:7. Ps.110:10.

Cf. Prov. 9:10.

Cf. 2Chr. 20:21.

Cf. Prov. 9:10.

Or, escape punishment.

Note: v21 is missing from the Catholic version (NJB).

Cf. Jn. 14:15.

Or, be not disobedient to. Cf. Js. 1:8.

Cf. Ps. 141:3. Prov.21:23.

Cf. Jas. 1:6,8.

congregation, because you came not in truth, to the fear of Yahuah: but your heart is full of deceit.

CHAPTER 2:

1 Yahuah's servants must look for trouble, 7 and be patient, and trust in him. 12 For woe to them that do not so. 15 But they that fear Yahuah, will do so.

Cf. Matt.4:11; 2Tim.3:12; 1Pet.4:12.

1 My son, if you come to serve Yahuah, prepare your soul for temptation. 2 Set your heart right, and constantly endure, and haste not in time of trouble. 3 Cleave unto Him, and depart not away, that you may be increased at your last end.

Cf. Jas. 12:4.

4 Whatsoever is brought upon you, take cheerfully, and be patient when you are changed to a low estate.

Cf. Wisd.3:6; Pro. 17:3.

5 For gold is tried in the fire, and acceptable men in the furnace of adversity. 6 Believe in Him, and He will help you, order your way right, and trust in Him. 7 You that fear Yahuah, wait for His mercy, and go not aside, lest you fall. 8 You that fear Yahuah, believe Him, and your reward shall not fail. 9 You that fear Yahuah, hope for good, and for everlasting joy and mercy. 10 Look at the generations of old, and see, did any ever trust in Yahuah, and were confounded? Or did any abide in His fear, and were forsaken? Or whom did He ever despise, that called upon Him? 11 For Yahuah is full of compassion, and mercy, longsuffering, and very full of pity, and forgives sins, and saves in time of affliction. 12 Woe be to fearful hearts, and faint hands, and the sinner that goes two ways. 13 Woe unto him that is faint hearted, for he believes not, therefore shall he not be defended.

Cf. Ps.37:25.

14 Woe unto you that have lost patience: and what will you do when Yahuah shall visit you? 15 They that fear Yahuah, will not disobey His Word, and they that love Him, will keep his ways.

Cf. Jas. 1:6,8.

16 They that fear Yahuah, will seek that which is well pleasing unto Him, and they that love Him, shall be filled with the Law. 17 They that fear Yahuah, will prepare their hearts, and humble their souls in His sight:

Cf. Jn. 14:20.

18 Saying, We will fall into the hands of Yahuah, and not into the hands of men: for as his majesty is, so is his mercy.

CHAPTER 3:

3 Children must honor, and help both their parents. 21 We may not desire to know all things 26 The incorrigible must perish. 30 Alms are rewarded.

1 Hear me your father, O children, and do thereafter, that you may be safe. 2 For Yahuah has given the father honor over the children, and has confirmed the authority of the mother over the sons. 3 Who so honors his father, makes an atonement for his sins. 4 And he that honors his mother, is as one that lays up treasure. 5 Who so honors his father, shall have joy of his own children, and when he makes his prayer, he shall be heard. 6 He that honors his father, shall have a long life, and he that is obedient unto Yahuah, shall be a comfort to his mother. 7 He that fears Yahuah, will honor his father, and will do service unto his parents, as to his masters. 8 Honor your father and mother, both in word and deed, that a blessing may come upon you from them. 9 For the blessing of the father establishes the houses of children, but the curse of the mother roots out foundations. 10 Glory not in the dishonor of your father,

Cf. Ex. 20:6; Dt. 5:10, Or, judgment.

Cf. Ex. 20:12.

Cf. Ex.20:12; Dt. 5:10.

Cf. Gen. 27:27; Dt. 33:1.

for your father's dishonor is no glory unto you. 11 For the glory of a man, is from the honor of his father, and a mother in dishonor, is a reproach to the children. 12 My son, help your father in his age, and grieve him not as long as he lives. 13 And if his understanding fail, have patience with him, and despise him not, when you are in your full strength. 14 For the relieving of your father shall not be forgotten: and instead of sins it shall be added to build you up. 15 In the day of your affliction it shall be remembered, your sins also shall melt away, as the ice in the fair warm weather.

16 He that forsakes his father, is as a blasphemer, and he that angers his mother, is cursed of Elohim. 17 My son, go on with your business in meekness, so shall you be beloved of him that is approved. 18 The greater you are, the more humble yourself, and you shall find favor before Yahuah. 19 Many are in high places and of renown: but mysteries are revealed unto the meek. 20 For the power of Yahuah is great, and He is honored of the lowly. 21 Seek not out the things

Or, in all your ability.

Cf. Phil. 2:3.

Cf. Ps.25:9,14. Note: v.19 is missing from the Catholic version (NJB).

that are too hard for you, neither search the things that are above your strength. 22 But what you are commanded, think thereupon with reverence, for it is not needful for you, to see with your eyes, the things that are in secret. 23 Be not curious in unnecessary matters: for more things are shown unto you, than men understand. 24 For many are deceived by their own vain opinion, and an evil suspicion has overthrown their judgment. 25 Without eyes you shall want light: profess not the knowledge therefore that you do not have. 26 A stubborn heart shall fare

Cf. Prov.25:27; Rom.12:3.

Cf. Phil. 4:8.

Note: v.25 is missing from the Catholic version (NJB).

evil at the last, and he that loves danger shall perish therein. 27 An obstinate heart shall be laden with sorrows, and the wicked man shall heap sin upon sin. 28 In the punishment of the proud there is no remedy: for the plant of wickedness has taken root in him. 29 The heart of the prudent will understand a parable, and an attentive ear is the desire of a wise man. 30 Water will quench a flaming fire, and alms make an atonement for sins.

31 And he that requits good turns, is mindful of that which may come hereafter: and when he falls he shall find a stay.

Or, the proud man is not healed by his punishment.

Cf. Ps. 40:2; Tob. 12:9; Dan. 4:24; Matt. 5:7.

CHAPTER 4:

1 We may not despise the poor or fatherless, 11 but seek for Wisdom, 20 and not be ashamed of some things, nor gainsay the truth, 30 nor be as lions in our houses.

1 My son, defraud not the poor of his living, and make not the needy eyes to wait long. 2 Make not an hungry soul sorrowful, neither provoke a man in his distress. 3 Add not more trouble to an heart that is vexed, and defer not to give

to him that is in need. 4 Reject not the supplication of the afflicted, neither turn away your face from a poor man. 5 Turn not away your eye from the needy, and give him no occasion to curse you: 6 For if he curse you in the bitterness of his soul, his prayer shall be heard of Him that made him. 7 Get yourself the love of the congregation, and bow your head to a great man. 8 Let it not grieve you to bow down your ear to the poor, and give him a friendly answer

Or, him that asks.

with meekness. 9 Deliver him that suffers wrong, from the hand of the oppressor, and be not faint hearted when you sit in judgment. 10 Be as a father unto the fatherless, and instead of a husband unto their mother, so shall you be as the son of the Most High, and He shall love you more than your mother does.

11 Wisdom exalts her children, and lays hold of them that seek her. 12 He that loves her, loves life, and they that seek her early, shall be filled with joy. 13 He that holds her fast shall inherit glory, and wheresoever she enters, Yahuah will bless. 14 They that serve her shall minister to the Holy one, and them that love her, Yahuah does love. 15 Who so gives ear unto her, shall judge the nations, and he that attends unto her, shall dwell securely. 16 If a man commit himself unto her, he shall inherit her, and his generation shall hold her in possession. 17 For at the first she will walk with him by crooked ways, and bring fear and dread upon him, and torment him with her discipline, until she may trust his soul, and try him by her Laws. 18 Then will

Or, in the sanctuary.

she return the straight way unto him, and comfort him, and show him her secrets. 19 But if he go wrong, she will forsake him, and give him over to his own ruin.

20 Observe the opportunity, and beware of evil, and be not ashamed when it concerns your soul. 21 For there is a shame that brings sin, and there is a shame which is glory and grace. 22 Accept no person against your soul, and let not the reverence of any man cause you to fall: 23 And refrain not to speak, when there is occasion to do good, and hide not your wisdom in her beauty. 24 For by speech wisdom shall be known, and learning by the word of the tongue. 25 In no wise speak against the truth, but be abashed of the error of your ignorance. 26 Be not ashamed to confess your sins, and force not the course of the river. 27 Make not yourself an underling to a foolish man, neither accept the person of the mighty. 28 Strive for the truth unto death, and Yahuah shall fight for you. 29 Be not hasty in your tongue, and in your deeds slack and remiss. 30 Be not as a lion in your house, nor frantic among

Greek, in time of saving.

Or, and strive not against the stream.

Or, give.

your servants. 31 Let not your hand be stretched out to receive, and shut when you should repay.

Cf. Acts 20:35, credits Yahusha for saying: "It is more blessed to give than to receive." He has no such quote in the Gospels but Yahusha Ben Sirach does.

CHAPTER 5:

1 We must not presume of our wealth and strength, 6 Nor of the mercy of Elohim to sin. 9 We must not be double tongued, 12 Nor answer without knowledge.

Cf. Luke 12:15; Matt. 6:21.

1 Set not your heart upon your goods, and say not, I have enough for my life.
2 Follow not your own mind, and your strength, to walk in the ways of your heart: 3 And say not, Who shall control me for my works? For Yahuah will surely revenge your pride.
4 Say not, I have sinned, and what harm has happened unto me? For Yahuah is long suffering, He will in no wise let you go.
5 Concerning propitiation, be not without fear to add sin unto sin. 6 And say not, His mercy is great, He will be pacified for the multitude of my sins: for mercy and wrath come from Him, and his indignation rests upon sinners. 7 Make no tarrying to turn to Yahuah, and put not off from day to day: for

Cf. Ecclus. 21:1.

suddenly shall the wrath of Yahuah come forth, and in your security you shall be destroyed, and perish in the day of vengeance. 8 Set not your heart upon goods unjustly gotten: for they shall not profit you in the day of calamity. 9 Move not with every wind, and go not into every way: for so does the sinner that has a double tongue. 10 Be steadfast in your understanding, and let your word be the same. 11 Be swift to hear, and let your life be sincere, and with patience give answer. 12 If you have understanding, answer your neighbor, if not, lay your hand upon your mouth.
13 Honor and shame is in talk; and the tongue of man is his fall. 14 Be not called a whisperer, and lie not in wait with your tongue: for a foul shame is upon the thief, and an evil condemnation upon the double tongue. 15 Be not ignorant of any thing, in a great matter or a small.

Cf. 16:13.

Cf. Prov. 10:2, 11.4; Ez. 7:19.

Cf. Jas. 1:19.

Cf. Prov. 6:2.

CHAPTER 6:

2 Do not extol your own conceit, 7 But make choice of a friend. 18 Seek wisdom betimes: 20 It is grievous to some, 28 yet the fruits thereof are pleasant. 35 Be ready to hear wise men.

1 Instead of a friend, become not an enemy; for [thereby] you shall inherit an ill name, shame, and reproach: even so shall a sinner that has a double tongue. 2 Extol not yourself in the counsel of your own heart, that your soul be not torn in pieces as a bull [straying alone.]

Cf. John 15. 3 You shall eat up your leaves, and loose your fruit, and leave yourself as a dry tree. 4 A wicked soul shall destroy him that has it, and shall make him to be laughed to scorn by his enemies. 5 Sweet language *Greeke, a sweet throat* will multiply friends: and a fair speaking tongue will increase kind greetings. 6 Be in peace with many: nevertheless have but one counsellor of a thousand. *Or, get him in the time of trouble.* 7 If you would get a friend, prove him first, and be not hasty to credit him. 8 For some man is a friend for his own occasion, and will not abide in the day of your trouble. 9 And there is a friend, who being turned to enmity, and strife, will discover your reproach.

10 Again some friends are a companion at the table, and will not continue in the day *Cf. 37.5. Prov. 18:24.* of your affliction. 11 But in your prosperity he will be as yourself, and will be bowled over by your servants. 12 If you be brought low, he will be against you, and will hide himself from your face. 13 Separate yourself from your enemies, and take heed of your friends. 14 A faithful friend is a strong defense: and he that has found such an one, has found a treasure. 15 Nothing does countervail a faithful friend, and his excellency is invaluable. 16 A faithful friend is the medicine of life, and they that fear Yahuah shall find him. 17 Who so fears Yahuah shall direct his friendship aright, for as he is, so shall his neighbor be also. 18 My son, gather up instruction from your youth: so shall you find wisdom until your old age. 19 Come unto her as one that plows, and sows, and wait for her good fruits, for you shall not toil much in laboring about her, but you shall eat of her fruits right soon. 20 She is very unpleasant to the unlearned: he that

Or, heart

Cf. Zec. 12:4

Or, coller.

Cf. Matt. 11:29.

is without understanding, will not remain with her. **21** She will lie upon him as a mighty stone of trial, and he will cast her from him ere it be long. **22** For wisdom is according to her name, and she is not manifest unto many. **23** Give ear, my son, receive my advice, and refuse not my counsel, **24** And put your feet into her fetters, and your neck into her chain. **25** Bow down your shoulder, and bear her, and be not grieved with her bonds. **26** Come unto her with your whole heart, and keep her ways with all your power. **27** Search and seek, and she shall be made known unto you, and when you get hold of her, let her not go. **28** For at the last you shall find her rest, and that shall be turned to your joy. **29** Then shall her fetters be a strong defense for you, and her chains a robe of glory. **30** For there is a golden ornament upon her, and her bands are purple lace. **31** You shall put her on as a robe of honor: and shall put her about you as a crown of joy. **32** My son, if you will, you shall be taught: and if you will apply your mind, you shall be prudent. **33** If you love to hear, you shall receive understanding: and if you bow your ear, you shall be wise. **34** Stand in the multitude of the elders, and cleave unto him that is wise. **35** Be willing to hear every godly discourse, and let not the parables of understanding escape you. **36** And if you see a man of understanding, get betimes unto him, and let your foot wear the steps of his door. **37** Let your mind be upon the ordinances of Yahuah, and meditate continually in His commandments: He shall establish your heart, and give you wisdom at your own desire.

Or, a ribbon of blue silk, Num. 15:38.

Cf. 8:9.

Cf. Ps. 1:2.

CHAPTER 7:

1 We are exhorted from sin, 4 from ambition, 8 presumption, 10 and fainting in prayer: 12 from lying and back-biting, 18 and how to esteem a friend: 19 A good wife: 20 a servant: 22 our cattle: 23 our children and parents: 31 Yahuah and his Priests: 32 the poor and those that mourn.

1 Do no evil, so shall no harm come unto you.

2 Depart from the unjust, and iniquity shall turn away from you. 3 My son, sow not upon the furrows of unrighteousness, and you shall not reap them seven fold. 4 Seek not of Yahuah pre-eminence, neither of the King the seat of honor. 5 Justify not yourself before Yahuah, and boast not of your wisdom before the king. 6 Seek not to be judge, being not able to take away iniquity, lest at any time you fear the person of the mighty, and lay a stumbling block in the way of your uprightness. 7 Offend not against the multitude of a city, and then you shall not cast yourself down among the people. 8 Bind not one sin upon another, for in one you shall not be unpunished. 9 Say not, Elohim will look upon the multitude of my oblations, and when I offer to the Most High Elohim, He will accept

Cf. Ps.142:2; Eccles. 7:17; Job 9:20; Luke 18:11.

it. 10 Be not faint hearted when you make your prayer, and neglect not to give alms. 11 Laugh no man to scorn in the bitterness of his soul: for there is one which humbles and exalts. 12 Devise not a lie against your brother: neither do the like to your friend. 13 Use not to make any manner of lie: for the custom thereof is not good. 14 Use not many words in a multitude of elders, and make not much babbling when you pray.

15 Hate not laborious work, neither husbandry, which the Most High has ordained. 16 Number not yourself among the multitude of sinners, but remember that wrath will not tarry long.

17 Humble your soul greatly: for the vengeance of the ungodly is fire and worms.

18 Change not a friend for any good by no means: neither a faithful brother for the gold of Ophir.

19 Forgo not a wise and good woman: for her grace is above gold. 20 Whereas your servant works truly, entreate him not evil, nor the hireling that bestows himself wholly for you.

21 Let your soul love a good servant, and defraud him not of liberty. 22 Have you

Cf. Jas. 1:6,8.

Greek: plough not.

Cf. Matt. 6:5,7; Or, vain repetition.

Greek: created.

Sirach is still noting the value of the precious gold of Ophir in 200 B.C.

Cf. Lev. 19:15.

cattle? Have an eye to them, and if they be for your profit, keep them with you. 23 Have you children? Instruct them, and bow down their neck from their youth. 24 Have you daughters? Have care of their body, and show not yourself cheerful toward them. 25 Marry your daughter, and so shall you have performed a weighty matter: but give her to a man of understanding.

Cf. Dt. 25:4.

26 Have you a wife after your mind? Forsake her not, but give not yourself over to a light woman. 27 Honor your father with your whole heart, and forget not the sorrows of your mother.

Or, hateful.

28 Remember that you were begot of them, and how can you recompense them the things that they have done for you? 29 Fear Yahuah with all your soul, and reverence his priests. 30 Love Him that made you with all your strength, and forsake not his ministers. 31 Fear Yahuah, and honor the priest: and give him his portion, as it is commanded you, the first fruits, and the trespass offering, and the gift of the shoulders, and the sacrifice of sanctification, and the first fruits of the holy things. 32 And stretch your hand unto the poor, that your blessing may be perfected. 33 A gift has grace in the sight of every man living, and for the dead detain it not. 34 Fail not to be with them that weep, and mourn with them that mourn.

Cf. Dt. 14:28-29; Tob. 1:6-8.

Cf. Dt. 15:10; Or, your liberality.

35 Be not slow to visit the sick: for that shall make you to be beloved. 36 Whatsoever you take in hand, remember the end, and you shall never do amiss.

CHAPTER 8:

1 Whom we may not strive with, 8 nor despise, 10 nor provoke, 15 nor have to do with.

1 Strive not with a mighty man, lest you fall into his hands. 2 Be not at variance with a rich man, lest he overweigh you: for gold

Cf. 31:6; Matt. 5:25.

has destroyed many, and perverted the hearts of kings. 3 Strive not with a man that is full of tongue, and heap not wood upon his fire. 4 Jest not with a rude man, lest your ancestors be disgraced. 5 Reproach not a man that turns from sin, but remember that we are all

Or, of an evil tongue.

Cf. Gal. 6.2; 1Cor. 2.6.

worthy of punishment.

6 Dishonor not a man in his old age: for even some of us wax old. 7 Rejoice not over your greatest enemy being dead, but remember that we die all. 8 Despise not the discourse of the wise, but acquaint yourself with their proverbs; for of them you shall learn instruction, and how to serve great men with ease. 9 Miss not the discourse of the elders: for they also learned of their fathers, and of them you shall learn understanding, and to give answer as need requires. 10 Kindle not the coals of a sinner, lest you be burnt with the flame of his fire. 11 Rise not up (in anger) at the presence of an injurious person, lest he lie in wait to entrap you in your words. 12 Lend not unto him that is mightier than yourself; for if you lend him, count it but lost.

Cf. Lev. 19:32.

Or, for thy mouth.

13 Be not surety above your power: for if you be surety, take care to pay it. 14 Go not to law with a judge, for they will judge for him according to his honor. 15 Travail not by the way with a bold fellow, lest he become grievous unto you: for he will do according to his own will, and you shall perish with him through his folly. 16 Strive not with an angry man, and go not with him into a solitary place: for blood is as nothing in his sight, and where there is no help, he will overthrow you. 17 Consult not with a fool; for he cannot keep counsel. 18 Do no secret thing before a stranger, for you know not what he will bring forth.

19 Open not your heart to every man, least he requite you with a shrewd turn. Answer as need requires. Judge, for they will judge for him according to his honor.

Or, opinion.

Cf. Gen. 4:8.

Cf. Prov. 22:24.

CHAPTER 9:

1 We are advised how to use our wives. 3 What women to avoid. 10 And not to change an old friend. 13 Not to be familiar with men in authority, 14 But to know our neighbors, 15 And to converse with wise men.

1 Be not jealous over the wife of your bosom, and teach her not an evil lesson against yourself. 2 Give not your soul unto a woman, to set her foot upon your

substance. 3 Meet not with an harlot, lest you fall into her snares. 4 Use not much the company of a woman that is a singer, lest you be taken with her attempts.

Or, play upon instruments.

5 Gaze not on a maid, that you fall not by those things, that are precious in her. 6 Give not your soul unto harlots, that you loose not your inheritance. 7 Look not round about you, in the streets of the city, neither wander you in the solitary places thereof. 8 Turn away your eye from a beautiful woman, and look not upon another's beauty: for many have been deceived by the beauty of a woman, for herewith love is kindled as a fire. 9 Sit not at all with another man's wife, nor sit down with her in your arms, and spend not your money with her at the wine, lest your heart incline unto her, and so through your desire you fall into destruction.

Cf. Gen. 34:22; 2Sam. 11:2; Judg. 10.17.

10 Forsake not an old friend, for the new is not comparable to him: a new friend is as new wine: when it is old, you shall drink it with pleasure. 11 Envy not the glory of a sinner: for you know not what shall be his end. 12 Delight not in the thing that the ungodly have pleasure in, but remember they shall not go unpunished unto their grave. 13 Keep far from the man that has power to kill, so shall you not doubt the fear of death: and if you come unto him, make no fault, lest he take away your life presently: remember that you go in the midst of snares, and that you walk upon the battlements of the city. 14 As near as you can, guess at your neighbor, and consult with the wise. 15 Let your talk be with the wise, and all your communication in the law of the Most High. 16 And let just men eat and drink with you, and let your glorying be in the fear of Yahuah. 17 For the hand of the artificer, the work shall be commended: and the wise ruler of the people, for his speech. 18 A man of an ill tongue is dangerous in his city, and he that is rash in his talk shall be hated.

CHAPTER 10:

1 The commodities of a wise ruler. 4 Elohim sets him up. 7 The inconveniences of pride, injustice, and covetousness. 14 What Elohim has done to the proud. 19 Who shall be honored, 29 And who not.

1 A wise judge will instruct his people, and the government of a prudent man is well ordered. 2 As the judge of the people is himself, so are his officers, and what manner of man the ruler of the city is, such are all they that dwell therein. 3 An unwise king destroys his people, but through the prudence of them which are in authority, the city shall be inhabited. 4 The power of the earth is in the hand of Yahuah, and in due time He will set over it one that is profitable. 5 In the hand of Elohim is the prosperity of man: and upon the person of the scribe shall he lay his honor. 6 Bear not hatred to your neighbor for every wrong, and do nothing at all by injurious practices. 7 Pride is hateful before Elohim, and man: and by both does one commit iniquity. 8 Because of unrighteous dealings, injuries, and riches got by deceit, the kingdom is translated from one people to another.

9 Why is earth and ashes proud? There is not a more wicked thing, then a covetous man: for such an one sets his own soul to sale, because while he lives, he casts away his bowels. 10 The physician cuts off a long disease, and he that is today a king, tomorrow shall die. 11 For when a man is dead, he shall inherit creeping things, beasts and worms. 12 The beginning of pride is, when one departs from Elohim, and his heart is turned away from his maker. 13 For pride is the beginning of sin, and he that hath it, shall pour out abomination: and therefore Yahuah brought upon them strange calamities, and overthrew them utterly. 14 Yahuah has cast down the thrones of proud princes, and set up the meek in their stead. 15 Yahuah hath plucked up the roots of the proud nations: and planted the lowly in their place. 16 Yahuah overthrew countries of the heathen: and destroyed them to the foundations of the earth.

17 He took some of them away, and destroyed them, and has made their

Cf. Prov. 29:12.

Or, face.

Cf. Lev. 19:17.

Cf. Luke 1:52.

Cf. Prov. 16:18.

memorial to cease from the earth. **18** Pride was not made for men, nor furious anger for them that are born of a woman. **19** They that fear Yahuah are a sure seed, and they that love Him, an honorable plant: they that regard not the Law, are a dishonorable seed, they that transgress the commandments, are a deceivable seed. **20** Among brethren he that is chief is honorable, so are they that fear Yahuah in his eyes.

Or, unstable generation.

Note: v. 21 is missing from the Catholic version (NJB).

Or, principality.

21 The fear of Yahuah goes before the obtaining of authority: but roughness and pride, is the loosing thereof. **22** Whether he be rich, noble, or poor, their glory is the fear of Yahuah. **23** It is not meet to despise the poor man that has understanding, neither is it convenient to magnify a sinful man. **24** Great men, and judges, and potentates shall be honored, yet is there none of them greater than he that fears Yahuah. **25** Unto the servant that is wise, shall they that are free do service: and he that has knowledge, will not grudge when he is reformed.

Cf. Prov. 17:2; 2Sam. 12:13.

26 Be not overwise in doing your business, and boast not yourself in the time of your distress. **27** Better is he that labors and abounds in all things, than he that boasts himself, and wants bread.

Cf. Prov. 12:9.

28 My son, glorify your soul in meekness, and give it honor according to the dignity thereof. **29** Who will justify him that sins against his own soul? And who will honor him that dishonors his own life? **30** The poor man is honored for his skill, and the rich man is honored for his riches. **31** He that is honored in poverty, how much more in riches? And he that is dishonorable in riches, how much more in poverty?

CHAPTER 11:

4 We may not vaunt or set forth ourselves, 8 Nor answer rashly, 10 Nor meddle with many matters. 14 Wealth and all things else, are from Elohim. 14 Brag not of thy wealth, 29 Nor bring every man into your house.

Or, of the lowly, Gen. 40:40; Dan. 6:3.

1 Wisdom lifts up the head of him that is of low degree, and makes him to sit among great men. 2 Commend not a man for his beauty, neither abhore a man for his outward appearance.

3 The bee is little among such as fly, but her fruit is the chief of sweet things.

4 Boast not of your clothing and raiment, and exalt not yourself in the day of honor: for the works of Yahuah are wonderful, and His works among men are hidden.

Cf. Act.12.21.

Greek: tyrants.

5 Many kings have sat down upon the ground, and one that was never thought of, has worn the crown. 6 Many mighty men have been greatly disgraced: and the honorable delivered into other men's hands.

Cf. 1Ki.15:28

7 Blame not before you have examined the truth: understand first, and then rebuke. 8 Answer not, before you have heard the cause: neither interrupt men in the midst of their talk. 9 Strive not in a matter

Cf. Dt.12:24.

Cf. Prov. 8:13.

that concerns you not: and sit not in judgment with sinners. 10 My son, meddle not with many matters: for if you meddle much, you shall not be innocent: and if you follow after, you shall not obtain, neither shall you escape by flying. 11 There is one that labors and takes pains, and makes haste, and is so much the more behind. 12 Again, there is another that is slow, and has need of help, wanting ability, and full of poverty, yet the eye of Yahuah looked upon him for good, and set him up from his low estate, 13 And lifted up his head from misery, so that many that saw it, marveled at him. 14 Prosperity and adversity, life and death, poverty and riches, come from Yahuah. 15 Wisdom, knowledge, and understanding of the Law, are of Yahuah: love, and the way of good works, are from Him. 16 Error and darkness had their beginning together with sinners: and evil shall wax old with them that glory therein. 17 The gift of Yahuah remains with the godly, and His favor brings prosperity forever. 18 There is that waxes rich by his wariness, and pinching, and this is the portion of

Or, in the judgment of sinners.

Or, escape hurt.

Cf. Matt. 19:12; 1Tim. 6:9; Prov. 10:13.

Cf. Job 1:12; Ez. 28.4.

Note: v. 15-16 are missing from the Catholic version (NJB).

Cf. Jas. 1:17.

Cf. Luke 12:15.

Cf. Prov. 6:10, 24:33.

his reward: 19 Whereas he says, I have found rest, and now will eat continually of my goods, and yet he knows not what time shall come upon him, and that he must leave those things to others, and die. 20 Be steadfast in your covenant, and be conversant therein, and wax old in your work. 21 Marvel not at the works of sinners, but trust in Yahuah, and abide in your labor: for it is an easy thing in the sight of Yahuah, on the sudden to make a poor man rich.

Cf. Luke 12:19. Or, passe.

Cf. Matt. 10:22.

22 The blessing of Yahuah is in the reward of the godly, and suddenly He makes His blessing to flourish. 23 Say not, what profit is there of my service? And what good things shall I have hereafter? 24 Again, say not, I have enough, and possess many things; and what evil can come to me hereafter? 25 In the day of prosperity, there is a forgetfulness of affliction: and in the day of affliction, there is no remembrance

Or, for a reward.

Cf. Mal. 3:14.

of prosperity. 26 For it is an easy thing unto Yahuah in the day of death, to reward a man according to his ways. 27 The affliction of an hour, makes a man forget pleasure: and in his end, his deeds shall be discovered.

28 Judge none blessed before his death: for a man shall be known in his children. 29 Bring not every man into your house, for the deceitful man has many trains. 30 Like as a partridge taken [and kept] in a cage, so is the heart of the proud; and like as a spy, watches he for your fall. 31 For he lies in wait, and turns good into evil, and in things worthy praise, will lay blame upon you. 32 Of a spark of fire, a heap of coals is kindled: and a sinful man lays wait for blood. 33 Take heed of a mischievous man, (for he works wickedness) lest he bring upon you a perpetual blot. 34 Receive a stranger into your house, and he will disturb you, and turn you out of your own.

CHAPTER 12:

2 Be not liberal to the ungodly.
10 Trust not your enemy, nor the wicked.

1 When you will do good, know to whom you do it, so shall you be thanked for your benefits. 2 Do good to the godly man, and you shall find a recompence, and if not from him, yet from the Most High. 3 There can no

good come to him that is always occupied in evil: nor to him that gives no alms. 4 Give to the godly man, and help not a sinner. 5 Do well unto him that is lowly, but give not to the ungodly: hold back your bread, and give it not unto him, lest he overmaster you thereby. For [else] you shall receive twice as much evil, for all the good you shall have done unto him. 6 For the Most High hates sinners, and will repay vengeance unto the ungodly, and keeps them against the mighty day of their punishment. 7 Give unto the good, and help not the sinner. 8 A friend cannot be known in prosperity, and an enemy cannot be hidden in adversity. 9 In the prosperity of a man, enemies will be grieved, but in his adversity, even a friend will depart.

Or, brass.

10 Never trust your enemy: for like as iron rusts, so is his wickedness. 11 Though he humble himself, and go crouching, yet take good heed, and beware of him, and you shall be unto him, as if you had wiped a looking glass, and you shall know that his rust has not been altogether wiped away.

Cf. Jas. 1:23.

12 Set him not by you, lest when he has overthrown you, he stand up in your place, neither let him sit at your right hand, lest he seek to take your seat, and you at the last remember my words, and be pricked therewith.

Cf. 2Cor. 6:14-18.

13 Who will pity a charmer that is bitten with a serpent, or any such as come nigh wild beasts?

14 So one that goes to a sinner, and is defiled with him in his sins, who will pity?

Or, mingled

15 For a while he will abide with you, but if you begin to fall, he will not tarry. 16 An enemy speaks sweetly with his lips, but in his heart he imagines how to throw you into a pit: he will weep with his eyes, but if he find opportunity, he will not be satisfied with blood.

Cf. Jer. 41:6.

17 If adversity come upon you, you shall find him there first, and though he pretend to help you, yet shall he undermine you.

Or, supplant.

18 He will shake his head and clap his hands, and whisper much, and change his countenance.

CHAPTER 13:

1 Keep not company with the proud, or a mightier than yourself. 15 Like will to like. 21 The difference between the rich and the poor. 25 A man's heart will change his countenance.

1 He that touches pitch, shall be defiled therewith, and he that has fellowship with a proud man, shall be like unto him. 2 Burden not yourself above your power, while you live, and have no fellowship with one that is mightier, and richer than yourself. For how agree the kettle and the earthen pot together? For if the one be smitten against the other, it shall be broken. 3 The rich man has done wrong, and yet he threatens withal: the poor is wronged, and he must entreat also. 4 If you be for his profit, he will use you: but if you have nothing, he will forsake you. 5 If you have any thing, he will live with you, yes he will make you bare, and will not be sorry for it. 6 If he has need of you, he will deceive you, and smile upon you, and put you in hope, he will speak you fair, and say, What do you want? 7 And he will shame you by his meats, until he has drawn you dry twice or thrice, and

Cf. Dt. 7:2; 2Cor. 6:14-18.

Greek: this shall smite against it, and be broken.

at the last he will laugh you to scorn: afterward when he sees you, he will forsake you, and shake his head at you. 8 Beware that you be not deceived, and brought down in your jolity. 9 If you be invited of a mighty man, withdraw yourself, and so much the more will he invite you. 10 Press not upon him, lest you be put back, stand not far off, lest you be forgotten. 11 Affect not to be made equal unto him in talk, and believe not his many words: for with much communication will he tempt you, and smiling upon you will get out your secrets. 12 But cruelly he will lay up your words, and will not spare to do you hurt, and to put you in prison. 13 Observe and take good heed, for you walk in peril of your overthrowing: when you hear these things, awake in your sleep. 14 Love Yahuah all your life, and call upon him for your salvation. 15 Every beast loves his like, and every man loves his neighbor. 16 All flesh consorts according to kind, and a man will cleave to his like: 17 What fellowship has the wolf with the lamb? So the sinner with the godly. 18 What agreement is there

Or, by your simplicity.

Or, forbear not, Or, but.

Note: v. 14 is missing from the Catholic version (NJB).

between the hyena and a dog? And what peace between the rich and the poor? 19 As the wild ass is the lions prey in the wilderness: so the rich eat up the poor. 20 As the proud hate humility: so does the rich abhor the poor. 21 A rich man beginning to fall, is held up of his friends: but a poor man being down, is thrust also away by his friends. 22 When a rich man is fallen, he has many helpers: he speaks things not to be spoken, and yet men justify him: the poor man slipped, and yet they rebuked him too: he spake wisely, and could have no place.

23 When a rich man speaks, every man holds his tongue, and look what he says, they extol it to the clouds: but if the poor man speak, they say, What fellow is this? And if he stumble, they will help to overthrow him. 24 Riches are good unto him that has no sin, and poverty is evil in the mouth of the ungodly. 25 The heart of a man changes his countenance, whether it be for good or evil: and a merry heart makes a cheerful countenance. 26 A cheerful countenance is a token of a heart that is in prosperity, and the finding out of parables, is a wearisome labor of the mind.

CHAPTER 14:

1 A good conscience makes men happy. 5 The ungenerous does good to none. 13 But do you good. 10 Men are happy that draw near to wisdom.

Cf. 19:16. and 25:8; Jas. 3.2, Or, sorrow.

1 Blessed is the man that has not slipped with his mouth, and is not pricked with the multitude of sins. 2 Blessed is he whose conscience has not condemned him, and who is not fallen from his hope in Yahuah. 3 Riches are not comely for the ungenerous: and what should an envious man do with money? 4 He that gathers by defrauding his own soul, gathers for others, that shall spend his goods riotously. 5 He that is evil to himself, to whom will he be good? He shall not take pleasure in his goods. 6 There is none worse than he that envies himself; and this is a recompense of his wickedness. 7 And if he does good, he does it unwillingly, and at the last he will declare his wickedness.

8 The envious man has a wicked eye, he turns away his face and despises men.

9 A covetous man's eye is not satisfied with his portion, and the iniquity of the wicked dries up his soul.

Cf. Prov. 17:20.

10 A wicked eye envies [his] bread, and he is ungenerous at his table. 11 My son, according to your ability do good to yourself, and give Yahuah his due offering.

12 Remember that death will not be long in coming, and that the covenant of the grave is not showed unto you. 13 Do good unto your friend before you die, and according to your ability, stretch out your hand and give to him.

Cf. Tobit 4:7.

Or, the feast day.

14 Defraud not yourself of the good day, and let not the part of a good desire overpass you.

15 Shall you not leave your travails unto another? And your labors to be divided by lot? 16 Give, and take, and sanctify your soul, for there is no seeking of dainties in the grave.

Cf. Isa.40:5; Jas. 1:10; 1Pet. 1:24.

17 All flesh waxes old as a garment: for the covenant from the beginning is; you shall die the death. 18 As of the green leaves on a thick tree, some fall, and some grow; so is the generation of flesh and blood, one comes to an end, and another is born. 19 Every work rots and consumes away, and the worker thereof shall go withal. 20 Blessed is the man that does meditate good things in wisdom, and that reasons of holy things by his understanding.

Cf. Ps. 1:2.

21 He that considers her ways in his heart, shall also have understanding in her secrets. 22 Go after her as one that traces, and lie in wait in her ways. 23 He that pries in at her windows, shall also hearken at her doors. 24 He that does lodge near her house, shall also fasten a pin in her walls. 25 He shall pitch his tent nigh unto her, and shall lodge in a lodging where good things are.

Or, stake.

26 He shall set his children under her shelter, and shall lodge under her branches. 27 By her he shall be covered from heat, and in her glory shall he dwell.

CHAPTER 15:

2 Wisdom embraces those that fear Yahuah. 7 The wicked shall not get her. 11 We may not charge Yahuah with our faults: 14 For He made, and left us to ourselves.

1 He that fears Yahuah will do good, and he that has the knowledge of the Law shall obtain her. 2 And as a mother shall she meet him, and receive him as a wife married of a virgin. 3 With the bread of understanding shall she feed him, and give him the water of wisdom to drink. 4 He shall be stayed upon her, and shall not be moved, and shall rely upon her, and shall not be confounded. 5 She shall exalt him above his neighbors, and in the midst of the congregation shall she open his mouth. 6 He shall find joy, and a crown of gladness, and she shall cause him to inherit an everlasting name. 7 But foolish men shall not attain unto her, and sinners shall not see her. 8 For she is far from pride, and men that are liars cannot remember her. 9 Praise is not seemly in the mouth of a sinner, for it was not sent him of Yahuah: 10 For praise shall be uttered in wisdom, and Yahuah will prosper it.

11 Say not, It is through Yahuah, that I fell away, for you ought not to do the things that He hates. 12 Say not, He has caused me to err, for He has no need of the sinful man. 13 Yahuah hates all abomination, and they that fear Elohim love it not. 14 He Himself made man from the beginning, and left him in the hand of his counsel, 15 If you will, to keep the Commandments, and to perform acceptable faithfulness. 16 He has set fire and water before you: stretch forth your hand unto whether you will.

17 Before man is life and death, and whether he likes, it shall be given him.

18 For the wisdom of Yahuah is great, and He is mighty in power, and beholds all things, 19 And his eyes are upon them that fear him, and he knows every work of man. 20 He has commanded no man to do wickedly, neither has he given any man license to sin.

Or, a parable. Or, he was not sent of, &c.

Or, rather a parable.

11-20: Cf. Jas. 1:13-15.

Cf. Gen. 1:20.

Cf. Jer. 21:8.

Cf. Ps. 33:16.

CHAPTER 16:

1 It is better to have none than many lewd children. 6 The wicked are not spared for their number. 12 Both the wrath and the mercy of Yahuah are great. 17 The wicked cannot be hid. 20 Yahuah's works are unsearchable.

1 Desire not a multitude of unprofitable children, neither delight in ungodly sons. 2 Though they multiply, rejoice not in them, except the fear of Yahuah be with them. 3 Trust not in their life, neither respect their multitude: for one that is just, is better than a thousand, and better it is to die without children, than to have them that are ungodly. 4 For by one that has understanding, shall the city be replenished, but the kindred of the wicked, shall speedily become desolate. 5 Many such things have I seen with mine eyes, and mine ear has heard greater things than these. 6 In the congregation of the ungodly, shall a fire be kindled, and in a rebellious nation, wrath is set on fire. 7 He was not pacified towards the old giants, who fell away in the strength of their foolishness. 8 Neither spared He the place where Lot sojourned, but abhored them for their pride. 9 He pitied not the people of perdition, who were taken away in their sins. 10 Nor the six hundred thousand footmen, who were gathered together in the hardness of their hearts. 11 And if there be one stiff-necked among the people, it is a marvel, if he escape unpunished; for mercy and wrath are with Him, He is mighty to forgive, and to pour out displeasure. 12 As His mercy is great, so is his correction also: he judges a man according to his works. 13 The sinner shall not escape with his spoils, and the patience of the godly shall not be frustrated. 14 Make way for every work of mercy: for every man shall find according to his works. 15 Yahuah hardened Pharaoh, that he should not know Him, that His powerful works might be known to the world. 16 His mercy is manifest to every creature, and he has separated his light from the darkness with an adamant. 17 Say not, I will hide myself from Yahuah: shall any remember me from above? I shall not be remembered among so many people: for what is my soul among

Or, tribe.

Cf. 21:10. Or, has been.

Cf. Gen. 6.4; 1 En. 5; Jub. 5; 1Pet. 2:4; Jude 1:6.

Cf. Gen. 19:24.

Cf. Num. 14:15; 16:20; 20:51.

Cf. 5:6.

Note: v. 15-16 are missing from the Catholic version (NJB).

Or, strong partition.

such an infinite number of creatures? 18 Behold, the heaven, and the heaven of heavens, the deep and the earth, and all that therein is, shall be moved when he shall visit. 19 The mountains also, and foundations of the earth shall be shaken with trembling, when Yahuah looks upon them. 20 No heart can think upon these things worthily: and who is able to conceive his ways?

Cf.
1Ki. 8:17;
2Chr. 6:18;
2Pet. 3:10.

21 It is a tempest, which no man can see: for the most part of his works are hidden. 22 Who can declare the works of his justice? Or who can endure them? For his Covenant is afar off, and the trial of all things is in the end. 23 He that wants understanding, will think upon vain things: and a foolish man erring, imagines follies. 24 My son, hearken unto me, and learn knowledge, and mark my words with your heart.

25 I will show forth doctrine in weight, and declare his knowledge exactly. 26 The works of Yahuah are done in judgment from the beginning: and from the time He made them, He disposed the parts thereof. 27 He garnished his works forever, and in his hand are the chief of them unto all generations: they neither labor, nor are weary, nor cease from their works.

28 None of them hinders another, and they shall never disobey His Word.

29 After this, Yahuah looked upon the earth, and filled it with his blessings. 30 With all manner of living things has He covered the face thereof, and they shall return into it again.

CHAPTER 17:

1 How Yahuah created and furnished man. 14 Avoid all sin: 19 For Yahuah sees all things. 25 Turn to Him while you live.

Cf. Gen. 1:27, 5:2; Wisd. 2:23, 7:1,6; 1Cor. 11:7; Col. 3:10.

Cf. Gen. 1:26; 1Cor. 11:7.

1 Yahuah created man of the earth, and turned him into it again. 2 He gave them few days, and a short time, and power also over the things therein. 3 He endued them with strength by themselves, and made them according to his image,

Or, of him.

4 And put the fear of man upon all flesh, and gave him dominion over beasts and fouls. 5 [They received the use of the five operations of Yahuah, and in the sixth place he imparted them understanding, and in the seventh, speech, an interpreter of the cogitations thereof.]

Note: v. 5 is missing from the Catholic version (NJB).

6 Counsel, and a tongue, and eyes, ears, and a heart, gave He them to understand. 7 Withal, he filled them with the knowledge of understanding, and showed them good and evil. 8 He set His eye upon their hearts, that He might show them the greatness of His works.

9 He gave them to glory in his marvelous acts forever, that they might declare his works with understanding.

Note: v. 9 is missing from the Catholic version (NJB).

10 And the elect shall praise His holy Name. 11 Beside this He gave them knowledge, and the law of life for an heritage. 12 He made an everlasting covenant with them, and showed them His judgments. 13 Their eyes saw the majesty of His glory, and their ears heard His glorious voice. 14 And He said unto them, Beware of all unrighteousness, and He gave every man commandment concerning his neighbor, 15 Their ways are ever before Him, and shall not be hid from His eyes. 16 Every man from his youth is given to evil, neither could they make to themselves fleshy hearts for stony. 17 For in the division of the nations of the whole earth, he set a ruler over every people, but Israel is Yahuah's portion. 18 Whom being his first born, He nourishes with discipline, and giving him the light of His love, does not forsake him. 19 Therefore all their works are as the sun before Him, and his eyes are continually upon their ways. 20 None of their unrighteous deeds are hid from Him, but all their sins are before Yahuah: 21 But Yahuah being gracious, and knowing his workmanship,

Cf. Ex. 20:16, 22:23.

Note: v. 16 is missing from the Catholic version (NJB).

Cf. Ez. 36:26.

Cf. Dt. 32:8; Rom.13:1; Deu.4:20, 10:15.

Note: v. 18 is missing from the Catholic version (NJB).

Cf. Ex. 4:22.

Note: v. 21 is missing from the Catholic version (NJB).

neither left nor forsook them, but spared them.

22 The alms of a man is as a signet with him, and he will keep the good deeds of man, as the apple of the eye, and give repentance to his sons and daughters.

Cf. 29:13.

23 Afterward he will rise up and reward them, and render their recompense upon their heads.

Cf. Matt. 25:35.

24 But unto them that repent, He granted them return, and comforted those that fail in patience.

Cf. Acts 3:19.

25 Return unto Yahuah, and forsake your sins, make your prayer before his face, and offend less.

Cf. Jer. 3:12. Or, lessen your offense.

26 Turn again to the Most High, and turn away from iniquity: for He will lead you out of darkness into the light of health,

Or, illumination.

and hate abomination vehemently. **27** Who shall praise the Most High in the grave, instead of them which live and give thanks?

Cf. Ps.6:6; Isa. 38:19.

28 Thanksgiving perishes from the dead, as from one that is not: the living and sound in heart, shall praise Yahuah. **29** How great is the loving kindness of Yahuah our Elohim, and his compassion unto such as turn unto Him in holiness?

30 For all things cannot be in men, because the son of man is not immortal. **31** What is brighter than the sun? Yet the light thereof fails: and flesh and blood will imagine evil.

Cf. Job 25:4-5.

32 He views the power of the height of heaven, and all men are but earth and ashes.

CHAPTER 18:

4 Yah's works are to be wondered.
9 Man's life is short. 11 Yah is
merciful. 15 Do not blemish your good
deeds with ill words. 22 Defer not to
be justified. 30 Follow not your lusts.

Cf.
Gen. 1:1.

Cf.
Ex. 20:3;
Isa.
46:9-10;
1Cor. 8:6;
1Tim. 2:5.

Note: v.3
is missing
from
Catholic
version
(NJB).

Cf.
Lev. 10:6;
44:23.

Cf.
Ps. 105.

Cf.
Ps. 90:10,
Jub. 5:8.

1 He that lives forever, created all things in general. 2 Yahuah only is righteous, and there is none other but He. 3 Who governs the world with the palm of His hand, and all things obey His will, for He is the King of All, by His power dividing holy things among them from profane. 4 To whom has He given power to declare His works? And who shall find out His noble acts? 5 Who shall number the strength of his majesty? And who shall also tell out His mercies? 6 As for the wonderous works of Yahuah, there may nothing be taken from them, neither may any thing be put unto them, neither can the ground of them be found out. 7 When a man has done, then he begins, and when he leaves off, then, he shall be doubtful. 8 What is man, and whereto serve he? What is his good, and what is his evil? 9 The number of a man's days at the most are an hundred years. 10 As a drop of water unto the sea, and a gravel stone in comparison of the sand, so are a thousand years to the days of eternity.

Cf.
Jub. 4:30;
Ps. 90:4;
2Pet. 3:8.

11 Therefore is Elohim patient with them, and pours forth His mercy upon them. 12 He saw and perceived their end to be evil, therefore he multiplied His compassion. 13 The mercy of man is toward his neighbor, but the mercy of Yahuah is upon all flesh: He reproves and nurtures, and teaches, and brings again as a shepherd his flock.

14 He has mercy on them that receive discipline, and that diligently seek after His judgments.

15 My son, blemish not your good deeds, neither use uncomfortable words when you give any thing.

Cf. 41:23.

16 Shall not the dew assuage the heat? So is a word better than a gift. 17 Lo is not a word better than a gift? But both are with a gracious man. 18 A fool will scold rudely, and a gift of the envious consumes the eyes. 19 Learn before you speak, and use medicine, or ever you be sick. 20 Before judgment examine yourself, and in the day of visitation you shall find mercy.

Medicine
does not
refer to
pharma-
keía
(φαρμα-
κεία) i.e.
sorcery in
scripture.
G5331.

Cf.
Jas. 1:5.

Cf. 1Cor.
11:28-31.

21 Humble yourself before

you be sick, and in the time of sins show repentance.

22 Let nothing hinder you to pay your vow in due time, and defer not until death to be justified.

23 Before you pray, prepare yourself, and be not as one that tempts Yahuah.

24 Think upon the wrath that shall be at the end; and the time of vengeance when He shall turn away His face.

Cf. 7:17, 36.

25 When you have enough remember the time of hunger, and when you are rich think upon poverty and need. **26** From the morning until the evening the time is changed, and all things are soon done before Yahuah. **27** A wise man will fear in every thing, and in the day of sinning he will beware of offense: but a fool will

Cf. Prov. 28:14.

not observe time. **28** Every man of understanding knows wisdom, and will give praise unto him that found her. **29** They that were of understanding in sayings, became also wise themselves, and poured forth exquisite parables.

30 Go not after your lusts, but refrain yourself from your appetites. **31** If you give your soul the desires that please her, she will make you a laughing stock to your enemies, that malign you.

Cf. Rom. 6:6, 13:14.

32 Take not pleasure in much good cheer, neither be tied to the expense thereof. **33** Be not made a begger by banqueting upon borrowing, when you have nothing in your purse, for you shall lie in wait for your own life: and be talked on.

CHAPTER 19:

2 Wine and women seduce wise men. 7 Say not all you hear. 17 Reprove your friend without anger. 22 There is no wisdom in wickedness.

1 A laboring man that is given to drunkeness shall not be rich, and he that condemns small things shall fall by little and little. 2 Wine and women will make men of understanding to fall away, and he that cleaves to harlots will become impudent. 3 Moths and worms shall have him to heritage, and a bold man shall be taken away. 4 He that is hasty to give credit is light minded, and he that sins shall offend against his own soul. 5 Who so takes pleasure in wickedness shall be condemned, but he that resists pleasures, crowns his life. 6 He that can rule his tongue shall live without strife, and he that hates babbling, shall have less evil. 7 Rehearse not unto another that which is told unto you, and you shall fare never the worse. 8 Whether it be to friend or foe, talk not of other men's lives, and if you can't without offense reveal them not. 9 For he heard and observed you, and when the time comes he will hate you.

10 If you have heard a word, let it die with you, and be bold it will not burst you. 11 A fool travails with a word, as a woman in labor of a child. 12 As an arrow that sticks in a man's thigh, so is a word within a fool's belly. 13 Admonish a friend, it may be he has not done it, and if he has [done it] that he do it no more. 14 Admonish your friend, it may be he has not said it, and if he has, that he speak it not again. 15 Admonish a friend: for many times it is a slander, and believe not every tale. 16 There is one that slips in his speech, but not from his heart, and who is he that has not offended with his tongue? 17 Admonish your neighbor before you threaten him, and not being angry give place to the Law of the Most High. 18 The fear of Yahuah is the first step to be accepted [of Him,] and wisdom obtains His love. 19 The knowledge of the Commandments of Yahuah, is the doctrine of life, and they that do things that please Him, shall receive the fruit of the tree of immortality.

20 The fear of Yahuah is all wisdom, and in all wisdom

Cf. Jos .22:11.

Or, of friend or foe.

Or, show his hatred.

Or, heart

Cf. Lev. 19:17; Matt. 18:15.

Or, reprove.

Or, willingly. , Jas. 3:2.

Or, reprove.

Or, of receiving him.

Note: v. 18-19 are missing from the Catholic version (NJB). i.e. Tree of Life, Cf. Rev. 2:7, 22:2; 2 Esd. 2:10-12, 8:52.

is the performance of the Law, and the knowledge of his omnipotence. 21 If a servant say to his master, I will not do as it pleases you, though afterward he does it, he angers him that nourishes him. 22 The knowledge of wickedness is not wisdom, neither at any time the counsel of sinners, prudence. 23 There is a wickedness, and the same an abomination, and there is a fool wanting in wisdom. 24 He that has small understanding and fears Elohim, is better than one that has much wisdom, and transgresses the Law of the Most High. 25 There is an exquisite subtilty, and the same is unjust, and there is one that turns aside to make judgment appear: and there is a wise man that justifies in judgment.

26 There is a wicked man that hangs down his head sadly; but inwardly he is full of deceit, 27 Casting down his countenance, and making as if he heard not: where he is not known, he will do you a mischief before you be aware. 28 And if for want of power he be hindered from sinning, yet when he finds opportunity he will do evil. 29 A man may be known by his look, and one that has understanding, by his countenance, when you meet him. 30 A man's attire, and excessive laughter, and gate, show what he is.

Note: v. 21 is missing from the Catholic version (NJB).

Or, judges.

Or, in black.

CHAPTER 20:

1 Of silence and speaking. 10 Of gifts, and gain. 18 Of slipping by the tongue. 24 Of lying. 27 Of diverse advertisements.

Or, seasonable.

1 There is a reproof that is not comely: again some man holds his tongue, and he is wise. 2 It is much better to reprove, than to be angry secretly, and he that confesses his fault, shall be preserved from hurt. 3 How good is it when you are reproved, to show repentance? For so shall you escape willful sin. 4 As is the lust of an eunuch to deflour a virgin; so is he *Cf. 30:20.* that executes judgment with violence. 5 There is one that keeps silence and is found wise: and another by much babbling becomes hateful. 6 Some man holds his tongue, because he has not to answer, and some *Cf. Eccle.3:7.* keep silent, knowing his time. 7 A wise man will hold his tongue till he see opportunity: but a babbler *Cf. 32:4.* and a fool will regard no time. 8 He that uses many words shall be abhored; and he that takes to himself authority therein, shall be hated. 9 There is a sinner that has good success in evil things; and there is a gain that turns to loss. 10 There is a gift that shall not profit you; and there is a gift whose recompense is double.

11 There is an abasement because of glory; and there is that lifts up his head from a low estate. 12 There is that buys much for a little, and repays it seven fold. 13 A wise man by his words makes himself beloved: but the graces of fools shall be poured out. 14 The gift of a fool shall do you no good when you have it; neither yet of the envious for his necessity: for he looks to receive many things for one. 15 He gives little and upbraided much; he opens his mouth like a crier; today he lends, and tomorrow will he ask it again: such an one is to be hated of Elohim and man. 16 The fool says, I have no friends, I have no thanks for all my good deeds: and they that eat my bread speak evil of me. 17 How oft, and of how many shall he be laughed to scorn? For he knows not right what it is to have; and it is all one unto him, as if he had it not.

18 To slip upon a pavement, is better than to slip with the tongue: so, the fall of the wicked shall come speedily. 19 An unseasonable tale

Cf. 6:5. Or, pleasant conceits. Lost, or spilt.

Greek: for, his eyes are many for one to receive.

Cf. Jas. 1:5.

Or, an unpleasant fellow.

Greek: shall not be pricked.

Cf. 25:2.

will always be in the mouth of the unwise. **20** A wise sentence shall be rejected when it comes out of a fool's mouth: for he will not speak it in due season. **21** There is that is hindered from sinning through want: and when he takes rest, he shall not be troubled. **22** There is that destroys his own soul through bashfulness, and by accepting of persons overthrows himself.

23 There is that for bashfulness promises to his friend, and makes him his enemy for nothing.

24 A lie is a foul blot in a man, yet it is continually in the mouth of the untaught. **25** A thief is better than a man that is accustomed to lie: but they both shall have destruction to heritage.

26 The disposition of a liar is dishonorable, and his shame is ever with him.

27 A wise man shall promote himself to honor with his words: and he that has understanding, will please great men. **28** He that tills his land, shall increase his heap: and he that pleases great men, shall get pardon for iniquity. **29** Presents and gifts blind the eyes of the wise, and stop up his mouth that he cannot reprove.

30 Wisdom that is hidden, and treasure that is hoarded up, what profit is in them both? **31** Better is he that hides his folly, than a man that hides his wisdom. **32** Necessary patience in seeking Yahuah, is better than he that leads his life without a guide.

Cf. Prov. 12:11, 28:19.

Cf. Ex. 23:8; Dt. 16:19. Or, as a muzzle in the mouth.

LeviteBible.com

CHAPTER 21:

1 Flee from sin as from a serpent.
4 His oppression will undo the rich.
9 The end of the unjust shall be naught. 12 The differences between the fool and the wise.

1 My son, have you sinned? Do so no more, but ask pardon for your former sins. 2 Flee from sin as from the face of a serpent: for if you come too near it, it will bite you: the teeth thereof, are as the teeth of a lion, slaying the souls of men.
3 All iniquity is as a two-edged sword, the wounds whereof cannot be healed.
4 To terrify and do wrong, will waste riches: thus the house of proud men shall be made desolate. 5 A prayer out of a poor man's mouth reaches to the ears of Elohim, and his judgment comes speedily. 6 He that hates to be reproved, is in the way of sinners: but he that fears Yahuah, will repent from his heart.
7 An eloquent man is known far and near, but a man of understanding knows when he slips. 8 He that builds his house with other men's money, is like one that gathers himself stones for the tomb of his burial.

Cf. Ps.41:4;
Luke 15:21.

Cf. Ex. 3:9,
22:23.

Greek: be converted.

9 The congregation of the wicked is like tow wrapped together: and the end of them is a flame of fire to destroy them.
10 The way of sinners is made plain with stones, but at the end thereof is the pit of hell. 11 He that keeps the Law of Yahuah, gets the understanding thereof: and the perfection of the fear of Yahuah, is wisdom. 12 He that is not wise, will not be taught: but there is a wisdom which multiplies bitterness.
13 The knowledge of a wise man shall abound like a flood: and his counsel is like a pure fountain of life.
14 The inner parts of a fool, are like a broken vessel, and he will hold no knowledge as long as he lives. 15 If a skilful man hear a wise word, he will commend it, and add unto it: but as soon as one of no understanding hears it, it displeases him, and he casts it behind his back.
16 The talking of a fool is like a burden in the way: but grace shall be found on the lips of the wise.
17 They inquire at the mouth of the wise man in the congregation, and they shall ponder his words in

Cf. 16:16.

Cf. Eccles.
1:18.
Or, witty.
Or, subtilty.

Cf. 33:5.

Cf.
Prov. 9:9.

their heart. **18** As is a house that is destroyed, so is wisdom to a fool: and the knowledge of the unwise, is as talk without sense.

Or, not to be inquired after.

19 Doctrine unto fools, is as fetters on the feet, and like manacles on the right hand. **20** A fool lifts up his voice with laughter, but a wise man does scarce smile a little. **21** Learning is unto a wise man, as an ornament of gold, and like a bracelet upon his right arm. **22** A foolish man's foot is soon in his [neighbor's] house: but a man of experience is ashamed of him. **23** A fool will peep in at the

Cf. 19:27-28.

door into the house, but he that is well nurtured, will stand without. **24** It is the rudeness of a man to hearken at the door: but a wise man will be grieved with the disgrace. **25** The lips of talkers will be telling such things as pertain not unto them: but the words of such as have understanding, are weighed in the balance. **26** The heart of fools is in their mouth, but the mouth of the wise is in their heart. **27** When the ungodly curse satan, he curses his own soul. **28** A whisperer defiles his own soul, and is hated wheresoever he dwells.

Cf. 28:13.

LeviteBible.com

CHAPTER 22:

1 Of the slothful man, 3 and a foolish daughter. 11 Weep rather for fools, than for the dead. 13 Meddle not with them. 16 The wise man's heart will not shrink. 20 What will lose a friend.

1 A slouthful man is compared to a filthy stone, and every one will hiss him out to his disgrace. 2 A slothful man is compared to the filth of a dunghill: every man that takes it up, will shake his hand. 3 An evil nurtured son is the dishonor of his father that begat him: and a [foolish] daughter is born to his loss. 4 A wise daughter shall bring an inheritance to her husband: but she that lives dishonestly, is her father's heaviness. 5 She that is bold, dishonors both her father and her husband, but they both shall despise her. 6 A tale out of season [is as] music in morning: but stripes and correction of wisdom are never out of time. 7 Who so teaches a fool, is as one that glues a potsherd together, and as he that wakes one from a sound sleep. 8 He that tells a tale to a fool, speaks to one in a slumber: when he has told his tale, he will say, What is the matter?

9 If children live honestly, and have wherewithal, they shall cover the baseness of their parents. 10 But children being haughty through disdain, and want of nurture, do stain the nobility of their kindred.

11 Weep for the dead, for he has lost the light: and weep for the fool, for he wants understanding: make little weeping for the dead, for he is at rest: but the life of the fool is worse than death.

12 Seven days do men mourn for him that is dead; but for a fool, and an ungodly man, all the days of his life. 13 Talk not much with a fool, and go not to him that has no understanding, beware of him lest you have trouble, and you shall never be defiled with his fooleries: depart from him, and you shall find rest, and never be disquieted with madness. 14 What is heavier than lead? And what is the name thereof, but a fool? 15 Sand, and salt, and a mass of iron is easier to bear than a man without understanding.

16 As timber girt and bound together in a building, cannot be loosed with shaking: so the heart that is established by advised counsel, shall fear at no time.

Cf. Prov. 13:22. Or, shall be the heir of her husband.

Note: v. 7-8 are missing from the Catholic version (NJB).

Or an art.

Cf. 38:16.

Cf. 12:12. Or, when he shakes off his filth. Or, wearied.

Cf. Prov. 27:3.

17 A heart settled upon a thought of understanding, is as a fair plastering on the wall of a gallery. 18 Pails set on an high place will never stand against the wind: so a fearful heart in the imagination of a fool, can not stand against any fear.

Or, of a polished wall.

19 He that pricks the eye, will make tears to fall: and he that pricks the heart, makes it to show her knowledge. 20 Who so casts a stone at the birds, frays them away, and he that upbraids his friend, breaks friendship. 21 Though you draw a sword on your friend, yet despair not, for there way be a returning (to favor.) 22 If you have opened your mouth against your friend, fear not, for there may be a reconciliation: except for upbraiding, or pride, or disclosing of secrets, or a treacherous wound, for these things every friend will depart. 23 Be faithful to your neighbor in his poverty, that you may rejoice in his prosperity: abide steadfast unto him in the time of his trouble, that you may be heir with him in his heritage: for a mean estate is not always to be condemned, nor the rich that is foolish, to be had in admiration. 24 As the vapor and smoke of a furnace goes before the fire: so reviling before blood. 25 I will not be ashamed to defend a friend: neither will I hide myself from him. 26 And if any evil happen unto me by him, every one that hears it will beware of him. 27 Who shall set a watch before my mouth, and a seal of wisdom upon my lips, that I fall not suddenly by them, and that my tongue destroy me not?

Cf. Ps. 141:3.

CHAPTER 23:

1 A prayer for grace to flee sin.
9 We may not use swearing: 14 But remember our parents. 16 Of three sorts of sin. 23 The adultress wife sins many ways.

1 O Yahuah, father and governor of all my whole life, leave me not to their counsels, and let me not fall by them. 2 Who will set scourges over my thoughts, and the discipline of wisdom over mine heart? That they spare me not for mine ignorances and it pass not by my sins: 3 Lest my ignorances increase, and my sins abound to my destruction, and I fall before my adversaries, and my enemy rejoice over me, whose hope is far from your mercy. 4 O Yahuah, father and Elohim of my life, give me not a proud look, but turn away from your servants always a haughty mind: 5 Turn away from me vain hopes, and concupiscence, and you shall hold him up that is desirous always to serve you. 6 Let not the greediness of the belly, nor lust of the flesh take hold of me, and give not over me your servant into an impudent mind. 7 Hear, O children, the discipline of the mouth:

Or, a giant like.

He that keeps it, shall never be taken in his lips. 8 The sinner shall be left in his foolishness: both the evil speaker and the proud shall fall thereby. 9 Accustom not your mouth to swearing: neither use yourself to the naming of the holy one. 10 For as a servant that is continually beaten, shall not be without a blue mark: so he that swears and names Elohim continually, shall not be faultless. 11 A man that uses much swearing shall be filled with iniquity, and the plague shall never depart from his house: If he shall offend, his sin shall be upon him: and if he acknowledge not his sin, he makes a double offense, and if he swear in vain, he shall not be innocent, but his house shall be full of calamities. 12 There is a word that is clothed about with death: Elohim grant that it be not found in the heritage of Jacob, for all such things shall be far from the godly, and they shall not wallow in their sins. 13 Use not your mouth to intemperate swearing, for therein is the word of sin.
14 Remember your father and your mother, when you sit among great men.

Cf. 27:15; Ex. 20:7; Matt. 5:33.

Greek: justified.

141

Be not forgetful before them, and so you by your custom become a fool, and wish that you had not been born, and curse the day of your nativity. **15** The man that is accustomed to scornful words, will never be reformed all the days of his life. **16** Two sorts of men multiply sin, and the third will bring wrath: a hot mind is as a burning fire, it will never be quenched till it be consumed: a fornicator in the body of his flesh, will never cease till he has kindled a fire. **17** All bread is sweet to a whoremonger, he will not leave off till he die. **18** A man that breaks wedlock, saying thus in his heart, Who sees me? I am compassed about with darkness: the walls cover me; and nobody sees me, what need I fear? The Most High will not remember my sins: **19** Such a man only fears the eyes of men, and knows not that the eyes of Yahuah are ten thousand times brighter than the sun, beholding all the ways of men, and considering the most secret parts.

20 He knew all things before ever they were created, so also after they were perfected, he looked upon them all: **21** This man shall be punished in the streets of the city, and where he suspected not, he shall be taken. **22** Thus shall it go also with the wife, that leaves her husband, and brings in an heir by another: **23** For first she has disobeyed the Law of the Most High: and secondly, she has trespassed against her own husband, and thirdly, she has played the whore in adultery, and brought children by another man. **24** She shall be brought out into the congregation, and inquisition shall be made of her children.

25 Her children shall not take root, and her branches shall bring forth no fruit. **26** She shall leave her memory to be cursed, and her reproach shall not be blotted out. **27** And they that remain, shall know that there is nothing better than the fear of Yahuah, and that there is nothing sweeter than to take heed unto the Commandment of Yahuah. **28** It is great glory to follow Yahuah, and to be received of him is long life.

Cf. 2Sam. 16:17.

Cf. Prov. 9:17.

Cf. Isa. 29:15; Job. 24:15.

Cf. Lev. 20:10; Dt. 22:22.

Or, a stranger.

Cf. Ex. 20:14.

Or, visitation.

Cf. Wisd. 4:3.

CHAPTER 24:

2 Wisdom does praise herself, show her beginning, 4 Her dwelling, 13 Her glory, 17 Her fruit, 26 Her increase, and perfection.

The praise of wisdom.

1 Wisdom shall praise herself, and shall glory in the midst of her people.
2 In the Congregation of the Most High, shall she open her mouth, and triumph before his power.
3 I came out of the mouth of the Most High, and covered the earth as a cloud. 4 I dwelt in high places, and my throne is in a cloudy pillar. 5 I alone compassed the circuit of heaven, and walked in the bottom of the deep. 6 In the waves of the sea, and in all the earth, and in every people, and nation, I got a possession. 7 With all these I sought rest: and in whose inheritance shall I abide?
8 So the creator of all things gave me a commandment, and He that made me, caused my tabernacle to rest: and said, Let your dwelling be in Jacob, and your inheritance in Israel.
9 He created me from the beginning before the world, and I shall never fail. 10 In the holy Tabernacle I served before Him: and so was I established in Sion.

Or, a mist.

Cf. Job 22:14.

Cf. Prov. 8:23.

Cf. Ex. 31:3.

11 Likewise in the beloved city he gave me rest, and in Jerusalem was my power. 12 And I took root in an honorable people, even in the portion of Yahuah's inheritance. 13 I was exalted like a cedar in Lebanon, and as a cypress tree upon the mountains of Hermon. 14 I was exalted like a palm tree in En-gedi, and as a rose-plant in Jericho, as a fair olive tree in a pleasant field, and grew up as a planetree by the water. 15 I gave a sweet smell like cinnamon, and aspalathus, and I yielded a pleasant odor like the best myrrh, as galbanum and onyx, and sweet storax, and as the sum of franckincense in the Tabernacle. 16 As the turpentine tree, I stretched out my branches, and my branches are the branches of honor and grace. 17 As the vine brought I forth pleasant savor, and my flowers are the fruit of honor and riches. 18 I am the mother of fair love, and fear, and knowledge, and holy hope, I therefore being eternal, am given to all my children which are named of him. 19 Come unto me all that be desirous of me, and fill yourselves with my fruits. 20 For my memorial

Cf. Ps. 132: 8. Or, holy.

Or, Cades Or, in the water.

Cf. Ex. 30:34.

Cf. John 15:1.

Note: v. 18 is missing from the Catholic version (NJB).

Or, chosen.

is sweeter than honey, and mine inheritance than the honeycomb. **21** They that eat me shall yet be hungry, and they that drink me shall yet be thirsty. **22** He that obeys me, shall never be confounded, and they that work by me, shall not do amiss. **23** All these things are **the book of the Covenant of the Most High Elohim**, even the Law which Moses commanded for an heritage unto the Congregations of Jacob. **24** Faint not to be strong in Yahuah; that He may confirm you, cleave unto Him: for Yahuah Almighty is Elohim alone, and besides him there is no other Saviour. **25** He fills all things with his wisdom, as Pison, and as Hiddekel in the time of the new fruits. **26** He makes the understanding to abound like Euphrates, and as Jordan in the time of the harvest. **27** He makes

Cf. Ps. 19:10-11.

Cf. Ex. 20:1, 24:1; Dt. 4:1, 29:2.

Note: v. 24 is missing from the Catholic version (NJB).

Cf. Gen. 2:11.

Cf. Jos. 3:15.

the doctrine of knowledge appear as the light, and as Gihon in the time of vintage. **28** The first man knew her not perfectly: no more shall the last find her out. **29** For her thoughts are more than the sea, and her counsels profounder than the great deep. **30** I also came out as a brook from a river, and as a conduit into a garden. **31** I said, I will water my best garden, and will water abundantly my garden bed: and lo, my brook became a river, and my river became a sea. **32** I will yet make doctrine to shine as the morning, and will send forth her light afar off.

33 I will yet pour out doctrine as prophecy, and leave it to all ages forever. **34** Behold that I have not labored for myself only, but for all them that seek wisdom.

Cf. 33:16.

SIRACH'S RIVERS FROM EDEN

The analogy here employed by Sirach is to the antediluvian Rivers From Eden truly matching our well-proven position on that topic. He provides information which clarifies these tributaries of antiquity. First, there are 5, not 4. For Wisdom is as the source River From Eden itself which feeds the 4 branches equaling 5 *[v.25]*. The Pison and Hiddekel *(Not Tigris)* Rivers are filled by that source river of Wisdom *[v.25]*. Understanding abounds like Euphrates/Parat *[v.26]*. Knowledge fills the Gihon *[v.27]*, but not Spring. "In the time of vintage" is the Ancient River from Eden never the Gihon Springs which fails to be a river *(Nahar)*, was right there in Sirach's time functioning as a spring, and is a straight line of all of 325 m. Thus, it surrounds nothing and never fits scripture for the ancient, vintage Gihon River. It also, is defined in Genesis 2 encompassing the whole land of Ethiopia. That's not Israel nor can that ever fit logically as it is not even the right continent.

Sirach, then, places the location of this entire river system on the bottom of the ocean floor. He expresses *"her counsels profounder than the great deep" [v.29]* locating them on the ocean deep. She came out initially, before the Flood as a brook, in comparison, from a river which Sirach already said the source river was Wisdom in analogy *[v.31]*. Just as Genesis 2:10 defines, Sirach reiterates the purpose of the Rivers from Eden to water the Garden of Eden, "my best garden." *[v.31]* Then, the flood happened and a brook became a river... it grew due to the Flood... a river became a sea... *[v.31]* The new world ocean formed in the Flood burying the Rivers from Eden on the ocean deep affirming the world was only 15% water before the Flood *(2nd Esdras 6:42-52)*. However, they are still there and still function

CHAPTER 25:

1 What things are beautiful, and what hateful. 6 What is the crown of age. 7 What things make men happy. 13 Nothing worse than a wicked woman.

1 In three things I was beautified, and stood up beautiful, both before Elohim and men: the unity of brethren, the love of neighbors, a man and a wife that agree together. 2 Three sorts of men my soul hates, and I am greatly offended at their life: a poor man that is proud, a rich man that is a liar, and an old adulterer that dotes. 3 If you have gathered nothing in your youth, how can you find any thing in your age? 4 Oh how comely a thing is judgment for gray hairs, and for ancient men to know counsel? 5 Oh how comely is the wisdom of old men, and understanding and counsel to men of honor? 6 Much experience is the crown of old men, and the fear of Elohim is their glory. 7 There be nine things which I have judged in my heart to be happy, and the tenth I will utter with my tongue: a man that has joy of his children, and he that lives to see the fall

Or, gloried. Cf. Gen. 13:2, 5. Rom. 12:10.

of his enemy. 8 Well is him that dwells with a wife of understanding, and that has not slipped with his tongue, and that has not served a man more unworthy than himself. 9 Well is him that has found prudence, and he that speaks in the ears of him that will hear.

Cf. 14:1, 19:16; Jas. 3:2.

10 Oh how great is he that finds wisdom! Yet is there none above him that fears Yahuah. 11 But the love of Yahuah passes all things for illumination: he that holds it, whereto shall he be likened? 12 The fear of Yahuah is the beginning of His love: and faith is the beginning of cleaving unto Him. 13 [Give me] any plague, but the plague of the heart: and any wickedness, but the wickedness of a woman.

Or, a friend.

Or, to whom.

Note: v. 12 is missing from the Catholic version (NJB).

14 And any affliction, but the affliction from them that hate me: and any revenge, but the revenge of enemies. 15 There is no head above the head of a serpent, and there is no wrath above the wrath of an enemy. 16 I had rather dwell with a lion and a dragon, than to keep house with a wicked woman. 17 The wickedness of a woman changes her face, and darkens her countenance

Cf. Prov. 21:19.

Or, like a bear.

like sackecloth.

18 Her husband shall sit among his neighbors: and when he hears it, shall sigh bitterly. **19** All wickedness is but little to the wickedness of a woman: let the portion of a sinner fall upon her. **20** As the climbing up a sandy way is to the feet of the aged, so is a wife full of words to a quiet man.

Or, scolding.

21 Stumble not at the beauty of a woman, and desire her not for pleasure. **22** A woman, if she maintain her husband, is full of anger, impudency, and much reproach. **23** A wicked woman abates the courage, makes a heavy countenance, and a wounded heart: a woman that will not comfort her husband in distress makes weak hands, and feeble knees. **24** Of the woman came the beginning of sin, and through her we all die. **25** Give the water no passage: neither a wicked woman liberty to wander abroad. **26** If she go not as you would have her, cut her off from your flesh, and give her a bill of divorce, and let her go.

*Cf. 42.2;
2Sam. 11:2.*

*Cf. Heb.
12:12.*

*Cf.
Gen. 3:6;
1Tim. 2:14.*

*Cf.
Dt. 24:1-3;
Matt. 5:32,
19:7; Mark
10:4.
Also,
Jer. 3:8:
Yahuah
gave Israel
a bill of
divorce for
playing the
harlot.*

CHAPTER 26:

1 A good wife, 4 and a good conscience do glad men. 6 A wicked wife is a fearful thing. 13 Of good and bad wives. 28 Of three things that are grievous. 29 Merchants and hucksters are not without sin.

1 Blessed is the man that has a virtuous wife, for the number of his days shall be double. **2** A virtuous woman rejoices her husband, and he shall fulfill the years of his life in peace. **3** A good wife is a good portion, which shall be given in the portion of them that fear Yahuah. **4** Whether a man be rich or poor, if he have a good heart towards Yahuah, he shall at all times rejoice with a cheerful countenance.

5 There be three things that my heart fears: and for the fourth I was sore afraid: the slander of a city, the gathering together of an unruly multitude, and a false accusation: all these are worse than death. **6** But a grief of heart and sorrow, is a woman that is jealous over another woman, and a scourge of the tongue which communicates withal. **7** An evil wife is a yoke shaken to and fro: he that has hold of her, is as though he held a scorpion. **8** A drunken woman and a wanderer

*Greek: an
evil report.*

*Or, a yoke
of oxen.*

abroad, causes great anger, and she will not cover her own shame. 9 The whoredom of a woman may be known in her haughty looks, and eyelids. 10 If your daughter be shameless, keep her in straightly: lest she abuse herself through over much liberty.

Cf. 44:11.

11 Watch over an impudent eye: and marvel not, if she trespass against you. 12 She will open her mouth as a thirsty traveler, when he has found a fountain: and drink of every water near her: by every hedge will she sit down, and open her quiver

Or stake.

against every arrow. 13 The grace of a wife delights her husband, and her discretion will fat his bones. 14 A silent and loving woman is a gift of Yahuah, and there is nothing so much worth, as a mind well instructed.

15 A shamefast and faithful woman is a double grace, and her continent mind cannot be valued. 16 As

Greek: in the highest places of Yahuah. Or, ornament.

the sun when it arises in the high heaven: so is the beauty of a good wife in the ordering of her house. 17 As the clear light is upon the holy candlestick: so is

Or, in constant age.

the beauty of the face in ripe age. 18 As the golden pillars are upon the sockets of silver: so are the fair feet with a constant heart.

Or, comely.
Or, breast.

19 My son, keep the flower of your age sound: and give not your strength to strangers. 20 When you have gotten a fruitful possession through all the field: sow it with your own seed, trusting in the goodness of your stock. 21 So your race which you leave shall be magnified, having the confidence of their good descent. 22 An harlot shall be accounted as spittle: but a married

Or, a swine.

woman is a tower against death to her husband.

23 A wicked woman is given as a portion to a wicked man: but a godly woman is given to him that fears Yahuah. 24 A dishonest woman contempts in shame, but an honest woman will reverence her husband.

25 A shameless woman shall be counted as a dog: but she that is shamefast will fear Yahuah. 26 A woman that honors her husband, shall be judged wise of all: but she that dishonors him in her pride, shall be counted ungodly of all. 27 A loud crying woman, and a scold, shall be sought out to drive away the enemies.

28 There be two things that grieve my heart: and the third makes me angry: a man of war that suffers poverty, and men of understanding that are not set by: and one that returns from righteousness to sin: Yahuah prepares such a one for the sword.

29 A merchant shall hardly keep himself from doing wrong: and an huckster shall not be freed from sin.

CHAPTER 27:

1 Of sins in selling and buying.
7 Our speech will tell what is in us.
16 A friend is lost by discovering his secrets. 25 He that digs a pit shall fall into it.

1 Many have sinned for a small matter: and he that seeks for abundance will turn his eyes away. 2 As a nail sticks fast between the joinings of the stones: so does sin stick close between buying and selling.

Cf. Prov. 28:21. Or, a thing indifferent.

Cf. Prov. 23:4. 1Tim. 6:9.

3 Unless a man hold himself diligently in the fear of Yahuah, his house shall soon be overthrown. 4 As when one sifts with a sieve, the refuse remains, so the filth of man in his talk.

Or, thought.

5 The furnace proves the potters vessel: so the trial of man is in his reasoning.

Cf. Prov. 27. 21.

6 The fruit declares if the tree has been dressed: so is the utterance of a conceit in the heart of man.

Cf. Matt. 7:16-20. "... know them by their fruits." (v. 6) NRSV: "...the fruit discloses the cultivation."

7 Praise no man before you hear him speak, for this is the trial of men. 8 If you follow righteousness, you shall obtain her, and put her on, as a glorious long robe. 9 The birds will resort unto their like, so will truth return unto them that practice in her. 10 As the lion lies in wait for the prey: so sin for them that work iniquity. 11 The discourse of a godly man is always with wisdom: but a fool changes as the moon. 12 If you be among the undiscreet, observe the time: but be continually among men of understanding. 13 The discourse of fools is irksome, and their sport is in the wantoness of sin.

Cf. Jas. 5:5.

14 The talk of him that swears much, makes the hair stand upright: and their quarrels make one stop his ears. 15 The strife of the proud is blood-shedding, and their revilings are grievous to the ear. 16 Who so discovers secrets, looses

his credit: and shall never find friend to his mind.

17 Love your friend, and be faithful unto him: but if you betray his secrets, follow no more after him.

18 For as a man has destroyed his enemy: so have you lost the love of your neighbor. 19 As one that lets a bird go out of his hand, so have you let your neighbor go; and shall not get him again.

20 Follow after him no more, for he is too far off, he is as a gazelle escaped out of the snare. 21 As for a wound it may be bound up, and after reviling there may be reconcilement: but he that betrays secrets is without hope. 22 He that winks with the eyes works evil, and he that knows him will depart from him. 23 When you are present he will speak sweetly, and will admire your words: but at the last

Cf. Prov. 10:10.

he will twist his mouth, and slander your sayings. 24 I have hated many things, but nothing like him, for Yahuah will hate him.

Or, alter his speech.

25 Who so casts a stone on high, casts it on his own head, and a deceitful stroke shall make wounds.

26 Who so digs a pit shall fall therein: and he that sets a trap shall be taken therein.

Cf. Ps. 7:15; Prov. 26:27; Eccles. 8:10.

27 He that works mischief, it shall fall upon him, and he shall not know whence it comes. 28 Mockery and reproach are from the proud: but vengeance as a lion shall lie in wait for them. 29 They that rejoice at the fall of the righteous shall be taken in the snare, and anguish shall consume them before they die.

Cf. Dt. 32:35; Rom. 12:19.

30 Malice and wrath, even these are abominations, and the sinful man shall have them both.

CHAPTER 28:

1 Against revenge. 8 Quarreling, 10 Anger, 15 And backbiting.

1 The vengeful shall find vengeance from Yahuah, and He will surely keep his sins (in remembrance.)

2 Forgive your neighbor the hurt that he has done

unto you, so shall your sins also be forgiven when you pray. 3 One man bears hatred against another, and does he seek pardon from Yahuah? 4 He shows no mercy to a man, which is like himself: and does he ask forgiveness of his own sins? 5 If he that is but

Cf. Matt. 6:14. Origin of Messiah's doctrine!

flesh nourish hatred, who will entreat for pardon of his sins? 6 Remember your end, and let enmity cease, [remember] corruption and death, and abide in the Commandments. 7 Remember the Commandments, and bear no malice to your neighbor: [remember] the Covenant of the highest, and wink at ignorance. 8 Abstain from strife, and you shall diminish your sins: for a furious man will kindle strife. 9 A sinful man disquiets friends, and makes debate among them that be at peace. 10 As the matter of the fire is, so it burns: and as a man's strength is, so is his wrath, and according to his riches his anger rises, and the stronger they are which contend, the more they will be inflamed. 11 An hasty contention kindles a fire, and an hasty fighting sheds blood. 12 If you blow the spark, it shall burn: if you spit upon it, it shall be quenched, and both these come out of your mouth. 13 Curse the whisperer, and double tongued: for such have destroyed many that were at peace. 14 A backbiting tongue has disquieted many, and driven them from nation to nation, strong cities has it pulled down, and overthrown the houses of great men.

15 A backbiting tongue has cast out virtuous women, and deprived them of their labors. 16 Who so hearkens unto it, shall never find rest, and never dwell quietly. 17 The stroke of the whip makes marks in the flesh, but the stroke of the tongue breaks the bones. 18 Many have fallen by the edge of the sword: but not so many as have fallen by the tongue. 19 Well is he that is defended from it, and has not passed through the venom thereof: who has not drawn the yoke thereof, nor has been bound in her bands.

20 For the yoke thereof is a yoke of iron, and the bands thereof are bands of brass. 21 The death thereof is an evil death, the grave was better than it. 22 It shall not have rule over them that fear Elohim, neither shall they be burnt with the flame thereof. 23 Such as forsake Yahuah shall fall into it, and it shall burn in them, and not be quenched, it shall be sent upon them as a lion, and devour them as a leopard. 24 Look that you hedge your possession

Cf. Lev. 19:17-18. "Thou shalt not avenge, nor bear any grudge.." "...love thy neighbour as thyself." Cf. Matt. 22:39-40. Note: Yahusha and Sirach were quoting Moses.

Cf. 8:1.

Cf. Prov. 26:21.

Cf. 21:28.

Or, third.

Cf. Luke 21:24; Prov. 18:21.

about with thornes, and bind up your silver and gold: 25 And weigh your words in a balance, and make a door and bar for your mouth. 26 Beware you slide not by it, lest you fall before him that lies in wait.

CHAPTER 29:

2. We must show mercy and lend: 4 but the borrower must not defraud the lender. 9 Give alms. 14 A good man will not undo his surety. 18 To be surety and undertake for others is dangerous. 22 It is better to live at home, than to sojourn.

1 He that is merciful, will lend unto his neighbor, and he that strengthens his hand, keeps the Commandments. 2 Lend to your neighbor in time of his need, and pay your neighbor again in due season.

Cf. Dt. 15:8; Matt.5:42; Luke 6:35.

3 Keep your word and deal faithfully with him, and you shall always find the thing that is necessary for you. 4 Many when a thing was lent them, reckoned it to be found, and put them to trouble that helped them. 5 Till he has received, he will kiss a man's hand: and for his neighbor's money he will speak softly: but when he should repay, he will prolong the time, and return words of grief, and complain of the time. 6 If he prevail, he shall hardly receive the half, and he will count as if he had found it: if not; he has deprived him of his money, and he has gotten him an enemy without cause: he pays him with cursings, and railings: and for honor he will pay him disgrace.

Or, if he be able.

7 Many therefore have refused to lend for other men's ill dealing, fearing to be defrauded. 8 Yet have patience with a man in poor estate, and delay not to show him mercy. 9 Help the poor for the commandments sake, and turn him not away because of his poverty. 10 Lose your money for your brother and your friend, and let it not rust under a stone to be lost. 11 Lay up your treasure according to the commandments of the Most High, and it shall bring you more profit than gold. 12 Shut up alms in your storehouses: and it shall deliver you from all affliction. 13 It shall fight for you against your enemies, better than a mighty shield and strong spear.

Cf. Dan. 4:24; Matt. 6:19-20; Luke 11:41, 12:33; Acts 10:4; 1Tim. 6:18,19; Job 4:8, 9,10.

14 An honest man is surety for his neighbor: but he that

Or, fail.

is impudent, will forsake him. 15 Forget not the friendship of your surety: for he has given his life for you. 16 A sinner will overthrow the good estate of his surety: 17 And he that is of an unthankful mind, will leave him in [danger] that delivered him. 18 Being surety has undone many of good estate, and shaked them as a wave of the sea: mighty men has it driven from their houses, so that they wandered among strange nations. 19 A wicked man transgressing the commandments of Yahuah, shall fall into being surety: and he that undertakes and follows other men's business for gain, shall fall into suits. 20 Help your neighbor according to your power, and beware that you yourself fall not into the same. 21 The chief thing for life is water and bread,

and clothing, and an house to cover shame. 22 Better is the life of a poor man in a mean cottage, than delicate fare in another man's house. 23 Be it little or much, hold you contented, that you hear not the reproach of your house. 24 For it is a miserable life to go from house to house: for where you are a stranger, you dare not open your mouth. 25 You shall entertain and feast, and have no thanks: moreover, you shall hear bitter words. 26 Come stranger, and furnish a table, and feed me of that you have ready. 27 Give place you stranger to an honorable man, my brother comes to be lodged, and I have need of my house. 28 These things are grievous to a man of understanding: the upbraiding of houseroom, and reproaching of the lender.

Cf. 39:26.

CHAPTER 30:

1 It is good to correct our children, 7 and not to pamper them. 14 Health is better than wealth. 22 Health and life are shortened by grief.

Cf. Prov. 13:24, 23:13. Of children.

1 He that loves his son, causes him oft to feel the rod, that he may have joy of him in the end. 2 He

that chastises his son, shall have joy in him, and shall rejoice of him among his acquaintance. 3 He that teaches his son, grieves the enemy: and before his friends he shall rejoice of him. 4 Though his father die, yet he is as though he were not dead: for he has

Or, good by him.

Or, kinsfolk.

Cf. Dt. 6:7.

left one behind him that is like himself. 5 While he lived, he saw and rejoiced in him: and when he died he was not sorrowful. 6 He left behind him an avenger against his enemies, and one that shall requite kindness to his friends.

Cf. Ps. 128.

7 He that pampers too much of his son, shall bind up his wounds, and his bowels will be troubled at every cry. 8 An horse not broken becomes headstrong: and a child left to himself will be willful.

9 Coddle your child, and he shall make you afraid: play with him, and he will bring you to heaviness. 10 Laugh not with him, lest you have sorrow with him, and lest you gnash your teeth in the end. 11 Give him no liberty in his youth, and wink not at his follies.

Or, astonished.

Cf. 7:23.

12 Bow down his neck while he is young, and beat him on the sides while he is a child, lest he wax stubborn, and be disobedient unto you, and so bring sorrow to your heart. 13 Chastise your son, and hold him to labor, lest his lewd behavior be an offense unto you. 14 Better is the poor being sound and strong of constitution, than

Of health.

a rich man that is afflicted in his body. 15 Health and good state of body are above all gold, and a strong body above infinite wealth. 16 There are no riches above a sound body, and no joy above the joy of the heart. 17 Death is better than a bitter life, or continual sickeness. 18 Delicates poured upon a mouth shut up, are as messes of meat set upon a grave. 19 What good does the offering unto an idol? For neither can it eat nor smell: so is he that is persecuted of Yahuah.

Sirach rebukes the practice of All Saints/ All Soul's Day!

Or, afflicted.

20 He sees with his eyes and groans, as an eunuch that embraces a virgin, and sighs. 21 Give not over your mind to heaviness, and afflict not yourself in your own counsel. 22 The gladness of the heart is the life of man, and the joyfulness of a man prolongs his days. 23 Love your own soul, and comfort your heart, remove sorrow far from you: for sorrow has killed many, and there is no profit therein. 24 Envy and wrath shorten the life, and carefulness brings age before the time. 25 A cheerful and good heart will have a care of his meat and diet.

Cf. Prov. 12:25, 15:13, 17:22.

Or, exultation.

Or, a noble.

CHAPTER 31:

1 Of the desire of riches. 12 Of moderation and excess in eating, or drinking wine.

1 Watching for riches, consumes the flesh, and the care thereof drives away sleep. 2 Watching care will not let a man slumber, as a sore disease breaks sleep. 3 The rich have great labor in gathering riches together, and when he rests, he is filled with his delicates. 4 The poor labors in his poor estate, and when he leaves off, he is still needy. 5 He that loves gold shall not be justified, and he that follows corruption, shall have enough thereof. 6 Gold has been the ruin of many, and their destruction was present. 7 It is a stumbling block unto them that sacrifice unto it, and every fool shall be taken therewith. 8 Blessed is the rich that is found without blemish, and has not gone after gold: 9 Who is he? And we will call him blessed: For wonderful things has he done among his people. 10 Who has been tried thereby, and found perfect? Then let him glory. Who might offend and has not offended, or done evil, and has not done it? 11 His goods shall be established, and the congregation shall declare his alms. 12 If you sit at a bountiful table, be not greedy upon it, and say not, There is much meat on it. 13 Remember that a wicked eye is an evil thing: and what is created more wicked than an eye? Therefore it weeps upon every occasion. 14 Stretch not your hand whithersoever it looks, and thrust it not with him into the dish. 15 Judge your neighbor by yourself: and be discreet in every point. 16 Eat as it becomes a man those things which are set before you: and devour not, lest you be hated. 17 Leave off first for manners sake, and be not unsatiable, lest you offend. 18 When you sit among many, reach not your hand out first of all. 19 A very little is sufficient for a man well nurtured, and he fetches not his wind short upon his bed. 20 Sound sleep comes of moderate eating: he rises early, and his wits are with him, but the pain of watching and choller, and pangs of the belly are with an unsatiable man. 21 And if you have been forced to eat, arise, go

Cf. 1Tim. 6:9,10.

Cf. Luke 12:15.

Cf. 8:2.

Cf. Luke 6:24.

Cf. Ps.111:9; Prov. 23:1. Greek: open not your throat upon it.

Or, before every thing that is presented.

Cf. 37:29.

Or, and lies not pussing and blowing.

forth, vomit, and you shall have rest. **22** My son, hear me, and despise me not, and at the last you shall find as I told you: in all your works be quick, so shall there no sickeness come unto you. **23** Who so is liberal of his meat, men shall speak well of him, and the report of his good housekeeping will be believed. **24** But against him that is ungenerous of his meat, the whole city shall murmur; and the testimonies of his greediness shall not be doubted of. **25** Show not your valiantness in wine, for wine has destroyed many. **26** The furnace proves the edge by dipping: so does wine the hearts of the proud by drunkenness. **27** Wine

Cf. Prov. 22: 9.

Cf. Isa. 5:22; Jude 13:8.

is as good as life to a man if it be drunk moderately: what life is then to a man that is without wine? For it was made to make men glad. **28** Wine measurably drunk, and in season, brings gladness of the heart and cheerfulness of the mind. **29** But wine drunken with excess, makes bitterness of the mind, with brawling and quarreling.

30 Drunkenness increases the rage of a fool till he offend, it diminishes strength, and makes wounds. **31** Rebuke not your neighbor at the wine, and despise him not in his mirth: Give him no despiteful words, and press not upon him with urging him (to drink.)

CHAPTER 32:

1 Of his duty that is chief or master in a feast. 14 Of the fear of Yahuah. 18 Of counsel. 20 Of a ragged and a smooth way. 23 Trust not any but yourself and to Elohim.

1 If you be made the master (of the feast) lift not yourself up, but be among them as one of the rest, take diligent care for them, and so sit down. **2** And when you have done all your office,

take your place that you may be merry with them, and receive a crown for your well ordering of the feast.

3 Speak you that are the elder, for it becomes you, but with sound judgment, and hinder not music.

4 Pour not out words where there is a musician, and show not forth wisdom out of time. **5** A concert of music in a banquet of wine, is as a signet of carbuncle

Cf. 20:7; Eccl. 3:7.

set in gold. 6 As a signet of an emerald set in a work of gold, so is the melody of music with pleasant wine.

7 Speak young man, if there be need of you: and yet scarcely when you are twice asked: 8 Let your speech be short, comprehending much in few words, be as one that knows, and yet holds his tongue. 9 If you be among great men, make not yourself equal with them, and when ancient men are in place, use not many words. 10 Before the thunder goes lightning: and before a shamefaced man shall go favor. 11 Rise up before, and be not the last: but get you home without delay. 12 There take your pastime, and do what you will: but sin not by proud speech 13 And for these things bless Him that made you, and has replenished you with his good things.

Cf.
Job 33:6.

14 Who so fears Yahuah, will receive His discipline, and they that seek Him early, shall find favor.

15 He that seeks the law, shall be filled therewith: but the hypocrite will be offended thereat. 16 They that fear Yahuah shall find judgment, and shall kindle justice as a light. 17 A sinful man will not be reproved, but finds an excuse according to his will. 18 A man of counsel will be considerate, but a strange and proud man is not daunted with fear, even when of himself he has done without counsel.

19 Do nothing without advice, and when you have once done, repent not.

20 Go not in a way wherein you may fall, and stumble not among the stones. 21 Be not confident in a plain way. 22 And beware of your own children. 23 In every good work trust your own soul: for this is the keeping of the commandments. 24 He that believes in Yahuah, takes heed to the commandment, and he that trusted in Him, shall fare never the worse.

Cf.
Rom. 14:5.

Cf.
Matt. 16:27.

Or, shall not be hurt.

LeviteBible.com

CHAPTER 33:

1 The safety of him that fears Yahuah. 2 The wise and the foolish. 7 Times and seasons are of Elohim. 10 Men are in His hands, as clay in the hands of the potter. 18 Chiefly regard yourself. 24 Of servants.

1 There shall no evil happen unto him that fears Yahuah, but in temptation even again He will deliver him. 2 A wise man hates not the Law, but he that is an hypocrite therein, is as a ship in a storm. 3 A man of understanding trusts in the Law, and the Law is faithful unto him, as an oracle.

Or, as the asking of urim.

4 Prepare what to say, and so you shall be heard, and bind up instruction, and then make answer. 5 The heart of the foolish is like a cartwheel: and his thoughts are like a rolling axeltree. 6 A stallion horse is as a mocking friend, he neighs under every one that sits upon him. 7 Why does one day excel another? When as all the light of every day in the year is of the Sun. 8 By the knowledge of Yahuah they were distinguished: and he altered seasons and feasts. 9 Some of them He made High Days, and hallowed them, and some of them he made ordinary days. 10 And all men are

Greeke: bowels. Cf. 21:16.

Or, ordained for the number of days.

from the ground, and Adam was created of earth. 11 In much knowledge Yahuah has divided them, and made their ways diverse. 12 Some of them He blessed, and exalted, and some of them He sanctified, and set near Himself: but some of them He cursed, and brought low, and turned out of their places. 13 As the clay is in the potter's hand to fashion it at his pleasure: so man is in the hand of Him that made him, to render to them as like him best. 14 Good is set against evil, and life against death: so is the godly against the sinner, and the sinner against the godly. 15 So look upon all the works of the Most High, and there are two and two, one against another. 16 I woke up last of all, as one that gathers after the grape-gatherers: by the blessing of Yahuah I profited, and filled my wine-press, like a gatherer of grapes.

17 Consider that I labored not for myself only, but for all them that seek learning; 18 Hear me, O great men of the people, and hearken with your ears rulers of the Congregation: 19 Give not your son, and wife, your brother and friend power

Cf. Gen. 1:27, 2:7.

Or, standings.

Cf. Isa. 45:9, 64:8; Jer. 18:6; Rom. 9:20-21.

Or, gleaneth.

Cf. 24:39.

over you while you live, and give not your goods to another, lest it repent you: and you entreat for the same again. **20** As long as you live and have breath in you, give not yourself over to any. **21** For better it is that your children should seek you, than that you should stand to their courtesy.

22 In all your works keep to yourself the pre-eminence, leave not a stain in your honor. **23** At the time when you shall end your days, and finish your life, distribute your inheritance. **24** Fodder, a wand, and burdens, are for the ass: and bread, correction, and work for a servant. **25** If you set your servant to labor, you shall find rest: but if you let him go idle, he shall seek liberty. **26** A yoke and a collar do bow the neck: so are tortures and torments for an evil servant. **27** Send him to labor that he be not idle: for idleness teaches much evil. **28** Set him to work, as is fit for him; if he be not obedient, put on more heavy fetters. **29** But be not excessive toward any, and without discretion do nothing. **30** If you have a servant, let him be unto you as yourself, because you have bought him with a price. **31** If you have a servant, treat him as a brother: for you have need of him, as of your own soul: if you treat him evil, and he run from you, which way will you go to seek him?

Or, sell not.

Or, look to their hands.

Of servants.

Cf. 7:20. Greeke: in blood.

CHAPTER 34:

1 Of dreams. 13 The praise and blessing of them that fear Yahuah. 18 The offering of the ancient, and prayer of the poor innocent.

1 The hopes of a man void of understanding are vain, and false: and dreams lift up fools. **2** Who so regards dreams, is like him that catches after a shadow, and follows after the wind. **3** The vision of dreams is the resemblance of one thing to another, even as the likeness of a face to a face. **4** Of an unclean thing, what can be cleansed? And from that thing which is false, what truth can come? **5** Divinations, and soothsayings, and dreams are vain: and the heart fancies as a woman's heart in travail. **6** If they be not sent from the Most High in your visitation, set not your heart upon them.

Of dreams.

Or, has his mind upon.

Cf. Prov. 27:19.

Cf. Job 14:4.

Or, regard them not.

7 For dreams have deceived many, and they have failed that put their trust in them. 8 The Law shall be found perfect without lies: and wisdom is perfection to a faithful mouth. 9 A man that has travailed knows many things: and he that has much experience, will declare wisdom. 10 He that has no experience, knows little: but he that has travailed, is full of prudence. 11 When I travailed, I saw many things: and I understand more, than I can express. 12 I was oft times in danger of death, yet I was delivered because of these things. 13 The spirit of those that fear Yahuah shall live, for their hope is in Him that saves them. 14 Who so fears Yahuah, shall not fear nor be afraid, for He is his hope. 15 Blessed is the soul of him that fears Yahuah: To whom does he look? And who is his strength? 16 For the eyes of Yahuah are upon them that love Him, He is their mighty protection, and strong stay, a defense from heat, and a cover from the

Cf. Ps. 33:18, 61:1-2.

sun at noon, a preservation from stumbling, and a help from falling. 17 He raises up the soul, and lightens the eyes: he gives health, life, and blessing. 18 He that sacrifices of a thing wrongfully gotten, his offering is ridiculous, and the gifts of unjust men are not accepted. 19 The Most High is not pleased with the offerings of the wicked, neither is he pacified for sin by the multitude of sacrifices. 20 Who so brings an offering of the goods of the poor, does as one that kills the son before his father's eyes. 21 The bread of the needy, is their life: he that defrauds him thereof, is a man of blood. 22 He that takes away his neighbor's living, slays him: and he that defrauds the laborer of his hire, is a bloodshedder. 23 When one builds, and another pulls down, what profit have they than but labor? 24 When one prays, and another curses, whose voice will Yahuah hear? 25 He that washes himself after the touching of a dead body, if he touch it again, what avails his washing? 26 So is it with a man that fasts for his sins, and goes again and does the same: who will hear his prayer, or what does his humbling profit him?

Cf. Prov. 21:27. Or, the mockeries.

Cf. Prov. 15:8.

Cf. 7:20; Dt. 24:14-15.

Cf. Num. 19:11-12.

CHAPTER 35:

1 Sacrifices pleasing Yahuah.
14 The prayer of the fatherless, of the
widow, and of the humble in spirit.
20 Acceptable mercy.

Cf. 1Sam.
15:22.
Jer.
7:3,5,6,7.

1 He that keeps the law, brings offerings enough: he that takes heed to the commandment, offers a peace offering. 2 He that requites a good turn, offers fine flour: and he that gives alms, sacrifices praise. 3 To depart from wickedness is a thing pleasing to Yahuah: and to forsake unrighteousness, is a propitiation. 4 You shall not appear empty before Yahuah: 5 For all these things [are to be done] because of the commandment. 6 The offering of the righteous makes the altar fat, and the sweet savor thereof is before the Most High. 7 The sacrifice of a just man is acceptable, and the memorial thereof shall never be forgotten. 8 Give Yahuah his honor with a good eye, and diminish not the first fruits of your hands. 9 In all your gifts show a cheerful countenance, and dedicate your tithes with gladness. 10 Give unto the Most High, according as he has enriched you, and as

Cf.
Ex. 23:15.
Dt. 16:16.

Cf.
2Cor. 9:7.
Or, set
apart.

you have gotten, give with a cheerful eye. 11 For Yahuah recompenses, and will give you seven times as much. 12 Do not think to corrupt with gifts, for such He will not receive: and trust not to unrighteous sacrifices, for Yahuah is judge, and with Him is no respect of persons. 13 He will not accept any person against a poor man: but will hear the prayer of the oppressed. 14 He will not despise the supplication of the fatherless: nor the widow when she pours out her complaint. 15 Do not the tears run down the widows cheeks? And is not her cry against him that causes them to fall? 16 He that serves Yahuah, shall be accepted with favor, and his prayer shall reach unto the clouds. 17 The prayer of the humble pierces the clouds: and till it come nigh he will not be comforted: And will not depart till the Most High shall behold to judge righteously, and execute judgment. 18 For Yahuah will not be slack, neither will the mighty be patient towards them, till he has smitten in sunder the loins of the unmerciful, and repaid vengeance to the heathen: Till he has

Cf.
Tob.4:8.

Cf. Prov.
6:30-31.

Or,
diminish
nothing
of thy
offerings.
Lev.
22:21-22;
Dt. 10:17,
15:21;
2Chr. 19:7;
Job 34:19;
Wisd. 6:7;
Acts 10:34;
Rom. 2:11;
Gal. 2:6;
Eph. 6:9;
Col. 3:25;
1Pet. 1:17.

Cf.
Ps. 2:9;
Rev. 2:27,
12:5,
19:15.

Or, cruell
oppress-
ors.

taken away the multitude of the proud, and broken the scepter of the unrighteous: 19 Till he has rendered to every man according to his deeds, and to the works of men according to their devices, till he has judged the cause of his people: and made them to rejoice in his mercy, 20 Mercy is seasonable in the time of affliction, as clouds of rain in the time of drought.

Greek: fair.

CHAPTER 36:

1 A prayer for the Church against the enemies thereof. 18 A good heart and a forward. 21 Of a good wife.

1 Have mercy upon us, O Yahuah Elohim of all, and behold us: 2 And send your fear upon all the nations that seek not after you.

Cf.
Jer. 10:25.
Or, upon.

3 Lift up your hand against the strange nations, and let them see your power. 4 As you were sanctified in us before them: so be magnified among them before us. 5 And let them know you, as we have known you, that there is no Elohim, but only you, O Elohim. 6 Show new signs, and make other strange wonders: glorify your hand and your right arm, that they may set forth your wonderous works. 7 Raise up indignation, and pour out wrath: take away the adversary and destroy the enemy. 8 Make the time short, remember the covenant, and let them declare your wonderful works. 9 Let him that escapes, be consumed by the rage of the fire, and let them perish that oppress the people. 10 Smite in sunder the heads of the rulers of the heathen, that say, There is none other but we. 11 Gather all the tribes of Jacob together, and inherit them, as from the beginning.

Greek:
oath.

12 O Yahuah have mercy upon the people, that **are called by your name**, and upon Israel, whom you have named your first born. 13 O be merciful unto Jerusalem your holy city, the place of your rest. 14 Fill Sion with your unspeakable oracles, and your people with your glory. 15 Give testimony unto those that you have possessed from the beginning, and raise up prophets that have been

Cf.
Dt. 4:20;
Jub. 22:10,
15.

His name
is **Yahu**ah
and His
people
are the
Yahudim,
יהודים, never
Jews but
Yah's.
Cf.
Ex. 4:22;
Jub. 2:20.

Or, that
it may
magnify
your
oracles.

Or, proph-
esies.

in your name. 16 Reward them that wait for you, and let your prophets be found faithful. 17 O Yahuah hear the prayer of your servants, according to the blessing of Aaron over your people, that all they which dwell upon the earth, may know that you are Yahuah, the eternal Elohim. 18 The belly devours all meats, yet is one meat better than another.

19 As the palate tastes diverse kinds of venison: so does an heart of understanding false speeches. 20 A froward heart causes heaviness: but a man of experience will recompense him. 21 A woman will receive every man, yet is one daughter better than another 22 The beauty of a woman cheers the countenance, and a man loves nothing better. 23 If there be kindness, meekness, and comfort in her tongue, then is not her husband like other men. 24 He that gets a wife, begins a possession, a help like unto himself, and a pillar of rest. 25 Where no hedge is, there the possession is spoiled: and he that hath no wife will wander up and down mourning. 26 Who will trust a thief well appointed, that skips from city to city? So [who will believe] a man that has no house? And lodges wheresoever the night takes him?

Or, suppliants.

Cf. Num. 6:22-27.

Cf. Job 34:3.

Or, common.

Or, to thrive.

CHAPTER 37:

1 How to know friends and counselors. 12 The discretion and wisdom of a godly man blesses him. 27 Learn to refrain your appetite.

1 Every friend says, I am his friend also: but there is a friend which is only a friend in name. 2 Is it not a grief unto death, when a companion and friend is turned to an enemy? 3 O wicked imagination, whence came you in to cover the earth with deceit? 4 There is a companion, which rejoices in the prosperity of a friend: but in the time of trouble will be against him. 5 There is a companion which helps his friend for the belly, and takes up the buckler against the enemy. 6 Forget not your friend in your mind, and be not unmindful of him in your riches.

Or, in the presence of the enemy.

7 Every counsellor extols counsel; but there is some that counsels for himself.

8 Beware of a counsellor, and know before what need he has (for he will counsel *Or, what use there is of him.* for himself) lest he cast the lot upon you: 9 And say unto you, Your way is good: and afterward he stand on the other side, to see what shall befall you.

10 Consult not with one that suspects you: and hide your counsel from such as envy you. 11 Neither consult with a woman touching her of whom she is jealous; neither with a coward in matters of war, nor with a merchant concerning exchange; nor with a buyer of selling; nor with an envious man of thankfulness; nor with an unmerciful man touching kindness; nor with the slothful for any work; nor with an hireling for a year, of finishing work; nor with an idle servant of much business: Hearken not unto these in any matter of counsel. 12 But be continually with a godly man, whom you know to keep the commandments *Cf. 2Cor. 16:14-18.* of Yahuah, whose mind is according to your mind,

and will sorrow with you, if you shall miscarry. 13 And let the counsel of your own heart stand: for there is no man more faithful unto you than it. 14 For a man's mind is sometimes wont to tell him more than seven watchmen, that sit above in an high tower. 15 And above all this pray to the Most High, that He will direct your way in truth. 16 Let reason go before every enterprise, and counsel before every action. 17 The countenance is a sign of changing of the heart. 18 Four manner of things appear: good and evil, life and death: but the tongue *Cf. Prov. 18:21.* rules over them continually. 19 There is one that is wise and teaches many, and yet is unprofitable to himself. 20 There is one that shows wisdom in words, and is hated: he shall be destitute of all food. 21 For grace is not given him from Yahuah: because he is deprived of all wisdom. 22 Another is wise to himself: and the fruits of understanding are commendable in his mouth. 23 A wise man instructs his people, and the fruits of his understanding fail not. 24 A wise man shall be filled with blessing, and all they that see him, shall count him happy. 25 The days of the life of man may be numbered: but the days of Israel are innumerable. 26 A wise man shall inherit glory among his people, and his name shall be perpetual. 27 My son prove your soul in your life, and see what is evil for it, and give not that

Or, credit.

unto it. 28 For all things are not profitable for all men, neither has every soul pleasure in every thing. 29 Be not unsatiable in any dainty thing: nor too greedy upon meats. 30 For excess of meats, brings sickness, and surfeiting will turn into choler. 31 By surfeiting have many perished, but he that takes heed, prolongs his life.

Or, variety of meats.

CHAPTER 38:

1 Honor due to the physician, and why. 16 How to weep and mourn for the dead. 24 The wisedom of the learned man, and of the Laborer and Artificer: with the use of them both.

1 Honor a physician with the honor due unto him, for the uses which you may have of him: for Yahuah has created him. 2 For of the Most High comes healing, and he shall receive honor of the King. 3 The skill of the physician shall lift up his head: and in the sight of great men he shall be in admiration. 4 Yahuah has created medicines out of the earth; and he that is wise will not abhore them. 5 Was not the water made sweet with wood, that the

Or, a gift.

Cf. Jub. 10:12-13. Note: Herbal remedies out of the earth, not lab made pharma-keía, φαρμακεία, or sorcery (G5331).

virtue thereof might be known? 6 And he has given men skill, that he might be honored in his marvelous works. 7 With such does he heal [men,] and take away their pains. 8 Of such does the apothecary make a confection; and of his works there is no end, and from him is peace over all the earth. 9 My son, in your sickness be not negligent: but pray unto Yahuah, and He will make you whole. 10 Leave off from sin, and order your hands right, and cleanse your heart from all wickedness. 11 Give a sweet savor, and a memorial of fine flower: and make a fat offering, as not being. 12 Then give place to the physician, for Yahuah has

Cf. Ex. 15:25.

Cf. Isa. 38:2.

9-15: Cf. Jas. 5:14.

Or, as a deadman.

created him: let him not go from you, for you have need of him. **13** There is a time when in their hands there is good success.

A physician that prays to Yahuah is a precious thing.

Or, curing.

14 For they shall also pray unto Yahuah, that he would prosper that, which they give, for ease and remedy to prolong life. **15** He that sins before his maker, let him fall into the hand of the physician. **16** My son, let tears fall down over the dead, and begin to lament, as if you had suffered great harm yourself: and then cover his body according to the custom, and neglect not his burial. **17** Weep bitterly, and make great moan, and use lamentation, as he is worthy, and that a day or two, lest you be evil spoken of: and then comfort yourself for your heaviness. **18** For of heaviness comes death, and the heaviness of the heart, breaks strength. **19** In affliction also sorrow remains: and the life of the poor, is the curse of the heart. **20** Take no heaviness to heart: drive it away, and remember the last end. **21** Forget it not, for there is no turning again: you shall not do him good, but hurt

Cf. Tob. 1:16-18.

Cf. Prov. 15:13, 17:22.

yourself. **22** Remember my judgment: for you also shall be so; yesterday for me, and today for you.

23 When the dead is at rest, let his remembrance rest, and be comforted for him, when his spirit is departed from him. **24** The wisdom of a learned man comes by opportunity of leisure: and he that has little business shall become wise. **25** How can he get wisdom that holds the plough, and that glories in the goad; that drives oxen, and is occupied in their labors, and whose talk is of bullocks? **26** He gives his mind to make furrows: and is diligent to give the cow fodder. **27** So every carpenter, and workmaster, that labors night and day: and they that cut and engrave seals, and are diligent to make great variety, and give themselves to counterfeit imagery, and watch to finish a work. **28** The smith also sitting by the anvil, and considering the iron work; the vapor of the fire wastes his flesh, and he fights with the heat of the furnace: the noise of the hammer and the anvil is ever in his ears, and his eyes

Or, the sentence upon him.

Cf. 2Sam. 12:20.

Greek: of the breed of bullocks.

look still upon the pattern of the thing that he makes, he sets his mind to finish his work, and watches to polish it perfectly. 29 So does the potter sitting at his work, and turning the wheel about with his feet, who is always carefully set at his work: and makes all his work by number. 30 He fashions the clay with his *Or, tempers it with his feet.* arm, and bows down his strength before his feet: he applies himself to lead it over; and he is diligent to make clean the furnace.

31 All these trust their hands: and every one is wise in his work. 32 Without these cannot a city be inhabited: and they shall not dwell where they will, nor go up and down.

33 They shall not be sought for in public counsel; nor sit high in the congregation: they shall not sit on the judge's seat, nor understand the sentence of judgment: they cannot declare justice, and judgment, and they shall not be found where parables are spoken. 34 But they will maintain the state of the world, and [all] their desire is in the work of their craft.

CHAPTER 39:

1 A description of him that is truly wise. 12 An exhortation to praise Yahuah for his works, which are good to the good, and evil to them that are evil.

1 But he that gives his mind to the Law of the Most High, and is occupied in the meditation thereof, will seek out the wisdom of all the ancient, and be occupied in prophecies. 2 He will keep the sayings of the renowned men: and where subtile parables are, he will be there also. 3 He will seek out the secrets of grave sentences, and be conversant in dark parables. 4 He shall serve among great men, and appear before princes: he will travail through strange countries, for he has tried the good, and the evil among men. 5 He will give his heart to resort early to Yahuah that made him, and

will pray before the Most High, and will open his mouth in prayer, and make supplication for his sins. 6 When the great Yahuah will, he shall be filled with the spirit of understanding: he shall pour out wise sentences, and give thanks unto Yahuah in his prayer.

7 He shall direct his counsel and knowledge, and in his secrets shall he meditate. 8 He shall show forth that which he has learned, and shall glory in the Law of the covenant of Yahuah.

9 Many shall commend his understanding, and so long as the world endures, it shall not be blotted out, his memorial shall not depart away, and his name shall live from generation to generation. 10 Nations shall show forth His wisdom, *Cf. 44:15.* and the congregation shall declare His praise. 11 If he die, he shall leave a greater name than a thousand: and *Or, gain unto it.* if he live, he shall increase it. 12 Yet I have more to say which I have thought upon, for I am filled as the moon at the full. 13 Hearken unto me, holy children, and bud *Or, rivers of water.* forth as a rose growing by the brook of the field: 14 And give you a sweet savor as frankincense, and flourish as a lilly, send forth a smell, and sing a song of praise, bless Yahuah in all His works. 15 Magnify His Name, and show forth His praise with the songs of your lips, and with harps, and in praising Him you shall say after this manner: 16 All the works of Yahuah are exceeding good, and whatsoever He commands, shall be accomplished in due *Cf. Gen.1:31; Mark 7:37.* season. 17 And none may say, What is this? Wherefore is that? For at time convenient they shall all be sought out: at His commandment the waters stood as an heap, and at the words of His mouth the receptacles of waters. *Cf. Gen.1:2; Jub. 2:7.* 18 At His commandment is done whatsoever pleases Him, and none can hinder when He will save. 19 The works of all flesh are before Him, and nothing can be hid from His eyes. 20 He sees from everlasting to everlasting, and there is nothing wonderful before Him. 21 A man need not to say, What is this? Wherefore is that? For He has made all things for their uses.

22 His blessing covered the dry land as a river, and watered it as a flood. 23 As

He has turned the waters into saltiness: so shall the heathen inherit His wrath. 24 As his ways are plain unto the holy, so are they stumbling blocks unto the wicked. 25 For the good, are good things created from the beginning: so evil things for sinners. 26 The principal things for the whole use of man's life, are water, fire, iron, and salt, flour of wheat, honey, milk, and the blood of the grape, and oil, and clothing. 27 All these things are for good to the godly: so to the sinners they are turned into evil. 28 There be spirits that are created for vengeance, which in their fury lay on sore strokes, in the time of destruction they pour out their force, and appease the wrath of Him that made them. 29 Fire, and hail, and famine, and death: all these were created for vengeance: 30 Teeth of wild beasts, and scorpions, serpents, and the sword, punishing the wicked to destruction. 31 They shall rejoice in His commandment, and they shall be ready upon earth when need is, and when their time is come, they shall not transgress His word. 32 Therefore from the beginning I was resolved, and thought upon these things, and have left them in writing. 33 All the works of Yahuah are good: and He will give every needful thing in due season. 34 So that a man cannot say, This is worse than that: for in time they shall all be well approved. 35 And therefore praise Yahuah with the whole heart and mouth, and bless the Name of Yahuah.

Cf. Hos. 14:10.

Or, vipers.

Cf. Gen.1:31.

CHAPTER 40:

1 Many miseries in a man's life.
12 The reward of unrighteousness, and the fruit of true dealing. 17 A virtuous wife, and an honest friend rejoice the heart, but the fear of Yahuah is above all. 28 A begger's life is hateful.

1 Great travail is created for every man, and an heavy yoke is upon the sons of Adam, from the day that they go out of their mother's womb, till the day that they return to the mother of all things. 2 Their imagination of things to come, and the day of death [trouble] their thoughts, and [cause] fear of heart: 3 From Him that sits on a throne of glory, unto him that is humbled in earth and ashes. 4 From Him that wears purple, and a crown, unto him that is clothed with a linen frock. 5 Wrath, and envy, trouble and unquietness, fear of death, and anger, and strife, and in the time of rest upon his bed, his night sleep does change his knowledge. 6 A little or nothing is his rest, and afterward he is in his sleep, as in a day of keeping watch, troubled in the vision of his heart, as if he were escaped out of a battle: 7 When all is safe, he awakes, and marvels that the fear was nothing.

Cf. Eccles. 1:3

Or, to the porter.

8 [Such things happen] unto all flesh, both man and beast, and that is seven fold more upon sinners. 9 Death and bloodshed, strife and sword, calamities, famine, tribulation, and the scourge: 10 These things are created for the wicked, and for their sakes came the flood. 11 All things that are of the earth shall return to the earth again: and that which is of the waters does return into the sea. 12 All bribery and injustice shall be blotted out: but true dealing shall endure forever. 13 The goods of the unjust shall be dried up like a river, and shall vanish with noise, like a great thunder in rain. 14 While he opens his hand he shall rejoice: so shall transgressors come to nought. 15 The children of the ungodly shall not bring forth many branches: but are as unclean roots upon a hard rock. 16 The weed growing upon every water, and bank of a river, shall be pulled up before all grass. 17 Bountifulness is as a most fruitful garden, and mercifulness endures forever. 18 To labor and to be content with that a

Cf. 39:29-30.

Cf. Gen. 7:11.

Cf. 41:10; Gen. 3:19; Eccles. 1:7.

Greek: bribes.

Cf. Mark 4:5, 16-17; Matt. 13:18–23; Luke 8:11–15; John 15:1-11.

Cf. Job 8:11, 16:12; Gen. 41:2.

Or, a garden that is blessed.

Cf.
Phil. 4:12;
1Tim. 6:6.

man has, is a sweet life: but he that finds a treasure, is above them both.

19 Children and the building of a city continue a man's name: but a blameless wife is counted above them both. 20 Wine and music rejoice the heart: but the love of wisdom is above them both. 21 The pipe and the harp make sweet melody: but a pleasant tongue is above them both. 22 Your eye desires favor and beauty: but more than both, corn while it is green. 23 A friend and companion never meet amiss: but above both is a wife with her husband. 24 Brethren and help are against time of trouble: but alms shall deliver more than them both. 25 Gold and silver make the foot stand sure: but counsel is esteemed above them both. 26 Riches and strength lift up the heart: but the fear of Yahuah is above them both: there is no want in the fear of Yahuah, and it needs not to seek help. 27 The fear of Yahuah is a fruitful garden, and covers him above all glory. 28 My son, lead not a begger's life: for better it is to die than to beg. 29 The life of him that depends on another man's table, is not to be counted for a life: for he pollutes himself with other men's meat, but a wise man well nurtured will beware thereof. 30 Begging is sweet in the mouth of the shameless: but in his belly there shall burn a fire.

Cf.
Isa. 4:15.
Or, a
garden that
is blessed.

CHAPTER 41:

1 The remembrance of death. 3 Death is not to be feared. 5 The ungodly shall be accursed. 11 Of an evil and a good name. 14 Wisdom is to be uttered. 16 Of what things we should be ashamed.

1 O death, how bitter is the remembrance of you to a man that lives at rest in his possessions, unto the man that has nothing to vex him, and that has prosperity in all things: yes unto him that is yet able to receive meat? 2 O death, acceptable is your sentence unto the needy, and unto him whose strength fails, that is now in the last age, and is vexed with all things, and to him that despairs and has lost patience. 3 Fear not the sentence of death, remember them that have been before you, and that come after, for this is the sentence of Yahuah over

Or, to
whom
everything
is trouble-
some.

all flesh. 4 And why are you against the pleasure of the Most High? There is no inquisition in the grave, whether you have lived ten, or a hundred, or a thousand years. 5 The children of sinners, are abominable children: and they that are conversant in the dwelling of the ungodly. 6 The inheritance of sinners' children shall perish, and their posterity shall have a perpetual reproach. 7 The children will complain of an ungodly father, because they shall be reproached for his sake. 8 Woe be unto you ungodly men which have forsaken the law of the Most High Elohim: for if you increase, it shall be to your destruction. 9 And if you be born, you shall be born to a curse: and if you die, a curse shall be your portion. 10 All that are of the earth shall return to earth again: so the ungodly shall go from a curse to destruction.

Cf. 40:11.

11 The mourning of men is about their bodies: but an ill name of sinners shall be blotted out. 12 Have regard for your name: for that shall continue with you above a thousand great treasures of gold. 13 A good life has but few days: but a good name endures forever.

14 My children, keep discipline in peace: for wisdom that is hid, and a treasure that is not seen, what profit is in them both? 15 A man that hides his foolishness is better than a man that hides his wisdom. 16 Therefore be modest according to my word: for it is not good to retain all modesty, neither is it altogether approved in everything. 17 Be ashamed of whoredom before father and mother, and of a lie before a prince and a mighty man: 18 Of an offense before a judge and ruler, of iniquity before a congregation and people, of unjust dealing before your partner and friend:

19 And of theft in regard of the place where you sojourn, and in regard of the truth of Elohim and His covenant, and to lean with your elbow upon the meat, and of scorning to give and take: 20 And of silence before them that salute you, and to look upon an harlot: 21 And to turn away your face from your kinsman, or to take away a portion or a gift, or to gaze upon another man's wife, 22 Or to be overbusy with his maid, and come

not near her bed, or of upbraiding speeches before friends; and after you have given, upbraide not: **23** Or of iterating and speaking again that which uou have heard, and of revealing of secrets. **24** So shall you be truly modest, and find favor before all men.

Cf. Jas. 1:5.

CHAPTER 42:

1 Whereof we should not be ashamed.
9 Be careful of your daughter.
12 Beware of a woman. 15 The works and greatness of Yahuah.

1 Of these things be not ashamed, and accept no person to sin thereby. **2** Of the Law of the Most High, and His Covenant, and of judgment to justify the ungodly: **3** Of reckoning with your partners, and travelers: or of the gift of the heritage of friends: **4** Of exactness of balance, and weights: or of getting much or little: **5** And of merchants indifferent selling, of much correction of children, and to make the side of an evil servant to bleed. **6** Sure keeping is good where an evil wife is, and shut up where many hands are.

7 Deliver all things in number and weight, and put all in writing that you give out, or receive in. **8** Be not ashamed to inform the unwise and foolish, and the extreme aged that contend with those that are young, thus shall you be truly learned and approved of all men living. **9** The father wakes for the daughter when no man knows, and the care for her takes away sleep; when she is young lest she pass away the flower of her age, and being married, lest she should be hated: **10** In her virginity lest she should be defiled, and gotten with child in her father's house; and having an husband, lest she should misbehave herself: and when she is married, lest she should be barren. **11** Keep a sure watch over a shameless daughter, lest she make you a laughing stock to your enemies, and a by-word in the city, and a reproach among the people, and make you ashamed before the multitude.

12 Behold not every body's beauty, and sit not in the midst of women. **13** For from garments comes a moth, and from women wickedness. **14** Better is the rudeness of a man, than a courteous woman, a woman I say, which brings shame and reproach.

Or, of your partner's speech.
Or, compan-ions.
Or, of the giving.

Or, without profit.

Or, deal for.

Or, rebuke.
Or, that is accused of fornication.

Cf. 25:23.

Cf. Gen. 3:6.

Or, wicked-ness.

Works of Creation

15 I will now remember the works of Yahuah, and declare the things that I have seen: in the words of Yahuah are His works.

16 The sun that gives light, looks upon all things: and the work thereof is full of the glory of Yahuah.

17 Yahuah has not given power to the saints to declare all His marvelous works, which the Almighty Yahuah firmly settled, that whatsoever is, might be established for His glory.

18 He seeks out the deep and the heart, and considers their crafty devices: For Yahuah knows all that may be known, and He beholds the signs of the world. 19 He declares the things that are past, and for to come, and reveals the steps of hidden things. 20 No thought escapes Him, neither any word is hidden from Him.

21 He has garnished the excellent works of His wisdom, and He is from everlasting to everlasting, unto Him may nothing be added, neither can He be diminished, and He has no need of any counsellor.

22 O how desirable are all His works: and that a man may see even to a spark.

23 All these things live and remain forever, for all uses, and they are all obedient.

24 All things are double one against another: and He has made nothing imperfect.

25 One thing establishes the good of another: and who shall be filled with beholding his glory?

Just as in Gen. 1, the sun comes first not the moon. It bears greater significance.

Or, the highest.

Cf. Job 41:4. Isa. 21:15.

All of His Creation remains.

Cf. Gen. 1:31.

CHAPTER 43:

1 The works of Elohim in heaven, and in earth, and in the sea, are exceeding glorious and wonderful.
29 Yet Yahuah Himself in His power and wisdom is above all.

1 The pride of the height, the clear firmament, the beauty of heaven, with His glorious show; 2 The sun when it appears, declaring at his rising, a marvelous instrument, the work of the Most High. 3 At noon it parches the country, and who can abide the burning heat thereof? 4 A man blowing a furnace is in works of heat, but the sun burns the mountains three times more; breathing out fiery vapors, and sending forth bright beams, it

The firmament remains.

Cf. 1En. 72. The sun begins the Bible day.

Or, vessel.

Greek: he stayed his course.

Cf. Gen.1.16; 1En. 72; Jub. 2:8-9. Sun is the measure for days, weeks, months, and years.

3 of the 7 Feasts begin with the moon. Ex. 12.

The term month is named after the moon but the moon cycle is not that of the month in scripture ever. It comes in 10 days too soon annually.

dims the eyes. 5 Great is Yahuah that made it, and at His commandment it runs hastily. 6 He made the moon also to serve in her season, for a declaration of times, and a sign of the world. 7 From the moon is the sign of Feasts, a light that decreases in her perfection. 8 The month is called after her name, increasing wonderfully in her changing, being an instrument of the armies above, shining in the firmament of heaven, 9 The beauty of heaven, the glory of the stars, an ornament giving light in the highest places of Yahuah. 10 At the commandment of the holy One, they will stand in their order, and never faint in their watches.

11 Look upon the rainbow, and praise Him that made it, very beautiful it is in the brightness thereof.

Cf. Gen. 9:13.

12 It compasses the heaven about with a glorious circle, and the hands of the Most High have bent it.

Cf. Isa. 40:12.

13 By His commandment He makes the snow to fall apace, and sends swiftly the lightnings of His judgment. 14 Through this the treasures are opened, and clouds fly forth as fouls. 15 By His great power He makes the clouds firm, and the hailstones are broken small. 16 At His sight the mountains are shaken, and at His will the South wind blows. 17 The noise of the thunder makes the earth to tremble: so does the Northern storm, and the whirlwind: as birds flying He scatters the snow, and the falling down thereof, is as the lighting of grashoppers. 18 The eye marvels at the beauty of the whiteness thereof, and the heart is astonished at the raining of it. 19 The hoarfrost also as salt He pours on the earth, and being congealed, it lies on the top of sharp stakes. 20 When the cold North-wind blows, and the water is congealed into ice, it abides upon every gathering together of water, and clothes the water as with a breastplate. 21 It devours the mountains, and burns the wilderness, and consumes the grass as fire. 22 A present remedy of all is a mist coming speedily: a dew coming after heat, refreshes. 23 By His counsel He appeases the deep, and plants islands therein.

Or, to groan as a woman in her travail.

i.e. semi-solid.

Or, it is as the point of sharp stakes.

Or, upon the heat.

24 They that sail on the sea, tell of the danger thereof, and when we hear it with our ears, we marvel thereat. 25 For therein be strange and wonderous works, variety of all kinds of beasts, and sea dragons created.

Cf. Ps.107:23.
Cf. Job 41.

26 By Him the end of them has prosperous success, and by his word all things consist. 27 We may speak much, and yet come short: wherefore in sum, He is all. 28 How shall we be able to magnify Him? For He is great above all His works. 29 Yahuah is terrible and very great, and marvelous is His power. 30 When you glorify Yahuah exalt Him as much as you can: For even yet will He far exceed, and when you exalt Him, put forth all your strength, and be not weary: For you can never go far enough.

Cf. Ps. 96:42.

31 Who has seen Him, that He might tell us? And who can magnify Him as He is? 32 There are yet hid greater things than these be, for we have seen but a few of His works: 33 For Yahuah has made all things, and to the godly has He given wisdom.

Cf. Ps. 106:2; John 1:18.

CHAPTER 44:

1 The praise of certain holy men: 16 Of Enoch, 17 Noah, 19 Abraham, 22 Isaac, 23 and Jacob.

The praise of the fathers.

1 Let us now praise famous men, and our Fathers that begat us. 2 Yahuah has wrought great glory by them, through His great power from the beginning. 3 Such as did bear rule in their kingdoms, men renowned for their power, giving counsel by their understanding, and declaring prophecies: 4 Leaders of the people by their counsels, and learning meet for the people, wise and eloquent in their instructions. 5 Such as found out musical tunes, and rejected verses in writing. 6 Rich men furnished with ability, living peaceably in their habitations. 7 All these were honored in their generations, and were the glory of their times.

Or, ditties.

8 There be of them, that have left a name behind them, that their praises might be reported. 9 And some there be, which have no memorial, who are perished as though they had never been, and are become as though they had

Cf.
Gen. 7:22.

never been born, and their children after them. 10 But these were merciful men, whose righteousness has not been forgotten. 11 With their seed shall continually remain a good inheritance, and their children are within the covenant.

Or, after
them.

12 Their seed stands fast, and their children for their sakes. 13 Their seed shall remain forever, and their glory shall not be blotted out. 14 Their bodies are buried in peace, but their name lives forevermore.

15 The people will tell of their wisdom, and the congregation will show forth their praise. 16 **Enoch** pleased Yahuah, and was translated, being an example of repentance, to all generations. 17 Noah was found perfect and righteous, in the time of wrath, he was taken in exchange (for the world) therefore was he left as a remnant unto the earth, when the flood came. 18 An everlasting Covenant was made with him, that all

Cf. 39:10.

Cf.
Gen. 5:24;
Heb. 11:5.

Cf. Gen.
6:9; 7:1;
Heb. 11:7.

flesh should perish no more by the flood. 19 **Abraham** was a great father of many people: in glory was there none like unto him: 20 Who **kept the Law of the Most High**, and was in covenant with Him, he established the Covenant in his flesh, and when he was proved, he was found faithful.

21 Therefore He assured him by an oath, that He would bless the nations in his seed, and that He would multiply him, as the dust of the earth, and exalt his seed as the stars, and cause them to inherit from sea to sea, and from the river unto the utmost part of the land.

22 With **Isaac** did He establish likewise [for Abraham his father's sake] the blessing of all men and the covenant, 23 And made it rest upon the head of **Jacob**. He acknowledged him in his blessing, and gave him an heritage, and divided his portions, among the twelve tribes did he part them.

Cf.
Gen. 9:11.

Cf.
Gen. 12:3,
15:5, 17:4.

Abraham
had
law and
kept it in
righteous-
ness.

Cf.
Gen. 21:4.

Cf. Gen.
22:16-18;
Gal. 3:8.

Cf. Gen.
27:28,
28:14.

CHAPTER 45:

1 The praise of Moses, 6 Of Aaron, 23 and of Phinehas.

1 And he brought out of him a merciful man, which

found favor in the sight of all flesh, even Moses beloved of Elohim and men, whose memorial is blessed: 2 He made him like to the glorious saints,

Cf.
Ex. 11:3.

and magnified him, so that his enemies stood in fear of him. 3 By his words he caused the wonders to cease, and he made him glorious in the sight of kings, and gave him a commandment for his people, and showed him part of his glory.

Cf. Ex. 6:7-9.

4 He sanctified him in his faithfulness, and meekness,

Cf. Num. 12:3.

and chose him out of all men. 5 He made him to hear His voice, and brought him

Cf. Rom. 8:2. Law of life as opposed to the law of sin and death which are not the same law.

into the dark cloud, and gave him commandments before his face, even the *law of life* and knowledge, that he might teach Jacob

Cf. Ex. 17:4.

his Covenants, and Israel his judgments. 6 He exalted Aaron an holy man like unto him, even his brother,

Cf. Ex. 4:28.

of the tribe of Levi. 7 An everlasting covenant he made with him, and gave him the priesthood among the people, he beautified him with comely ornaments,

Greek: he blessed.

and clothed him with a robe of glory. 8 He put upon him perfect glory: and strengthened him with rich

Greek: vessels or instruments.

garments, with breeches, with a long robe, and the ephod: 9 And he compassed him with pomegranates, and with many golden bells round about, that as he went, there might be a sound, and a noise made that might be heard in the Temple, for a memorial to the children

Cf. Ex. 28:35.

of his people. 10 With an holy garment, with gold and blue silk, and purple the work of the embroiderer; with a breastplate of judgment, and with urim and thummim. 11 With twisted scarlet, the work of the cunning workman, with precious stones graven like seals, and set in gold, the work of the jeweler, with a writing engraved for a memorial, after the number of the tribes of Israel.

12 He set a crown of gold upon the miter, wherein was engraved holiness an ornament of honor, a costly work, the desires of the eyes goodly and beautiful. 13 Before him there were none such, neither did ever any stranger put them on, but only his children, and his children's children perpetually. 14 Their sacrifices shall be wholly consumed every day twice continually.

15 Moses consecrated him, and annointed him with holy oil, this was appointed unto him by an everlasting covenant, and to his seed so long as the heavens should remain, that they should

Cf. Numbers 3:7-8; 8:26; 18:5-6. Levites, and no one else, were anointed to keep Bible Canon to the First Century.

minister unto him, and execute the office of the priesthood, and bless the people in his name. 16 He chose him out of all men living to offer sacrifices to Yahuah, incense and a sweet savor, for a memorial, to make reconciliation for his people. 17 He gave unto him His commandments, and authority in the statutes of judgments, that he should teach Jacob the testimonies, and inform Israel in His laws. 18 Strangers conspired together against him, and maligned him in the wilderness, even the men that were of Dathan's, and Abiram's side, and the congregation of Core with fury and wrath.

19 This, Yahuah saw and it displeased Him, and in His wrathful indignation, were they consumed: He did wonders upon them, to consume them with the fiery flame. 20 But he made Aaron more honorable, and gave him an heritage, and divided unto him the first fruits of the increase, especially he prepared bread in abundance: 21 For they eat of the sacrifices of Yahuah, which he gave unto him and his seed: 22 Howbeit in the land of the people he had no inheritance, neither had he any portion among the people, for Yahuah himself is his portion and inheritance. 23 The third in glory is Phinehas the son of Eleazar, because he had zeal in the fear of Yahuah, and stood up with good courage of heart, when the people were turned back, and made reconciliation for Israel. 24 Therefore, was there a covenant of peace made with him, that he should be the chief of the sanctuary, and of his people, and that he, and his posterity should have the dignity of the priesthood forever. 25 According to the covenant made with David son of Jesse, of the tribe of Judah, that the inheritance of the king should be to his posterity alone: so the inheritance of Aaron should also be unto his seed.

26 Elohim give you wisdom in your heart to judge His people in righteousness, that their good things be not abolished, and that their glory may endure forever.

i.e. Bible Canon.
Cf. Dt. 17:10, 21:5.

Cf. Num. 16:12. Korah.

Cf. Num. 17:8.

Cf. Dt. 12:12, 18:10.

Cf. Num. 25:12, 13:1.

Bible Canon follows a bloodline from Aaron, passed to the Sons of Zadok specifically since the First Temple.

CHAPTER 46:

1 The praise of Joshua, 9 Of Caleb, 13 Of Samuel.

Yahusha:
יהושע
Yahushua:
יהושוע
Rendered both ways in Hebrew. Same name as Messiah.

1 Joshua the son of Nun was valiant in the wars, and was the successor of Moses in prophesies, who according to his name was made great for the saving of the elect of Elohim, and taking vengeance of the enemies that rose up against them, that he might set Israel in their inheritance. **2** How great glory got he when he did lift up his hands, and stretched out his sword against the cities?

Cf. Num. 27:18; Dt. 34:9; Jos. 1:2, 12:7.

Cf. Jos. 10:12-14.

3 Who before him so stood to it? For Yahuah Himself brought his enemies unto him. **4** Did not the sun go back by his means? And was not one day as long as two? **5** He called upon the Most High Yahuah, when the enemies pressed upon him on every side, and the great Yahuah heard him. **6** And with hailstones of mighty power he made the battle to fall violently upon the nations, and in the descent (of Bethoron) he destroyed them that resisted, that the nations might know all their strength, because he fought in the sight of Yahuah, and he followed the mighty one.

7 In the time of Moses also, he did a work of mercy, he and **Caleb** the son of Jephunneh, in that they withstood the Congregation, and withheld the people from sin, and appeased the wicked murmuring. **8** And of six hundred thousand people on foot, they two were preserved to bring them into the heritage, even unto the land that flows with milk and honey. **9** Yahuah gave strength also unto Caleb, which remained with him unto his old age, so that he entered upon the high places of the land, and his seed obtained it for an heritage. **10** That all the children of Israel might see that it is good to follow Yahuah. **11** And concerning **the Judges**, every one by name, whose heart went not a whoring, nor departed from Yahuah, let their memory be blessed. **12** Let their bones flourish out of their place, and let the name of them that were honored, be continued upon their children. **13** **Samuel the Prophet** of Yahuah, beloved of his Lord, established a kingdom, and anointed princes over his people. **14** By the Law of Yahuah he judged the Congregation,

Cf. Num. 26:65; Dt. 35:36.

Cf. 49:12.

Cf. 1Sam. 1:10,16:19.

and Yahuah had respect unto Jacob. 15 By his faithfulness he was found a true Prophet, and by his word he was known to be faithful in vision. 16 He called upon the mighty Yahuah, when his enemies pressed upon him on every side, when he offered the sucking lamb. 17 And Yahuah thundered from heaven, and with a great noise made his voice to be heard. 18 And he destroyed the rulers of the Tyrians, and all the princes of the Philistines. 19 And before his long sleep he made protestations in the sight of Yahuah, and his anointed, I have not taken any man's goods, so much as a shoe, and no man did accuse him. 20 And after his death he prophesied, and showed the King his end, and lift up his voice from the earth in prophecy, to blot out the wickedness of the people.

Cf. 1Sam. 7:9.

Cf. 1Sam. 12:3.

Cf. 1.Sam. 28:18-19.

CHAPTER 47:

1 The praise of Nathan, 2 Of David, 12 Of Solomon his glory, and infirmities. 23 Of his end and punishment.

1 And after him rose up **Nathan** to prophesy in the time of David. 2 As is the fat taken away from the peace offering, so was **David** chosen out of the children of Israel. 3 He played with lions as with kids, and with bears as with lambs. 4 Slew he not a giant when he was yet but young? And did he not take away reproach from the people, when he lifted up his hand with the stone in the sling, and beat down the boasting of Goliath?
5 For he called upon the Most High Yahuah, and he gave him strength in his right hand to slay that mighty warrior, and **set up the horn of his people:**
6 So the people honored him with ten thousands, and praised him in the blessings of Yahuah, in that He gave him a crown of glory. 7 For he destroyed the enemies on every side, and brought to nought the Philistines his adversaries, and **broke their horn** in sunder unto this day. 8 In all his works he praised the Holy One Most High, with words of glory, with his whole heart he sang songs, and loved Him that made him. 9 He set singers also before the altar, that by their voices they might make sweet melody, and

Cf. 2Sam. 12:1.

Or, he smote lions. Cf. 1Sam. 17:34.

Cf. 1.Sam.17. 49,50,51.

Cf. 1 En. 90:9-16. Enoch prophesied this horn of the lineage of David as Messiah. The "horn" represents true authority.

Cf. 1Sam. 18:7.

Cf. 2Sam. 5:7. Or, condemned.

Cf. 1Chr. 16:4.

Or, perfectly.

daily sing praises in their songs. 10 He beautified their feasts, and set in order the solemn times, until the end, that they might praise His Holy Name, and that the Temple might sound from morning. 11 Yahuah took away his sins, and **exalted his horn forever**: he gave him a covenant of kings, and a throne of glory in Israel. 12 After him rose up a wise son, and for his sake he dwelt at large. 13 **Solomon** reigned in a peaceable time, and was honored; for Elohim made all quiet round about him, that he might build an house in His Name, and prepare His Sanctuary forever. 14 How wise were you in your youth, and as a flood filled with understanding. 15 Your soul covered the whole earth, and you filled it with dark parables.

16 Your name went far unto the lands, and for your peace you were beloved. 17 The countries marveled at you for your songs, and proverbs, and parables, and interpretations. 18 By the Name of Yahuah Elohim, which is called Yahuah Elohim of Israel, you did gather gold as tin, and did multiply silver as lead.

Cf. 1 En. 90:9-16. Enoch prophesied this horn of the lineage of David as Messiah.

Cf. 1Sam. 12:13. Or, of a kingdom.

Cf. 1Ki. 4:21, 24.

Cf. 1Ki. 4:29-30.

Cf. 1Ki. 4:31-32. **Note:** Sirach historically affirms Solomon wrote at least 3 books in Song of Songs, Proverbs and Ecclesiastes. He quotes Wisdom of Solomon as well.

19 You did bow your loins unto women, and by your body you were brought into subjection. 20 You did stain your honor, and pollute your seed, so that you brought wrath upon your children, and were grieved for your folly. 21 So the kingdom was divided, and out of **Ephraim** ruled a rebellious kingdom. 22 But Yahuah will never leave off His mercy, neither shall any of His works perish, neither will He abolish the posterity of His elect, and the seed of him that loves Him He will not take away: wherefore He gave a remnant unto Jacob, and out of him a root unto David. 23 Thus rested Solomon with his fathers, and of his seed he left behind him **Rehoboam**, even the foolishness of the people, and one that had no understanding; who turned away the people through his counsel: there was also **Jeroboam** the son of Nebat, who caused Israel to sin, and showed Ephraim the way of sin: 24 And their sins were multiplied exceedingly, that they were driven out of the land. 25 For they sought out all wickedness, till the vengeance came upon them.

Cf. 1Ki. 10:27.

Cf. 1Ki. 11:1. Or, in.

Cf. 1Ki. 12:15-17.

Cf. 2Sam. 7:15.

Cf. 1Ki.12:10-11,13-14, 28, 30.

CHAPTER 48:

1 The praise of Elijah, 12 of Elisha, 17 and of Ezekiel.

1 Then stood up **Elijah** the Prophet as fire, and his word burnt like a lamp. 2 He brought a sore famine upon them, and by his zeal he diminished their number. 3 By the word of Yahuah he shut up the heaven, and also three times brought down fire. 4 O Elijah, how were you honored in your wonderous deeds! And who may glory like unto you! 5 Who did raise up a dead man from death, and his soul from the place of the dead by the word of the Most High. 6 Who brought kings to destruction, and honorable men from their bed. 7 Who heard the rebuke of Yahuah in Sinai, and in Horeb the judgment of vengeance.

8 Who anointed kings to take revenge, and Prophets to succeed after him:

9 Who wast taken up in a whirlwind of fire, and in a chariot of fiery horses: 10 Who was ordained for reproofs in their times, to pacify the wrath of Yahuah's judgment before it broke forth into fury, and to turn the heart of the father unto the son, and to restore the tribes of Jacob. 11 Blessed are they that saw you, and slept in love, for we shall surely live. 12 Elijah it was, who was covered with a whirlwind: and **Elisha** was filled with his spirit: while he lived he was not moved [with the presence] of any prince, neither could any bring him into subjection. 13 No word could overcome him, and after his death his body prophesied.

14 He did wonders in his life, and at his death were his works marvelous. 15 For all this the people repented not, neither departed they from their sins, till they were spoiled and carried out of their land, and were scattered through all the earth: yet there remained a small people, and a ruler in the house of David: 16 Of whom, some did that which was pleasing to Elohim, and some multiplied sins. 17 **Ezekiel** fortified his city, and brought in water into the midst thereof: he dug the hard rock with iron, and made wells for waters. 18 In his time Sennacherib came up, and sent Rabshakeh, and lift up his hand against Sion, and boasted proudly. 19 Then trembled their hearts and hands, and they

---

Cf. 1Ki. 17:1.

Or, made heaven to hold up. 1Ki. 18:38. 2Ki. 1:10,12.

Sirach generally affirms souls are not in Heaven in scripture upon death but in chambers within the Earth.

Cf. 1Ki. 17:21-22. Or, grave.

Cf. 2Ki. 1:16. Or, seat.

Cf. 1Ki. 19:15.

Cf. 1Ki. 19:16.

Cf. 2Ki. 2:11.

Or, written of. Mal.4.3. Or, establish.

Or, were adorned with love.

Cf. 2Ki. 2:11,15.

Or, Nothing. Cf. 2Ki. 13:21.

Cf. 2Ki. 18:11-12.

Cf. 2Ki. 18:2.

Cf. 2Ki. 18:13.

were in pain as women in travail. 20 But they called upon Yahuah which is merciful, and stretched out their hands towards Him, *Or, hand.* and immediately the Holy One heard them out of heaven, and delivered them by the ministry of **Isaiah.** 21 He smote the host of the Assyrians, and his Angel destroyed them. 22 For Ezekiel had done the thing that pleased Yahuah, and was strong in the ways of David his father, as Isaiah the Prophet, who was great and faithful in his vision, had commanded him. 23 In his time the sun went backward, and he lengthened the king's life. 24 He saw by an excellent spirit what should come to pass at the last, and he comforted them that mourned in Sion. 25 He showed what should come to pass forever, and secret things or ever they came.

Cf. 2Ki. 19:35; Isa. 37:36; Tob. 1:18.

Cf. 2Ki. 20:10; Isa. 38:8.

CHAPTER 49:

1 The praise of Josiah, 4 Of David and Hezekiah, 6 Of Jeremiah, 8 Of Ezekiel, 11 Zerubbabel, 12 Yahusha the son of Yosedec. 13 Of Nehemiah, Enoch, Seth, Shem, and Adam.

1 The remembrance of **Josiah** is like the composition of the perfume that is made by the art of the apothecary: it is sweet as honey in all mouths, and as music at a banquet of wine. 2 He behaved himself uprightly in the conversion of the people, and took away the abominations of iniquity. 3 He directed his heart unto Yahuah, and in the time of the ungodly he established the worship of Elohim. 4 All, except David and Hezekiah, and Josiah, were defective: for they forsook the Law of the Most High, (even) the kings of Judah failed: 5 Therefore He gave their power unto others, and their glory to a strange nation. 6 They burnt the chosen city of the sanctuary, and made the streets desolate according to the prophecy of **Jeremiah:** 7 For they entreated him evil, who nevertheless was a prophet sanctified in his mother's womb, that he might root out and afflict and destroy, and that he might build up also and plant. 8 It was Ezekiel who saw the glorious vision, which was shown him upon the chariot of the cherubim 9 For he made mention of

Cf. 2Ki. 22:1, 23:2; 2Chr. 3:34.

Or, prospered.

Cf. 2Ki. 23:4.

Or, horn. Horn = power, Cf. 1 En. 90:9-16.

Cf. 2Ki. 25:9. Or, by the hand of Jeremiah.

Cf. Jer. 1:5, 38:6.

Cf. Eze. 1:3,15.

Cf. Eze.13:11, 38:11,16, 46:12 Hag. 2:24; Ezra 3:2. Or, did good.

the enemies under [the figure of] the rain, and directed them that went right.

10 And of the twelve prophets let the memorial be blessed, and let their bones flourish again out of their place: *Cf. Eze. 13:13, 38:22.* for they comforted Jacob, and delivered them by assured hope. 11 How shall we magnify **Zerubbabel**? *Cf. Zach. 3:1; Ezra 3:2; Hag 1:12, 2:3.* Even he was as a signet on the right hand. 12 So was **Yahusha** the son of Yosedec: who in their time builded the house, and set up an Holy Temple *Cf. Neh. 7:1. Second Temple.* to Yahuah, which was prepared for everlasting

glory. 13 And among the elect was **Nehemiah** whose renown is great, who raised up for us, the walls that were fallen, and set up the gates *Cf. Gen. 5:24; Heb. 11:5.* and the bars, and raised up our ruins again. 14 But upon the earth was no man created like **Enoch**, for he was taken from the earth. 15 Neither was there a man born like unto **Joseph**, a governor of his brethren, a stay of the people, whose *Cf. Gen. 41:44, 42:6, 45:8.* bones were regarded of Yahuah. 16 **Shem** and **Seth** were in great honor among men, and so was **Adam** above every living thing in *Cf. Gen. 5:3, 11:10.* the creation.

CHAPTER 50:

1 Of Simon the son of Onias.
22 How the people were taught to praise Elohim, and pray. 27 The conclusion.

1 Simon the high priest the son of Onias, who in his life repaired the house again, and in his days fortified the Temple: 2 And by him was built from the foundation the double height, the high fortress of the wall about the Temple. 3 In his days the cistern to receive water *Cf. 1Ki. 7:23.* being in compass as the sea, was covered with plates of

brass. 4 He took care of the Temple that it should not fall, and fortified the city against being besieged.

5 How was he honored in the midst of the people, in his coming out of the *Greek: the house of the veil.* sanctuary? 6 He was as the morning star in the midst of a cloud: and as the moon at the full. 7 As the sun shining upon the Temple of the Most High, and as the rainbow giving light in the bright clouds. 8 And as the flower of roses in the spring of the year, as lillies by the rivers of waters,

and as the branches of the frankincense tree in the time of summer. 9 As fire and incense in the censer, and as a vessel of beaten gold set with all manner of precious stones, 10 And as a fair olive tree budding forth fruit, and as a cypress tree which grows up to the clouds. 11 When he put on the robe of honor, and was clothed with the perfection of glory, when he went up to the holy altar, he made the garment of holiness honorable.

12 When he took the portions out of the priest's hands, he himself stood by the hearth of the altar, compassed with his brethren round about, as a young cedar in Lebanon, and as palm trees compassed they him round about. 13 So were all the sons of Aaron in their glory, and the oblations of Yahuah in their hands, before all the congregation of Israel. 14 And finishing the service at the altar, that he might adorn the offering of the Most High Almighty, 15 He stretched out his hand to the cup, and poured of the blood of the grape, he poured out at the foot of the altar, a sweet smelling savor unto the Most High King of all. 16 Then shouted the sons of Aaron, and sounded the silver trumpets, and made a great noise to be heard, for a remembrance before the Most High. 17 Then all the people together hasted, and fell down to the earth upon their faces to worship their Yahuah Elohim Almighty the Most High. 18 The singers also sang praises with their voices, with great variety of sounds was there made sweet melody.

Or, trumpets beaten forth with the hammer.

19 And the people besought Yahuah the Most High by prayer before Him that is merciful, till the solemnity of Yahuah was ended, and they had finished his service. 20 Then he went down, and lifted up his hands over the whole congregation of the children of Israel, to give the blessing of Yahuah with his lips, and to rejoice in His name. 21 And they bowed themselves down to worship the second time, that they might receive a blessing from the Most High.

22 Now therefore bless the Elohim of all, which only does wonderous things everywhere, which exalts our days from the womb,

and deals with us according to His mercy. **23** He grant us joyfulness of heart, and that peace may be in our days in Israel forever. **24** That He would confirm His mercy with us, and deliver us at His time. **25** There be two manner of nations which my heart abhores, and the third is no nation. **26** They that sit upon the mountain of **Samaria**, and they that dwell amongst the **Philistines**, and that foolish people that dwell in **Shechem**.

27Yahusha the son of Sirach of Jerusalem has written in this book, the instruction of understanding and knowledge, who out of his heart poured forth wisdom. **28** Blessed is he that shall be exercised in these things, and he that lays them up in his heart, shall become wise. **29** For if he do them, he shall be strong in all things, for the light of Yahuah leads him, who gives wisdom to the godly: blessed be Yahuah forever. Amen. Amen.

CHAPTER 51:

1 I will thank you, O Yahuah and king, and praise you O Elohim my Saviour, I do give praise unto your name: **2** For you are my defender, and helper, and have preserved my body from destruction, and from the snare of the slanderous tongue, and from the lips that forge lies, and have been my helper against my adversaries. **3** And have delivered me according to the multitude of your mercies, and greatness of your name, from the teeth of them that were ready to devour me, and out of the hands of such as sought

after my life, and from the manifold afflictions which I had: **4** From the choking of fire on every side, and from the midst of the fire, which I kindled not: **5** From the depth of the belly of hell, from an unclean tongue, and from lying words.

6 By an accusation to the king from an unrighteous tongue, my soul drew near even unto death, my life was near to the hell beneath: **7** They compassed me on every side, and there was no man to help me: I looked for the succour of men, but there was none: **8** Then I thought upon your mercy, O Yahuah, and upon your acts of old, how you deliver such as wait for you, and save them out of the hands of the enemies: 9 Then I lifted up my supplication from the earth, and prayed for deliverance from death. 10 I called upon Yahuah the father of my Lord, that he would not leave me in the days of my trouble, and in the time of the proud when there was no help. 11 I will praise your Name continually, and will sing praise with thanksgiving, and so my prayer was heard: 12 For you saved me from destruction, and deliver me from the evil time: therefore will I give thanks and praise you, and bless your Name, O Yahuah. 13 When I was yet young, *Or, went astray.* or ever I went abroad, I desired wisdom openly in my prayer. 14 I prayed for her before the Temple, and will seek her out even to the end: 15 Even from the flower till the grape was ripe, has my heart delighted in her, my foot went the right way, from my youth up I sought after her. 16 I bowed down mine ear a little and received her, and received much learning. 17 I profited therein, [therefore] will I ascribe the glory unto Him that gives me wisdom:

18 For I purposed to do after her, and earnestly I followed that which is good, so shall I not be confounded: 19 My soul has wrestled with her, and in my doings I was exact, I stretched forth my hands to the heaven above, and bewailed my ignorances of her. 20 I directed my soul unto her, and I found her *Or, I got understanding.* in pureness, I have had my heart joined with her from the beginning, therefore shall I not be forsaken. 21 My heart was troubled in seeking her: therefore have I gotten a good possession. *Or, bowels.* 22 Yahuah has given me a tongue for my reward, and I will praise Him therewith. 23 Draw near unto me you unlearned, and dwell in the house of learning.

24 Wherefore are you slow, and what say you of these things, seeing your souls are very thirsty? 25 I opened my mouth, and said, buy her for yourselves without *Cf. Isa. 55:1.* money. 26 Put your neck under the yoke, and let your soul receive instruction, she is hard at hand to find.

27 Behold with your eyes, how that I have had but little labor, and have gotten unto me much rest. 28 Get learning with a great sum of money, and get much gold *Cf. 6:18.*

by her. **29** Let your soul rejoice in His mercy, and be not ashamed of His praise. **30** Work your work before, and in His time He will give you your reward.

Jeremiah 10
Directly Condemns
The Practice of the
Christmas Tree as
idolatry.

JEREMIAH'S WITNESSES

REPENTANCE IN CAPTIVITY

THE
Levite
BIBLE
LeviteBible.com

Copy of Ishtar gates in
Babylon ruins , Iraq.

THE BOOK OF
BARUCH

THE SCRIBE FOR JEREMIAH

WITH THE RESTORED
NAME OF YAHUAH

THE
Levite
BIBLE
LeviteBible.com

CHAPTER 1:

1 Baruch wrote a book in Babylon. 5 The Yahudim there wept at the reading of it. 7 They send money and the book, to the brethren at Jerusalem.

Jeremiah (36) had Baruch write his words in the 4th year and Baruch read them at the Jerusalem Temple in the 5th year of Yehoiakim. Baruch was then taken into captivity in Babylon with Yechonias and wrote his own words there in the 5th year of Bablonian captivity sharing them with the son of Yoachim again, but this time not at the Temple.

Cf. 90 A.D.: Josephus, Wars 1.7.4f; Jos., ibid., 6.4. [81]

Or, Yoacim.

Or, and vowed vowes.

Or, Yoacim.

1 And these are the words of the book, which Baruch the son of Nerias, the son of Maasias, the son of Sedecias, the son of Asadias, the son of Chelcias, wrote in Babylon, 2 In the fifth year, and in the seventh day of the month, what time as the Chaldeans took Jerusalem, and burnt it with fire. 3 And Baruch did read the words of this book, in the hearing of Yechonias, the son of Yoachim king of Yahuda, and in the ears of all the people, that came to [hear] the book. 4 And in the hearing of the nobles, and of the king's sons, and in the hearing of the elders, and of all the people from the lowest unto the highest, even of all them that dwelt at Babylon, by the river Sud. 5 Whereupon they wept, fasted, and prayed before Yahuah. 6 They made also a collection of money, according to every man's power. 7 And they sent it to Jerusalem unto Yoachim the High Priest the son of Chelcias, son of Salom, and to the Priests, and to all the people which were found with him at Jerusalem, 8 At the same time, when he received the vessels of the house of Yahuah that were carried out of the Temple, to return them into the land of Yahuda the tenth day of the month Sivan, [namely] silver vessels, which Sedecias the son of Yosias king of Yahuda had made, 9 After that Nebuchadnezzar king of Babylon had carried away Yechonias, and the Princes, and the captives, and the mighty men, and the people of the land from Jerusalem, and brought them unto Babylon: 10 And they said, Behold, we have sent you money, to buy you burnt offerings, and sin offerings, and incense, and prepare manna, and offer upon the Altar of Yahuah our Elohim, 11 And pray for the life of Nebuchadnezzar king of Babylon, and for the life of Belshazzar his son, that their days may be upon earth as the days of heaven. 12 And Yahuah will give us strength, and lighten our eyes, and we shall live under the shadow

Sivan is Babylonian. The Bible names it only the Third Month. The 10th day gives them enough time to prepare for Shavuot on the 15th. Note: It would be 4 days too late for the erroneous 6th of the Rabbis.

Or, prisoners

Cf. Jer. 24:1. [81]

Greek: corruptly for Mancha, a meat offering.

Cf. Dan. 5:2. Belshazzar... father Nebuchad-nezzar. Scholars who attempt to ignore this book because it says what Daniel says have destroyed their crediblity.

"Herodotus says that the Persians called Cyrus, their father." Ezra was referred to as πατήρ patir (Father or Priest) Eza as well in 4Q550 a fragment from 1st Esd., not Esther. Many scholars confuse this dynamic and some even place Esther as a father falsely [64].

1:15-2:17: Cf. Dan. 9:7-19 [81]

Cf. 2:6.

Baruch also uses the word father (pater) broadly.

Cf. Dan. 9:5.

of Nebuchadnezzar king of Babylon, and under the shadow of Belshazzar his son, and we shall serve them many days, and find favor in their sight. 13 Pray for us also unto Yahuah our Elohim, (for we have sinned against Yahuah our Elohim, and unto this day the fury of Yahuah, and his wrath is not turned from us) 14 And you shall read this book, which we have sent unto you, to make confession in the house of Yahuah, upon the feasts and solemn days. 15 And you shall say, To Yahuah our Elohim belongs righteousness, but unto us the confusion of faces, as it is come to pass this day unto them of Yahuda, and to the inhabitants of Jerusalem, 16 And to our kings, and to our princes, and to our Priests, and to our Prophets, and to our fathers. 17 For we have sinned before Yahuah, 18 And disobeyed Him, and have not hearkened unto the voice of Yahuah

our Elohim, to walk in the commandments that he gave us openly: 19 Since the day that Yahuah brought our forefathers out of the land of Egypt, unto this present day, we have been disobedient unto Yahuah our Elohim, and we have been negligent in not hearing His voice.

20 Wherefore the evils cleaved unto us, and the curse which Yahuah appointed by Moses His servant, at the time that he brought our fathers out of the land of Egypt, to give us a land that flows with milk and honey, like as it is to see this day. 21 Nevertheless we have not hearkened unto the voice of Yahuah our Elohim, according unto all the words of the Prophets, whom he sent unto us. 22 But every man followed the imagination of his own wicked heart, to serve strange gods, and to do evil in the sight of Yahuah our Elohim.

Baruch uses the word father (pater) broadly again.

Cf. Dt. 28:15.

CHAPTER 2:

The prayer and confession which the Yahudim at Babylon made, and sent in that book unto the brethren in Jerusalem.

1 Therefore Yahuah has made good His word, which He pronounced against us, and against our judges that judged Israel, and against our kings, and against our princes, and against the men of Israel and Yahudah, 2 To bring upon us great plagues, such as never happened under the whole heaven, as it came to pass in Jerusalem, according to the things that were written in the Law of Moses, 3 That a man should eat the flesh of his own son, and the flesh of his own daughter.

4 Moreover, He has delivered them to be in subjection to all the kingdoms that are round about us, to be as a reproach and desolation among all the people round about, where Yahuah has scattered them. 5 Thus, we were cast down and not exalted, because we have sinned against Yahuah our Elohim, and have not been obedient unto His voice. 6 To Yahuah our Elohim appertains righteousness:

Cf. 90 A.D.: Josephus, Wars 6.3.4 and 4.5.1-2. [81]

Cf. Dt. 28:53; Jer. 19:9. [81]

Cf. Jer. 42:18. [81]

Greek: were beneath and not above.

but unto us and to our father's open shame, as appears this day. 7 For all these plagues are come upon us, which Yahuah has pronounced against us, 8 Yet have we not prayed before Yahuah, that we might turn every one from the imaginations of his wicked heart. 9 Wherefore Yahuah watched over us for evil, and Yahuah has brought it upon us: for Yahuah is righteous in all His works, which He has commanded us. 10 Yet we have not hearkened unto his voice, to walk in the commandments of Yahuah, that He has set before us.

11 And now O Yahuah Elohim of Israel, that has brought your people out of the land of Egypt with a mighty hand, and high arm, and with signs and with wonders, and with great power, and has gotten yourself a name, as appears this day: 12 O Yahuah our Elohim, we have sinned, we have done ungodly, we have dealt unrighteously in all your ordinances. 13 Let your wrath turn from us: for we are but a few left among the heathen, where you have scattered us. 14 Hear

Cf. 1:15.

Cf. Dan. 9:15; Jer. 32:21. [81]

Cf. 90 A.D.: Josephus, Wars 6.9.3. [81]

Cf. Jer. 42:2. [81]

our prayers, O Yahuah, and our petitions, and deliver us for your own sake, and give us favor in the sight of them which have led us away: 15 That all the earth may know that you are Yahuah our Elohim, because Israel and his posterity is called **by your name. 16** O Yahuah look down from your holy house, and consider us: bow down your ear, O Yahuah, to hear us. 17 Open your eyes and behold: for the dead that are in the graves, whose souls are taken from their bodies, will give unto Yahuah neither praise nor righteousness. 18 But the soul that is greatly vexed, which goes stooping feeble, and the eyes that fail, and the hungry soul will give you praise and righteousness O Yahuah. 19 Therefore we do not make our humble supplication before you, O Yahuah our Elohim, for the righteousness of our fathers, and of our kings. 20 For you have sent out your wrath and indignation upon us, as you have spoken by your servants the prophets, saying, 21 Thus says Yahuah, bow down your shoulders to serve the

i.e.
Yahudim,
יהודים, or
Yah's, never
Jews.

Cf.
Dt. 26:15;
Isa. 63:15.

Cf.
Ps. 6:5,
115:17.
Isa. 38:18-
19. Greek:
spirit or life.

Cf.
Dan. 9:20.

king of Babylon: so shall you remain in the land that I gave unto your fathers. 22 But if you will not hear the voice of Yahuah to serve the king of Babylon, 23 I will cause to cease out of the cities of Yahudah, and from without Jerusalem the voice of mirth, and the voice of joy: the voice of the bridegroom, and the voice of the bride, and the whole land shall be desolate of inhabitants. 24 But we would not hearken unto your voice, to serve the king of Babylon: therefore have you made good the words that you spake by your servants the prophets, namely that the bones of our kings, and the bones of our fathers should be taken out of their places. 25 And lo, they are cast out to the heat of the day, and to the frost of the night, and they died in great miseries, by famine, by sword, and by pestilence. 26 And the house which is called by your name (have you laid waste) as it is to be seen this day, for the wickedness of the house of Israel, and the house of Yahudah. 27 O Yahuah our Elohim, you have dealt with

Cf.
Jer. 27:7-8.
90 A.D.:
Josephus,
Wars,
2.17.3. [81]

Cf.
Jer. 34:9-
10. [81]

Cf.
90 A.D.:
Josephus,
Wars 6.9.3.
[81]

Cf.
90 A.D.:
Josephus,
Wars 6.3.4
and 4.5.1-2.
[81]

Cf.
90 A.D.:
Josephus,
Wars 6.9.2-
3. [81]

Cf.
90 A.D.:
Josephus,
Wars 1.7.4f;
Jos., ibid.,
6.4. [81]

us after all your goodness, and according to all that great mercy of yours.

28 As you spoke by your servant Moses in the day when you did command him to write your Law, before the children of Israel, saying, 29 If you will not hear my voice, surely this very great multitude shall be turned into a small [number] among the nations, where I will scatter them. 30 For I knew that they would not hear me: because it is a stiff-necked people: but in the land of their captivities, they shall remember themselves,

Cf. Lev. 26:14; Dt. 28:15. Greek: this great swarm. 90 A.D.: Josephus, Wars 6.9.3. [81]

Or, come to themselves.

31 And shall know that I am Yahuah their Elohim: For I give them an heart, and ears to hear. 32 And they shall praise me in the land of their captivity, and think upon My Name, 33 And return from their stiff neck, and from their wicked deeds: for they shall remember the way of their fathers which sinned before Yahuah. 34 And I will bring them again into the land which I promised with an oath unto their fathers, Abraham, Isaac, and Jacob, and they shall be lords of it, and I will increase them, and they shall not be diminished.

Gr. back.

35 And I will make an everlasting covenant with them, to be their Elohim, and they shall be my people: and I will no more drive my people of Israel out of the land that I have given them.

CHAPTER 3:

3 The rest of their prayer and confession contained in that book, which Baruch wrote and sent to Jerusalem. 30 Wisdom was shown first to Jacob, and was seen upon the earth.

1 O Yahuah Almighty, Elohim of Israel, the soul in anguish, the troubled spirit cries unto you. 2 Hear O Yahuah, and have mercy: for you are merciful, and have pity upon us, because we have sinned before you. 3 For you endure forever, and we perish utterly. 4 O Yahuah Almighty, Elohim of Israel, hear now the prayers of the dead Israelites, and of their children, which have sinned before you, and not hearkened unto the voice of their Elohim: for the

which cause these plagues cleave unto us. **5** Remember not the iniquities of our forefathers: but think upon your power and your name, now at this time. **6** For you are Yahuah our Elohim, and you, O Yahuah, will we praise. **7** And for this cause you have put your fear in our hearts, to the intent that we should call upon your Name, and praise you in our captivity: for we have called to mind all the iniquity of our forefathers that sinned before you. **8** Behold, we are yet this day in our captivity, where you have scattered us, for a reproach and a curse, and to be subject to payments, according to all the iniquities of our fathers which departed from Yahuah our Elohim. **9** Hear, Israel, the **commandments of life**, give ear to understand wisdom. **10** How happens it, Israel, that you are in your enemies land, that you are waxen old in a strange country, that you are defiled with the dead? **11** That you are counted with them that go down into the grave? **12** You have forsaken the fountain of wisdom. **13** For if you had walked in the way of Elohim, you should have dwelled in peace forever. **14** Learn where is wisdom, where is strength, where is understanding, that you may know also where is length of days, and life, where is the light of the eyes and peace. **15** Who has found out her place? Or who has come into her treasures? **16** Where are the princes of the heathen become, and such as ruled the beasts upon the earth.

17 They that had their pastime with the fouls of the air, and they that hoarded up silver and gold wherein men trust, and made no end of their getting? **18** For they that wrought in silver, and were so careful, and whose works are unsearchable, **19** They are vanished, and gone down to the grave, and others are come up in their steads. **20** Young men have seen light, and dwelt upon the earth: but the way of knowledge have they not known, **21** Nor understood the paths thereof; nor laid hold of it: their children were far off from that way. **22** It has not been heard of in Canaan: neither has it been seen in Theman.

Cf. Dt. 30:1.

Cf. 90 A.D.: Josephus, Wars 6.9.3. [81]

Cf. Job 28; 12:20.

23 The Agarenes that seek wisdom upon earth, the merchants of Merran, and of Theman, the authors of *Or, expounders.* fables, and searchers out of understanding: none of these have known the way of wisdom, or remember her paths. 24 O Israel, how great is the house of Elohim? And how large is the place of His possession? 25 Great, and has no end: high, and unmeasurable. 26 There were the giants, *Cf. Gen. 6:1-4; Jub.5; 1En. 6-9.* famous from the beginning, that were of so great stature, and so expert in war. 27 Those did not Yahuah choose, neither gave He the way of knowledge unto them. 28 But they were destroyed, because they had no wisdom, and perished through their own foolishness. 29 Who has gone up into heaven and taken her, and brought her down from the clouds? 30 Who has gone over the sea, and found her, and will bring her for pure gold?

31 No man knows her way, nor thinks of her path. 32 But He that knows all things, knows her, and has found her out with His understanding: He that prepared the earth for evermore, has filled it with four-footed beasts. 33 He that sends forth light, and it goes: calls it again, and it obeys Him with fear. 34 The stars shined in their watches, and rejoiced: when He called them, they say, Here we are, and so with cheerfulness they showed light unto Him that made them. 35 This is our Elohim, and there shall none other be accounted of in comparison of Him. 36 He has found out all the way of knowledge, and has given it unto Jacob His servant, and to Israel His beloved. 37 Afterward did He show *Cf. Prov. 8:31; John 1:14.* Himself upon earth, and conversed with men.

CHAPTER 4:

1 The book of Commandments, is that Wisdom which was commended in the former chapter. 25 The Yahudim are moved to patience, and to hope for the deliverance.

1 This is the Book of the Commandments of Elohim: and the Law that endures forever: all they that keep it shall come to life: but such as leave it, shall die. 2 Turn, O Jacob, and take heed of it: walk in the presence of the light thereof, that you may be illuminated. 3 Give not your honor to another, nor the things that are profitable unto you, to a strange nation.

4 O Israel, happy are we: for things that are pleasing to Elohim, are made known unto us. 5 Be of good cheer, My people, the memorial of Israel. 6 You were sold to the nations, not for [your] destruction: but because you moved Elohim to wrath, you were delivered unto the enemies. 7 For you provoked Him that made you, by sacrificing unto devils, and not to Elohim. 8 Ye have forgotten the everlasting Elohim, that brought you up, and you have grieved Jerusalem that nursed you.

Cf. Dt. 30:19.

Greek: to the shining, before the light thereof.

Cf. 1Cor. 10:20.

9 For when she saw the wrath of Elohim coming upon you, she said; Hearken, O you that dwell about Sion: Elohim has brought upon me great mourning. 10 For I saw the captivity of my sons and daughters, which the everlasting brought upon them. 11 With joy did I nourish them: but sent them away with weeping and mourning. 12 Let no man rejoice over me a widow, and forsaken of many, who for the sins of my children, am left desolate: because they departed from the Law of Elohim. 13 They knew not His statutes, nor walked in the ways of His Commandments, nor trod in the paths of discipline in his righteousness. 14 Let them that dwell about Sion come, and remember you the captivity of my sons and daughters, which the everlasting has brought upon them. 15 For he has brought a nation upon them from far: a shameless nation, and of a strange language, who neither reverenced old man, nor pitied child. 16 These have carried away the dear beloved children of the widow, and left her that

Or, of His discipline in righteousness.

was alone, desolate without daughters. 17 But what can I help you? 18 For He that brought these plagues upon you, will deliver you from the hands of your enemies. 19 Go your way, O my children, go your way: for I am left desolate. 20 I have put off the clothing of peace, and put upon me the sackcloth of my prayer. I will cry unto the everlasting in my days. 21 Be of good cheer, O my children, cry unto Yahuah: and He shall deliver you from the power and hand of the enemies. 22 For my hope is in the Everlasting that He will save you, and joy is come unto me from the Holy One, because of the mercy which shall soon come unto you from the Everlasting our Saviour. 23 For I sent you out with mourning and weeping: but Elohim will give you to me again, with joy and gladness forever. 24 Like as now the neighbors of Sion have seen your captivity: so shall they see shortly your salvation from our Elohim, which shall come upon you with great glory, and brightness of the Everlasting. 25 My children, suffer patiently the wrath that is come upon you from Elohim: for your enemy has persecuted you: but shortly you shall see his destruction, and shall tread upon his neck. 26 My delicate ones have gone rough ways, and were taken away as a flock caught of the enemies. 27 Be of good comfort, O My children, and cry unto Elohim: for you shall be remembered of Him that brought these things upon you. 28 For as it was your mind to go astray from Elohim: so being returned seek Him ten times more. 29 For He that has brought these plagues upon you, shall bring you everlasting joy again with your salvation. 30 Take a good heart, O Jerusalem: for He that gave you that name, will comfort you. 31 Miserable are they that afflicted you, and rejoiced at your fall. 32 Miserable are the cities which your children served: miserable is she that received your sons. 33 For as she rejoiced at your ruin, and was glad of your fall: so shall she be grieved for her own desolation. 34 For I will take away the rejoicing of her

Or, prosperity. Or, in the time of my affliction. Ps. 116:2, 137:7, 2Esd. 9:38-10:28. Cf. Song Sol. 2:21-22. [81]

Or, my dearlings.

Cf. 1En. 89:56-67.

great multitude, and her pride shall be turned into mourning. 35 For fire shall come upon her from the Everlasting, long to endure: and she shall be inhabited of devils for a great time. 36 O Jerusalem, look about you toward the East, and behold the joy that comes unto you from Elohim. 37 Lo, your sons come whom you sent away: they come gathered together from the East to the West, by the word of the Holy One, rejoicing in the glory of Elohim.

CHAPTER 5:

1 Jerusalem is moved to rejoice, 5 and to behold their return out of captivity with glory.

1 Put off, O Jerusalem, the garment of your mourning and affliction, and put on the comeliness of the glory that comes from Elohim forever. 2 Cast about a double garment of the righteousness which comes from Elohim, and set a crown on your head of the glory of the Everlasting. 3 For Elohim will show your brightness unto every country under heaven. 4 For your name shall be called of Elohim forever, The peace of righteousness, and the glory of Yahuah's worship. 5 Arise, O Jerusalem, and stand on high, and look about toward the East, and behold your children gathered from the West unto the East by the word of the Holy One, rejoicing in the remembrance of Elohim. 6 For they departed from you on foot, and were led away of their enemies: but Elohim brings them unto you exalted with glory, as children of the kingdom. 7 For Elohim has appointed that every high hill, and banks of long continuance should be cast down, and valleys filled up, to make even the ground, that Israel may go safely in the glory of Elohim. 8 Moreover, even the woods, and every sweet smelling tree, shall overshadow Israel by the commandment of Elohim. 9 For Elohim shall lead Israel with joy, in the light of His glory, with the mercy and righteousness that comes from Him.

Cf. Song Sol. 11:3. [81]

Cf. Song Sol. 6:5. [81]

Cf. Song Sol. 9:6-7. [81]

*Ruins of the former city of Heliopolis, the city of
god Baal, Baalbek modern-day Lebanon.*

LETTER OF
JEREMIAH

BARUCH 6 IN 1611 KJV
THE EPISTLE OF JEREMIAH

WITH THE RESTORED NAME OF YAHUAH

THE Levite BIBLE
LeviteBible.com

CHAPTER 1:

1 The cause of the captivity is their sin. 3 The place whereto they were carried, is Babylon: the vanity of whose idols and idolatry are set forth at large in this Chapter.

1 A copy of an Epistle which Jeremiah sent unto them which were to be led captives into Babylon, by the king of the Babylonians, to certify them as it was commanded him of Elohim. 2 Because of the sins which you have committed before Elohim, you shall be led away captives unto Babylon by Nebuchadnezzar king of the Babylonians. 3 So when you be come unto Babylon, you shall remain there many years, and for a long season, namely **seven generations:** and after that I will bring you away peaceably from thence. 4 Now shall you see in Babylon gods of silver, and of gold, and of wood, born upon shoulders, which cause the nations to fear.

5 Beware therefore that you in no wise be like to strangers, neither be you afraid of them, when you see the multitude before them, and behind them, worshipping them. 6 But you say in your hearts, O

Yahuah, we must worship you. 7 For mine Angel is with you, and I myself caring for your souls. 8 As for their tongue, it is polished by the workman, and they themselves are guilded and laid over with silver, yet are they but false and cannot speak. 9 And taking gold, as it were for a virgin that loves to go carefree, they make crowns for the heads of their gods.

10 Sometimes also the Priests convey from their gods gold and silver, and bestow it upon themselves.

11 Yes, they will give thereof to the common harlots, and deck them as men with garments [being] gods of silver, and gods of gold, and wood. 12 Yet cannot these gods save themselves from rust and moths, though they be covered with purple raiment. 13 They wipe their faces because of the dust of the Temple, when there is much upon them. 14 And he that cannot put to death one that offends him, holds a scepter as though he were a judge of the country.

15 He has also in his right hand a dagger, and an axe: but cannot deliver himself

Cf. Jer. 25:12-13: "seventy years." Generations equals decades in this context and this is a Sabbath of decades. 2Chr. 36:21 affirms this.

Cf. Jub. 12:5; Isa. 44:8-10, 46:5, 7; Ps. 115:4; Wis. 13:10.

Cf. Jer. 10:3-10.

Cf. Jer. 10:3-10.

Or, which prostitute them-selves openly.

In the Sumerian Gilgamesh Epic, the giant carried a dagger and hatchet or axe. [63] Also, Sumerian god Bel Marduk, or Ba'al in Canaan, 12th Century archae-ology confirms daggers and axes in the Temple of Ba'al in Lachish, Israel. [62]

from war and thieves.

16 Whereby they are known not to be gods, therefore fear them not. 17 For like as a vessel that a man uses, is nothing worth when it is broken: even so it is with their gods: when they be set up in the Temple, their eyes be full of dust, through the feet of them that come in.

18 And as the doors are made sure on every side, upon him that offends the king, as being committed to suffer death: even so the priests make fast *Or, courts.* their temples, with doors, with locks and bars, lest their gods be spoiled with robbers. 19 They light them candles, yes, more than for themselves, whereof they cannot see one. 20 They are as one of the beams of the temple, yet they say, their *Greek: licked.* hearts are gnawed upon by things creeping out of the earth, and when they eat them and their clothes, they feel it not. 21 Their faces are blacked, through the smoke that comes out of the temple. 22 Upon their bodies and heads, sit bats, swallows, and birds, and the cats also. 23 By this you may know that they are no gods:

therefore fear them not.

24 Notwithstanding the gold that is about them, to make them beautiful, except they wipe off the rust they will not shine: for neither when they were molten did they feel it. 25 The things wherein there is no breath, are bought for *Or, any price.* a most high price. 26 They are born upon shoulders, having no feet, whereby *Cf. Isa. 46:7; Jub. 12:5.* they declare unto men that they be nothing worth.

27 They also that serve them, are ashamed: for if they fall to the ground at any time, they cannot rise up again of themselves: neither if one set them upright can they move of themselves: neither if they be bowed down, can they make themselves straight: but they set gifts *Or, offerings.* before them as unto dead men. 28 As for the things that are sacrificed unto them, their priests sell and abuse: in like manner their wives lay up part thereof in salt: but unto the poor and *Or, spend.* impotent, they give nothing of it. 29 Menstruous women, and women in childbed eat their sacrifices: by these things you may *Cf. Lev. 12:4.* know that they are no gods: fear them not. 30 For how

can they be called gods? Because women set meat before the gods of silver, gold, and wood. 31 And the priests sit in their temples, having their clothes rent, and their heads and beards shaven, and nothing upon their heads. 32 They roar and cry before their gods: as men do at the feast when one is dead. 33 The priests also take off their garments, and clothe their wives and children. 34 Whether it be evil that one does unto them, or good: they are not able to recompense it: they can neither set up a king, nor put him down. 35 In like manner, they can neither give riches nor money: though a man make a vow unto them, and keep it not, they will not require it.

36 They can save no man from death, neither deliver the weak from the mighty. 37 They cannot restore a blind man to his sight, nor help any man in his distress. 38 They can show no mercy to the widow: nor do good to the fatherless. 39 Their gods of wood, and which are overlaid with gold, and silver, are like the stones that be hewn out of the mountain: they that worship them shall be confounded. 40 How should a man then think and say that they are gods? When even the Chaldeans themselves dishonor them. 41 Who if they shall see one dumb that cannot speak, they bring him and entreat Bel that he may speak, as though he were able to understand.

i.e. Ba'al or Bel Marduk.

Or, bid him call upon Bel.

42 Yet they cannot understand this themselves, and leave them: for they have no knowledge.

Or, sense. Cf. Jer. 10:8, 14, 21: "brutish (old Eng. for stupid) and foolish."

43 The women also with cords above them, sitting in the ways, burn bran for perfume: but if any of them drawn by some that pass by, lie with him, she reproaches her fellow that she was not thought as worthy as herself, nor her cord broken.

44 Whatsoever is done among them is false: how may it then be thought or said that they are gods? 45 They are made of carpenters, and goldsmiths, they can be nothing else, than the workman will have them to be. 46 And they themselves that made them, can never continue long,

how should then the things that are made of them, be gods? 47 For they left lies and reproaches to them that come after.

48 For when there comes any war or plague upon them, the priests consult with themselves, where they may be hidden with them. 49 How then cannot men perceive, that they be no gods, which can neither save themselves from war nor from plague? 50 For seeing they be but of wood, and overlaid with silver and gold: it shall be known hereafter that they are false. 51 And it shall manifestly appear to all nations and kings, that they are no gods: but the works of men's hands, and that there is no work of Elohim in them.

52 Who then may not know that they are no gods?

53 For neither can they set up a king in the land, nor give rain unto men. 54 Neither can they judge their own cause, nor redress a wrong being unable: for they are as crows between heaven and earth. 55 Whereupon when fire falls upon the house of gods of wood, or laid over with gold or silver, their priests will fly away, and escape: but they themselves shall be burnt asunder like beams. 56 Moreover they cannot withstand any king or enemies: How can it then be thought or said that they be gods? 57 Neither are those gods of wood, and laid over with silver or gold able to escape either from thieves or robbers. 58 Whose gold, and silver, and garments wherewith they are clothed, they that are strong do take, and go away withal: neither are they able to help themselves. 59 Therefore it is better to be a king that shows his power, or else a profitable vessel in an house, which the owner shall have use of, than such false gods: or to be a door in an house to keep such things safe as be therein, than such false gods: or a pillar of wood in a palace, than such false gods. 60 For sun, moon, and stars, being bright and sent to do their offices, are obedient. 61 In like manner the lightning when it breaks forth is easy to be seen, and after the same manner the

*Cf.
Ps. 115:4;
Wisd. 13:10.*

Or, the same wind. wind blows in every country. 62 And when Elohim commands the clouds to go over the whole world: they do as they are bidden:

63 And the fire sent from above to consume hills and woods, does as it is commanded: but these are like unto them neither in show, nor power.

64 Wherefore it is neither to be supposed nor said, that they are gods, seeing they are able, neither to judge causes, nor to do good unto men. 65 Knowing therefore that they are no gods, fear them not. 66 For they can neither curse nor bless kings. 67 Neither can they do signs in the heavens among the heathen: nor shine as the sun, nor give light as the moon. 68 The beasts are better than they: for they can get under a cover, and help themselves.

69 It is then by no means manifest unto us that they are gods: therefore fear them not. 70 For as a scarecrow in a garden of cucumbers keeps nothing: so are their gods of wood, and laid over with silver and gold. 71 And likewise their gods of wood, and laid over with silver and gold, are like to a white thorn in an orchard that every bird sits upon: as also to a dead body, that is cast into the dark. 72 And you shall know them to be no gods, by the bright purple that rots upon them: and they themselves afterward shall be eaten, and shall be a reproach in the country. *Or purple and brightness.*

73 Better therefore is the just man that has no idols: for he shall be far from reproach.

2ND CHRONICLES'
WITNESS

AFFIRMING BIBLE HISTORY

Illustration of Ancient Assyrian soldiers.

THE
Levite
BIBLE
LeviteBible.com

PRAYER OF
MANASSEH

KING OF YAHUDAH REPENTS IN CAPTIVITY

WITH THE RESTORED
NAME OF YAHUAH

THE
Levite
BIBLE
LeviteBible.com

CHAPTER 1:

The prayer of Manasseh, King of Yahudah, when he was held captive in Babylon.

1 O Yahuah, Almighty Elohim of our Fathers, Abraham, Isaac, and Jacob, and of their righteous seed: 2 Who has made heaven and earth, with all the ornament thereof: 3 Who has bound the sea by the word of your Commandment: who has shut up the deep, and sealed it by your terrible and glorious Name, 4 Whom all men fear, and tremble before your power: 5 For the majesty of your glory cannot be born, and your anger threatening towards sinners is importable:

Cf. Jer. 5:22; Job 26:10.

6 But your merciful promise is beyond measure and unsearchable: 7 For you are the Most High Yahuah, of great compassion, long suffering, very merciful, and repents of the evils of men. You, O Yahuah, according to your great goodness has promised repentance, and forgiveness to them that have sinned against you: and of your infinite mercies have appointed repentance unto sinners that they may be saved. 8 You therefore, O

Or, cast out by entreaty.

Yahuah, that are the Elohim of the just, has not appointed repentance to the just, as to Abraham, and Isaac, and Jacob, which have not sinned against you: but you have appointed repentance unto me that am a sinner: 9 For I have sinned above the number of the sands of the sea. My transgressions, O Yahuah, are multiplied: my transgressions are multiplied, and I am not worthy to behold and see the height of heaven, for the multitude of mine iniquity. 10 I am bowed down with many iron chains, that I cannot lift up my head, neither have any release: For I have provoked your wrath, and done evil before you, I did not your will, neither kept I your Commandments: I have set up abominations, and have multiplied offenses. 11 Now therefore I bow the knee of my heart, beseeching you of grace: 12 I have sinned, O Yahuah, I have sinned and I acknowledge my iniquities: 13 Wherefore I humbly beseech you, forgive me, O Yahuah, forgive me, and destroy me not with my iniquities. Be not angry with me forever, by reserving evil

Or, turns a reproach to the foolish.

Or, neither take my breath.

for me, neither condemn me into the lower parts of the earth. For you are the Elohim, even the Elohim of them that repent:

14 And in me you will show all your goodness: for you will save me that am unworthy, according to your great mercy. 15 Therefore, I will praise you forever all the days of my life: for all the powers of the heavens do praise you, and yours is the glory forever and ever, Amen.

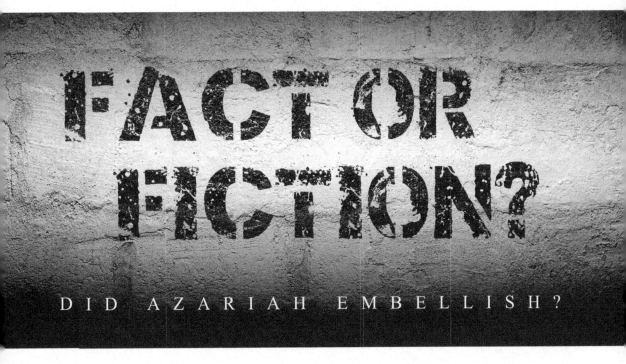

Imagine our righteous anger when we read a commentary from an illiterate scholar who referred to this account as embellishment? It is incredible that scholar did not even bother to read the "Prayer of Manasseh" from the Dead Sea Scrolls which matches this one in content and yet would call it such in ignorance *(See Introduction: Historicity of Manasseh)*. Unfortunately, this is the age in which we live. When one reads this prayer, it seems inspired just from a simple reading. When one tests it and we find it's historicity to the oldest fragments of most Bible texts found, it is outlandish that anyone calling themselves a scholar of the Bible would claim such.

2nd Chronicles 33:19 records this prayer was written and recorded by the Prophets and who could call themselves a Bible scholar and forget that? The fact that Prayer of Manasseh was found in Qumran among the documents of the Temple Priests proves it was not a recent writing but the ancient one copied over per the tradition.

THE
Levite
BIBLE

VOLUME 2
COMING
SOON

BIBLIOGRAPHY:

Translation Originally From:
1611 King James Version

Other General Sources of Note:
The Complete Dead Sea Scrolls in English. Revised Edition. By Geza Vermes. Penguin Books. London, NY. Revised 2004. Originally Published 1962. Page number in reference. [22]
The Book of Jubilees: The Torah Calendar. By Timothy Schwab and Anna Zamoranos. 2021. Based on the Original Translation, R.H. Charles, 1903. Free eBook: www.bookofjubilees.org.
2nd Esdras: The Hidden Book of Prophecy. By Timothy Schwab and Anna Zamoranos. 2021. Based on the Original 1611 King James Version. Free eBook at www.2esdras.org.
The Book of First Enoch: The Oldest Book In History. By Timothy Schwab and Anna Zamoranos. 2021. Based on the Original Translation by R.H. Charles, 1912. Free eBook at www.firstenoch.org.

Cited, Numbered Sources:
1. "The Canon of Scripture." Blue Letter Bible citing "What Everyone Needs To Know About The Bible." By Don Stewart. The Basic Bible Study Series. Publisher Dart Press, Orange, California. https://www.blueletterbible.org/faq/canon.cfm
2. Clark Pinnock, Biblical Revelation, Grand Rapids: Baker Book House, 1973, p. 104. Quoted by Blue Letter Bible.
3. 2014 Lecture at University of Chicago Divinity School sponsored by Jewish Federation of Chicago. Rachel Elior. Professor, Hebrew University of Jerusalem. https://www.youtube.com/watch?v=wLit979B60Y&t=3621s
4. Strong's Concordance "Awan" #H5770. Blue Letter Bible. (Note Ancient Hebrew never had a "V" so the word is Awan not Avan).
5. 1. "Where to See Some of the World's Oldest and Most Interesting Maps." By Jennifer Billock. Smithsonian Magazine. July 18, 2017.
2. "Geography and Ethnography: Perceptions of the World in Pre-Modern Societies." By Kurt A. Raaflaub & Richard J. A. Talbert. 2009. John Wiley & Sons. p. 147. 3. Map from: Wikimedia Commons. Map of the World from Sippar (Tell Abu Habba), Iraq, 6th century BCE. On display at the British Museum in London. By Osama Shukir Muhammed Amin.
6. "Books of Enoch Collection." By Scriptural Research Institute. 2020. p. 106.
7. "Rapha." Abarim Publications.
8. "The Dead Sea Scrolls and the Christian Myth." By John M. Allegro. 1992.
9. "The Mystery of the Essenes." By H. Spencer Lewis, F.R.C. From "The Mystical Life of Jesus." Rosicrucian Digest No. 2. 2007. p. 3.
10. "Natural History." Pliny the Elder. Book V. p. 277.
11. "The Life of Flavius Josephus." 1:2. The Genuine Works of Flavius Josephus the Jewish Historian. Translated from the Original Greek, according to Havercamp's accurate Edition.
12. 1770, Bonne Map of Israel. Rigobert Bonne 1727 – 1794. AdobeStock.
13. Madaba Mosaic Map(left), c. 6th century A.D. St. George's Church. Jordan. AdobeStock.
14. 1836, Tanner Map of Palestine, Israel, Holy Land. AdobeStock.
15. NASA/Goddard Space Flight Center Scientific Visualization Studio U.S. Department of Commerce, National Oceanic and Atmospheric Administration, National Geophysical Data Center, 2006, 2-minute Gridded Global Relief Data (ETOPO2v2). Horace Mitchell (NASA/GSFC): Lead Animator.
16. 1845, Chambers Map of Palestine, Israel, Holy Land. AdobeStock.
17. 1852, Philip Map of Palestine, Israel, Holy Land. AdobeStock.
18. Ein Gedi Photos: Chalcolithic Temple, Essene Synagogue, Tile mosaic Peacock symbols. AdobeStock.

19. *Antiquities of the Jews – Book VIII, Chapter 6:4 and 7:1. Flavius Josephus.*

20. *"Enoch and Qumran Origins: New Light on a Forgotten Connection." Gabriele Boccaccini, Editor. William B. Erdemans Publishing Co. Grand Rapids, MI and Cambridge, UK. 2005. p. 137.*

21. *"The Complete Dead Sea Scrolls In English Revised Edition." "The Damascus Document." Translated By Geza Vermes, 2004, Penguin Classics Books. London, England. First Published 1962. Revised Edition 2004. p. 139.3. Flavius Josephus, Antiquities of the Jews, 18:16.*

22. *The Complete Dead Sea Scrolls in English. Revised Edition. By Geza Vermes. Penguin Books. London, NY. Revised 2004. Originally Published 1962. Page number in reference.*

23. *"The World's Largest Caldera Discovered In The Philippine Sea." By David Bressan. Forbes Magazine. Oct. 21, 2019.*

24. *"Dudael." Wikipedia. Feb. 24, 2022.*

25. *Strong's Concordance. Blue Letter Bible.*

26. *Ancient Hebrew Research Center. By Jeff A. Benner. Ancient-Hebrew.org. 2019.*

27. *Philippines #1 in Gold in History. The Search for King Solomon's Treasure. The Lost Isles of Gold and the Garden of Eden. By Timothy Schwab and Anna Zamoranos. 2020. 1. "Ancient Mining: Classical Philippine Civilization." Wikipedia. Extracted August 9, 2019. and "Cultural Achievements of Pre-Colonial Philippines." Wikipedia. Extracted August 9, 2019. 2. "The Edge of Terror: The Heroic Story of American Families Trapped in the Japanese-occupied Philippines." By Scott Walker. Thomas Dunne Books. St. Martin's Press. New York. Chap. 3 - The Gold Miners, 1901-1937. p. 44. 3. "Philippine Civilization and Technology," By Paul Kekai Manansala. Asia Pacific University. 4. "Encyclopedic Dictionary of Archaeology – Philippines, the." Compiled by Barbara Ann Kipfer, Ph.D. Kluwer Academic/ Plenum Publishers. New York, London, Moscow. 2000. p. 436. 5. "Miners Shun Mineral Wealth of the Philippines." By Donald Greenlees. NY Times. May 14, 2008. Citing The Fraser Institute. 6. "Trillion – Dollar Philippine Economic Goldmine Emerging From Murky Pit." By Ralph Jennings. Forbes Magazine. Apr. 5, 2015. 7. "Mining for Gold in the Philippines." By Nicole Rashotte. Gold Investing News. Sept. 10th, 2019.*

28. *Philippines #1 in Pearl. The Search for King Solomon's Treasure. The Lost Isles of Gold and the Garden of Eden. By Timothy Schwab and Anna Zamoranos. 2020. 1. "This $100 Million Pearl Is The Largest and Most Expensive in the World." By Roberta Naas. Forbes Magazine. Aug 23, 2016. 2. "Pinoy in Canada Discovers Strange Family Heirloom is Actually a Giant Pearl Worth $90 Million." Buzzooks.com. May 23, 2019.*

29. *Romblon Philippines Strongest Onyx. The Search for King Solomon's Treasure. The Lost Isles of Gold and the Garden of Eden. By Timothy Schwab and Anna Zamoranos. 2020. 1. "ROMBLON: 8 Awesome Places You Should Visit in Romblon!" Our Awesome Planet. Sept. 7, 2016. 2. "The Romblon Marble." Ellaneto Tiger Marble Trader, Romblon. 2010. 3. "Marvelous Marble" By Robert A. Evora. Manila Standard. Jan. 16, 2014.*

30. *"The Center of the Center of Marine Biodiversity on Earth." 1. "Environmental Biology of Fishes." K.E. Carpenter and V.G. Springer. 2005. 72: 467-480. 2. "Center of the Center of Marine Diversity." CNN. Apr. 30, 2012. 3. "100 Scientists Declare RP as World's 'Center of Marine Biodiversity." By Katherine Adraneda. June 8, 2006. The Philippine Star reporting on "Philippines Environmental Monitor, 2005" by the World Bank.*

31. *"Havilah." Hitchcock's Dictionary of Bible Names from BibleHub.org and KingJamesBibleDictionary.com, Strong's Concordance #H2341. Blue Letter Bible.*

32. "Eve - Havah." Strong's Concordance #H2332. Blue Letter Bible.

33. "Alabaster, Mineral." and "Marble, Rock." By Editors of Encyclopaedia Britannica. Encyclopaedia Britannica. Updated Jan. 24, 2018 and Jan. 24, 2020.

34. "Indonesia's Mountains of Fire." By Daniel Quinn. Indonesia Expat. June 30, 2014. Indonesia's Volcanological Survey. Laporan Kebencanaan Geologi. Apr. 2, 2019.

35. Wikipedia.

41. "The giant undersea rivers we know very little about" By Richard Gray. BBC News. July 6, 2017. Citing Dan Parsons, PhD, Sedimentologist, University of Hull, UK.

42. "The Thanksgiving Hymns (iQH, 1Q36,4Q427-32). Hymn 14." The Complete Dead Sea Scrolls. By Geza Vermes. Penguin Classics. P. 278.

43. "Chapter Eight. Traditions Common To 4 Ezra And The Dead Sea Scrolls." By E.J.C. Tigchelaar and F. García Martínez. Qumranica Minora I. Qumran Origins and Apocalypticism. Series: Studies on the Texts of the Desert of Judah, Volume: 63. Publisher: Brill. 01 Jan 2007. 153–168.

44. F. García Martínez, "Qumran Origins and Early History: A Groningen Hypothesis," Folia Orientalia 25 (1989): 113–36.

53. "Commentary on Habakkuk." The Complete Dead Sea Scrolls in English. Revised Edition. By Geza Vermes. Penguin Books. London, NY. Revised 2004. Originally Published 1962. p. 510-511.

54. Commentary on Nahum, P. 505. The Complete Dead Sea Scrolls in English. Geza Vermes. Penguin Classics. Revised Edition. Published 1962. Revised 2004.

55. Commentary on Habukkuk, P. 515.The Complete Dead Sea Scrolls in English. Geza Vermes. Penguin Classics. Revised Edition. Published 1962. Revised 2004.

56. "Blessings (iQSb=iQ28b), The Blessing of the Prince of the Congregation." The Complete Dead Sea Scrolls in English. Geza Vermes. Penguin Classics. Revised Edition. Published 1962. Revised 2004. p. 389. 100 B.C. dating: J. T. Milik (DJD, I, 118-29).

60. "Antiquities of the Jews – Book XI." Josephus. Chapter 3.1. Chapter 11.133.

61. "Euergetes" Encyclopedia of The Bible citing R.H. Charles, The Apocrypha and Pseudepigrapha of the Old Testament, I (1963), 293. Bible Gateway.

62. "3,000-year-old Canaanite temple discovered in buried city in Israel." By Tom Metcalfe. Live Science. Feb. 24, 2020.

63. "The Gilgamesh Epic And Old Testament Parallels." By Alexander Heidel. Tablet VIII, Col. 11:4-5, p. 62; Tablet IX, 15-16. p.65; Tablet X, Col. 3:40-44, p.76.

64. "Cyrus the Great, King of Persia." By Richard N. Frye. Fact-checked by The Editors of Encyclopaedia Britannica. Apr 1, 2023.

65. "Psittacosis." Centers forr Disease Control nd Prevention. Last Reviewed: March 17, 2022. Content Source: National Center for Immunization and Respiratory Diseases.

66. Satpathy G, Behera HS, Ahmed NH. Chlamydial eye infections: Current perspectives. Indian Journal of Ophthalmology 2017;65:97-102

67. "Fish bile and cautery: trachoma treatment in art." By Johnson HA. Journal of the Royal Society of Medicine. 2005 Jan;98(1):30-2.

68. "Raphael, רפאל." Abarim Publications.

69. "Nineveh and Babylon." Austen Henry Layard. P. 168. London, 1853. On the spot drawing of Plate 6 (cropped) from bas-relief from the Palace of Sennacherib in Tobit's era. The fish is believed to be a mangar fish from the Tigris-Euphrates basin.

70. Özgür, M.E. (2016). The Luciobarbus esocinus (Heckel, 1843) from the Euphrates River Basin:

An introduction about its past, present and future. Proceedings of the 2nd International Congress on Applied Ichthyology & Aquatic Environment 10 - 12 November 2016, Messolonghi, Greece. Cited on Wikipedia.

71. "River Monsters: Discover the Largest Fish in the Euphrates River." by Brandi Allred A-Z Animals. Feb. 6, 2023.

72. "Prison of Solomon." Wikipedia. Citing Encyclopaedia Iranica, & Tehran Times.

73. "Antiquities of the Jews." By Flavius Josephus. Book 4:22.

74. Origen's "Letter to Africanus." By N.R.M. de Lange, Cambridge Studia Patristrica. Vol. XVI. PATRISTICA. STUDIA. Oxford 1975. p. 244.

75. "Letter to Africanus." Translated by Frederick Crombie. From Ante-Nicene Fathers, Vol. 4. Edited by Alexander Roberts, James Donaldson, and A. Cleveland Coxe. (Buffalo, NY: Christian Literature Publishing Co., 1885.) Revised and edited for New Advent by Kevin Knight.

76. "The Genuine Works of Flavius Josephus The Jewish Historian." Translated from the Original Greek, according to Havercamp's accurate Edition. By William Whiston M.A. University of Cambridge. London. 1737.

77. "Baruch Is There, Just Sometimes As Part of Jeremiah." By Tom Nash. Catholic Answers.

78. Bar 3:36 (Athenagoras, Legatio pro Christianis 9,2 [98,11–12 P.]). Cf. Cyprian, Testimonia ad
Quirinium 2,6 (CChr.SL 3,1, 35,17–36,20 Weber); Lactantius, Divinae institutiones 4,13,8 (SC 377, 114,30–34 Monat); Bernard Pouderon, "Les citations scripturaires dans l'oeuvre d'Athénagore: leurs sources et leur statut," Vetera Christianorum 31 (1994): (111–153) 112; Sean A. Adams, Baruch and the Epistle of Jeremiah: A Commentary on the Greek Texts of Codex Vaticanus (Septuagint Commentary Series; Leiden: Brill, 2014), 17.

79. "Baruch and the Epistle of Jeremiah." By Sean A. Adams. Brill. 2014. p. 17.

80. Decretum Gelasianum. https://www.tertullian.org/decretum_eng.htm.

81. The Apocrypha and Pseudepigripha of the Old Testametn In English. R. H. Charles, D.Litt., D.D. Vol. 1. Oxford at the Claredon Press. 1913.

82. "Of the Thundering Legion." By William Whiston. London. 1726. pp. 47-63.

83. "Apocrypha: Biblical Literature." Written and fact-checked by The Editors of Encyclopaedia Britannica. Last Updated: May 12, 2023.

84. "On the Patristic Old Testament Canon." By Admin. Classical Chritianity. Eastern Orthodoc For Today. Dec. 21, 2011.

85. "Susanna" Early Jewish Learning citing "Introduction to the Old Testament," By James King West. p. 458.

86. "Bel and The Dragon" Early Jewish Learning citing "Introduction to the Old Testament," By James King West. p. 458.

87. "The Pope and the Mithras Cult: Part II." By Jon Sorensen. Catholic Answers. Sept. 23, 2013.

88. "HAS 'Esther' BEEN FOUND AT QUMRAN? '4QProto-Esther' AND THE 'Esther' CORPUS." By Sidnie White Crawford. Revue de Qumrân 17, no. 1/4 (65/68) (1996): 307–25.

89. Bibilical Intertextuality Forum. intertextual. bible.

90. The Instructor (Book II), Chapter 1. The Paedagogus (Clement of Alexandria). Translated by William Wilson. From Ante-Nicene Fathers, Vol. 2. Edited by Alexander Roberts, James Donaldson, and A. Cleveland Coxe. (Buffalo, NY: Christian Literature Publishing Co., 1885.) Revised and edited for New Advent by Kevin Knight.

91. "Deuterocanonical Books In The New Testament." ScriptureCatholic.com.

92. "Polycarp and Paul: An Analysis of Their Literary and Theological Relationship In Light of Polycarp's Use Of Biblical and Extra-Biblical Literature." By Kenneth Berding, Brill. 2002. p.105.

93. "The Epistle of St. James." By Joseph B. Mayor, M.A. OAMB, LITT.D. DuBL. Macmillan and Co. London, NY. 1897. pp.76-77.

94. "An Analysis of 4Q Instruction" By Torleif Elgvin. Doctoral Thesis Submitted to the Senate of the Hebrew University of Jerusalem. 1997. 5.1.3. p. 172.

95. "Mystery" in the Wisdom of Solomon and 4QInstruction. By Benjamin Wold. Journal for the Study of the Pseudepigrapha. Sage Journals, Vol. 31, Iss. 1. Sept. 9, 2021.

96. "Book of (The) Wisdom of Solomon." McClintock and Strong Biblical Cyclopedia. The Cyclopedia of Biblical, Theological, and Ecclesiastical Literature. James Strong and John McClintock; Haper and Brothers; NY; 1880.

97. Deuterocanonical and Cognate Literature Yearbook 2019.

98. "Torah and Divine Revelation in Three Jewish Texts: 4QInstruction, Wisdom of Solomon and the Fourth Gospel." By Jeffrey Hubbard. Journal for the Study of the New Testament 44, no. 4 (June 1, 2022): 561–79.

99. "The Wisdom of Solomon." By The Rev. J. A. F. Gregg, M.A, Cambridge University Press. 1909.

100. "Adam, The Angels and Eternal Life: Genesis 1-3 in the Wisdom of Solomon and 4QInstruction." Matthew Goff. Florida State University.

101. "4QInstruction." By Matthew J. Goff. Wisdom Literature From the Ancient World; No. 2. Society of Biblical Literature. 2013.

102. "The Apocalypse of Baruch." By Rev. Canon R.H. Charles, D.D. Society For Promoting Christian Knowledge. London. NY. 1918.

103. "Baruch" by P. P. Saydon, revised by T. Hanlon, in A New Catholic Commentary on Holy Scripture, ed. Reginald C. Fuller, Thomas Nelson, Inc. Publishers, 1953, 1975, §504j. The same source states that "[t]here is also evidence that Baruch was read in Jewish synagogues on certain festivals during the early centuries of the Christian era (Thackeray, 107-11)", i.e. Henry St. John Thackeray, The Septuagint and Jewish Worship, 1923.

104. "Baruch and the Epistle of Jeremiah." By Sean A. Adams. Brill. 2014. p. 1.

105. VanderKam, James C. "The scrolls, the Apocrypha, and the Pseudepigrapha." Hebrew Studies, vol. 34, annual 1993, pp. 35+. Gale Academic OneFile. Accessed 1 June 2023.

106. Collins, John J. Dead Sea Discoveries 17, no. 2 (2010): 231–33. http://www.jstor.org/stable/20787404.

107. Dead Sea Scrolls Translated. The Qumran Texts In English. By Florentino Garcia Martinez Wilfred G. E. Watson Translator E. Jf. Brill Leiden, New York, Cologne. 1994.

108. "Nicene and Post-Nicene Fathers." Ser. 2. Vol. 1. Church History of Eusebius. Bk. 3. Ch. 39.

109. Christian Stadel. "The Judaeo-Syriac Version of Bel and the Dragon: An Edition with Linguistic Comments." Mediterranean Language Review 23 (2016): 1–31.

110. "The Lives of the Twelve Caesars." By C. Suetonius Tranquillus. The Life of Vespasian 5.6. p. 281. Loeb Classical Library, 1914.

111. A Collation of Variants from 967 to Ziegler's Critical Edition of Susanna, Daniel, Bel et Draco. By Tim McLay. p. 121-125.

INCREASING INSIGHT
THE REMNANT IS AWAKENING

The Days Daniel 12:4 Predicted Are Upon Us! Will You Join The Many Thousands Who Are Restoring Ancient Knowledge? Now, 8 Substantial Works Of Revelation!

Apocrypha: Vol. 1
7" x 10"

2nd Esdras:
7" x 10"

▶ **YouTube** *The God Culture*   f *The God Culture - Original*

International:
amazon

Philippines:
Shopee

eBooks:
issuu
PAPERTURN

The Book of Jubilees:
7" x 10"

Bible History Illustrated:
7" x 10"

First Enoch:
7" x 10"

www.OphirInstitute.com

REST: Sabbath
6" x 9" Paperback

The Full Case:
6" x 9" Paperback

Coffee Table Book:
10" x 12" Hardcover